Politics

Damien K. Picariello
Editor

Politics in Gotham

The Batman Universe and Political Thought

Editor
Damien K. Picariello
University of South Carolina Sumter
Sumter, SC, USA

ISBN 978-3-030-05775-6 (hardcover) ISBN 978-3-030-05776-3 (eBook)
ISBN 978-3-030-42869-3 (softcover)
https://doi.org/10.1007/978-3-030-05776-3

Library of Congress Control Number: 2019931028

Cover credit: Tim Flach / Getty Images
Cover designed by Fatima Jamadar

This Palgrave Macmillan imprint is published by the registered company Springer Nature Switzerland AG
The registered company address is: Gewerbestrasse 11, 6330 Cham, Switzerland

Praise for *Politics in Gotham*

"A compelling and fascinating collection on the politics of Gotham City and how they mirror our world today. Food for thought as well as good ol' fashioned comic-book debate!"

—Marc Andreyko, *Writer of* Manhunter, Batwoman, *and* Torso

"80 years of Batman across various media provides a fertile ground to explore the politics of narrative, gender, justice and heroism as they play out in the streets of Gotham. With essays ranging from the timely (addressing #FAKENEWS) to the timeless (Machiavelli and Batman), and from gendered heroes (Batgirl and feminism) to archetypal villains (Scarecrow and the politics of fear) this collection should be on the bookshelf of everyone interested in superheroes and politics. *Politics in Gotham* is a timely and welcome addition to the literature on Batman."

—Matthew J. Costello, *Professor of Political Science, Saint Xavier University, USA*

"*Politics in Gotham* represents another significant engagement with the superhero genre and makes a rigorous contribution to the growing scholarship in the area. For those interested in the complex politics surrounding a character like Batman this is a much-needed assessment of one of the most popular and enigmatic icons of popular culture."

—Neal Curtis, *Associate Professor of Media and Communication, University of Auckland, New Zealand*

"Batman finally faces an opponent he can't vanquish with a convenient Ka-Pow! on the jaw. And this team of political science professors wields the mightiest weapon of all: a willingness to take the dark knight seriously. They dare to look at Batman as if he were real and operating in an actual community. Enlisting the aid of Plato, Machiavelli, and other crossover allies, they cut into the vigilante heart of the superhero formula, exploring Gotham as a dark mirror reflecting our own very real world's concerns for law, justice, and democracy. Rather than dismissing superheroes as fluff, these academics honor the genre with a respectfully laser-sharp lens. Every Batman fan deserves this book."

—Chris Gavaler, *Associate Professor of English, Washington & Lee University, USA, and author of* Superhero Comics *(2017)*

"[I]f the idea of a political and philosophical examination of Batman and his city appeals to you, then this book would make a fine addition to your library...*Politics in Gotham* is a very thoughtful and thought-provoking series of analyses of political themes present in or implied by the Batman mythos. The idea of using Batman's world as a jumping point to explore various political topics is a brilliant idea and provides a fascinating and truly unique reading experience."

—Derek McNeil, DCComicsNews.com

"Each essay in this collection is erudite and learned, not just about its topic but about its medium. In short, this is an exemplary volume for the study of film, politics, theory, and the popular."

—Davide Panagia, *Professor of Political Science, UCLA, USA*

"Several years ago I taught a course entitled 'Batman: The Dark Knight and American Politics.' *Politics in Gotham: The Batman Universe and Political Thought* is the text that I wish I could have had for that course. For anyone who harbors doubts about the utility and appropriateness of using 'popular culture' as a lens to examine the issues of American politics and political thought in general, *Politics in Gotham* will dispel those doubts. The task is always to choose good material and then connect that material to serious questions and great works. This text succeeds beautifully in both.

Professor Damien Picariello has assembled a collection of essays of stunning variety and depth. The authors use both the pre-existing comic book material and its cinematic versions (primarily Christopher Nolan's remarkable trilogy, *Batman Begins*, *The Dark Knight* and *The Dark Knight Rises*) as the springboard for probing enduring questions of American politics and political life. None of the essays in this volume are superfluous, superficial or unworthy of the most serious reading; each explores the original material with interpretive ingenuity and connects that material with the deeper things."

—Jeffrey J. Poelvoorde, *Associate Professor of Politics, Converse College, USA*

"The adventures of Batman along with his enemies and friends become a resource for reflection on the deepest questions of political life in an engaging series of essays in this volume. Punishment, violence, judgment, legitimacy, vigilantism, perfectionism, even feminism, all surface as the authors find in Batman's universe the inescapable challenges that haunt all political communities concerned with peace and justice. As such, Batman comes to speak not only to the city of Gotham, but to our contemporary political world. This volume will be of interest not only to fans of Batman, but to anyone who cares about how to address the presence of evil in our political lives."

—Arlene W. Saxonhouse, *Caroline Robbins Professor of Political Science and Women's Studies, University of Michigan, USA*

"Thought-provoking, rigorous, and inspired, *Politics in Gotham* is at once a celebration of the deep, rich mythology of the Dark Knight and a daring interrogation of its implications in today's world. This book serves as a compelling and urgent symposium on Batman and what he means—and has the potential to mean—in today's world."

—Scott Snyder, *Writer of* Batman, Justice League, *and* American Vampire

"Reading *Politics in Gotham: The Batman Universe and Political Thought* brought back the halcyon days of our "Dark Knight Trilogy" of films, when pundits and political analysts from every extreme of the political spectrum were claiming Batman as one of their own. Maybe because he has no super-powers, Batman can be a cypher upon whom everyone who identifies with the character can impose their own feelings, personalities, beliefs, and philosophies. Perhaps the result of reading too much into the character and his Gotham tales or over-thinking the comic books, graphic novels, and movies too much, both political experts and laymen seem to have a field day discussing the political implications of Batman and all he stands for. The result is actually a lot of fun which simultaneously offers plenty of food for thought. There's much in this book that I agree with, and much that I disagree with. But being the comic book/super-hero geek I am, this tome could fuel enough heated and passionate conversations with all my geek friends to last us a full year on the comic con circuit."

—Michael Uslan, *Executive Producer and originator of the Batman movie franchise*

"Damien Picariello has assembled a top-notch collection of essays that student and professor alike will enjoy immensely. *Politics in Gotham* uses the Batman universe to help explain central issues in political life and thought in a way that is as pedagogically useful as it is just plain fun to read."

—Justin S. Vaughn, *Co-editor of* Poli Sci Fi: An Introduction to Political Science through Science Fiction *(2016)*

"This new collection on Batman and political theory includes thought-provoking essays on heroism, feminism, sovereignty, policing, and the politics of fear. The volume also features perceptive contributions on Christopher Nolan's *Dark Knight* trilogy. While the recent expansion in comics scholarship has been largely driven by researchers in literary studies, media studies, and cultural studies, Damien K. Picariello's book makes it clear that political theorists have a great deal to offer when it comes to the study of Batman, superheroes, and popular culture."

—Kent Worcester, *Professor of Political Science, Marymount Manhattan College, USA, and coeditor of* A Comics Studies Reader *(2008) and* The Superhero Reader *(2013)*

Contents

1 **Introduction: "I Don't Want Batman as President"** 1
Damien K. Picariello

2 **Justice Unmasked** 7
Alan I. Baily

3 ***The Dark Knight*: Toward a Democratic Tragedy** 23
Steven Johnston

4 **The Heroism of *Sober Expectations*** 39
Damien K. Picariello

5 **Deconstructing Batman's Legitimacy: The Radical Political Critique of Christopher Nolan's Batman Cycle** 57
William J. Berger

6 **Batman the Noble Dog: The Costs of Spiritedness for the Individual and Society** 75
Ian J. Drake and Matthew B. Lloyd

7 **The Dark Prince of the Republic: Machiavelli, Batman, and Gotham City** 91
Anthony Petros Spanakos

8 **The Lion, the Fox, and the Bat: The Animal Nature of Machiavelli's *The Prince* and Batman** 107
Daniel V. Goff

9 **Criminal Justice in Gotham: The Role of the Dark Knight** 123
Mark D. White

10 **The Retributive Knight** 141
Mohamad Al-Hakim

11 **Politics as "the Product of Everything You Fear": Scarecrow as Phobia Entrepreneur** 159
Christina M. Knopf

12 **#FAKENEWS in Gotham City** 177
Salvatore James Russo

13 **Batgirls and the Politics of Feminism in Gotham** 195
Carolyn Cocca

14 **Dawn of Justice: Revisioning, Accountability, and Batman in the Twenty-first Century** 213
Aidan Diamond

Index 233

Notes on Contributors

Mohamad Al-Hakim is Assistant Professor of Philosophy at Florida Gulf Coast University. He specializes in political, legal, and moral philosophy with special focus on hate crimes and social justice.

Alan I. Baily is Associate Professor in the Department of Government at Stephen F. Austin State University. He has published essays on Plato, *The Big Lebowski*, Thomas Carlyle, and Christopher Lasch. He lives in Nacogdoches, Texas, with his wife Meredith, their seven pets, and at least one bat.

William J. Berger is a fellow with the philosophy, politics, and economics program at the University of Pennsylvania. He works on topics of inequality, polarization, and trust that lie on the intersection of empirical and normative political science. He has been crafting this chapter, in some form, since the 1992 premier of Batman: The Animated Series.

Carolyn Cocca is Professor of Politics, Economics, and Law at the State University of New York, College at Old Westbury. She teaches courses about US politics, law, and gender studies and is a recipient of the State University of New York Chancellor's Award for Excellence in Teaching. She has served as Director of the College at Old Westbury Women's Center and obtained and directed a US$200,000 grant from the US Department of Justice's Office of Violence Against Women to train all campus units to have a coordinated and effective response to sexual assault, domestic and dating violence, and stalking, as well as establishing educational programs geared toward preventing such violence. She is the author of *Jailbait: The Politics of Statutory Rape Laws in the United States* and the editor of *Adolescent Sexuality*. She has written numerous articles and book chapters about gender, sexuality, and the law as well as about gender, sexuality, and superhero comics, and her latest book, *Superwomen: Gender, Power, and Representation,* won the 2017 Will Eisner Comic Industry Award in the Best Academic/Scholarly Work category.

Aidan Diamond is a PhD student at the University of Southern California, where she studies comparative media. Her work, which has been published in *Studies in Comics* and the *Journal of Graphic Novels and Comics*, as well as *The Ascendance of Harley Quinn*, focuses on graphic narrative and body politics. Since 2015, she has presented in Canada, America, the United Kingdom, and Australia. In 2016, she co-organized the *Mixing Visual Media in Comics* conference in St. John's, Newfoundland, with Nancy Pedri and Lauranne Poharec. This is her first work on film.

Ian J. Drake is Associate Professor of Jurisprudence at Montclair State University in New Jersey. He obtained his PhD in American history from the University of Maryland at College Park. His teaching interests include the American judiciary and legal system, the US Supreme Court and constitutional history, the history and contemporary study of law and society, broadly construed, and political theory. Prior to earning his PhD in history, Drake practiced law in the areas of insurance and tort law.

Daniel V. Goff is a Marine Corps CH-53E pilot and assigned to the USMC's Strategic Initiatives Group at the Pentagon. As a student in Salve Regina's Humanities PhD program LtCol Goff studies the moral and ethical implications of human enhancement with special emphasis on the military considerations and interpretations of transhumanist philosophy.

Steven Johnston is Neal A. Maxwell Presidential Chair at the University of Utah. He is the author of *Wonder and Cruelty: Ontological War in 'It's a Wonderful Life'* (Lexington Books, Politics, Literature & Film series, 2019); *Lincoln: The Ambiguous Icon* (Rowman & Littlefield, Modernity and Political Thought series, 2018); *American Dionysia: Violence, Tragedy, and Democratic Politics* (2015); *The Truth about Patriotism* (2007); and *Encountering Tragedy: Rousseau and the Project of Democratic Order* (1999).

Christina M. Knopf is Assistant Professor of Communication and Media Studies at the State University of New York (SUNY) Cortland. She is the author of *The Comic Art of War: A Critical Study of Military Cartoons, 1805–2014, with a Guide to Artists* (2015). She also has articles appearing in several journals and multiple anthologies, including *Cultures of War in Graphic Novels: Violence, Trauma, and Memory* (2018), *Working Class Comic Book Heroes: Class Conflict and Populist Politics in Comics* (University Press of Mississippi, 2018), and *The Ten Cent War: Comic Books, Propaganda, and World War II* (2017). Knopf has a PhD in political communication and cultural sociology from the University at Albany.

Matthew B. Lloyd has been collecting, reading, and studying comics for nearly 40 years. He holds an MA from the University of Louisville in Art History with a concentration in Ancient Art. He is a reviewer for DCComicsNews.com.

Damien K. Picariello is Assistant Professor of Political Science at the University of South Carolina Sumter. He teaches courses on American politics, film and politics, and political theory. His written work focuses on literature, film, and politics, as well as ancient, modern, and American political thought. It is his considered opinion that *The Dark Knight Rises* is the best of the trilogy.

Salvatore James Russo (Tulane University, BA, Fordham University School of Law JD, University of Mississippi, MA, PhD) is Assistant Professor of Political Science and Constitutional Law at California State University-Dominguez Hills. His research focuses on influences on political behavior, including legal institutions, mass media, and religion, as well as Southern Politics.

Anthony Petros Spanakos is Professor and Chair of Political Science and Law at Montclair State University. He is writing a book on domestic political change in Brazil and Venezuela and researching on the changes in global politics resulting from the emergence of countries like China and Brazil. His research has been published in *Comparative Political Studies, Latin American Politics and Society, Latin American Perspectives*, and *East Asian Policy*, as well as other academic journals. He is the co-editor of *Reforming Brazil* (2004) and *Conceptualising Comparative Politics* (2015) and a special issue on "the Legacy of Hugo Chavez" of *Latin American Perspectives* (2017). He is also the co-editor of the *Conceptualising*

Comparative Politics book series for Routledge. He was a Fulbright Fellow (Brazil 2002, Venezuela 2008) and a visiting research fellow at the East Asian Institute (2009).

Mark D. White is Chair of the Department of Philosophy at the College of Staten Island/City University of New York (CUNY) in New York City, where he teaches courses in philosophy, economics, and law. He is the author of seven books, including *Batman and Ethics*, and editor or co-editor of nearly 20 more, including *Batman and Philosophy* (with Robert Arp).

List of Figures

Fig. 4.1	"This is not how man was supposed to live," Rā's al Ghūl tells Bruce Wayne	46
Fig. 4.2	Harvey Dent tells Batman: "You thought we could be decent men in an indecent time. But you were wrong...the only morality in a cruel world is chance"	50
Fig. 4.3	A celebration to honor Harvey Dent and the Dent Act	51
Fig. 5.1	The Joker confronts Batman. Screengrabs generated by Yosef Washington for the author	61
Fig. 5.2	Batman becomes what Gotham needs him to be	67
Fig. 5.3	Bane as a populist rhetorician	68
Fig. 11.1	Scarecrow in the *Arkham Knight* videogame wears a gas mask and suicide-bomber vest reminiscent of terrorist imagery. (Screen shot from video game trailer)	167
Fig. 11.2	Scarecrow is an anarchist in the *Injustice 2* videogame; his crow-feathered costume suggests misfortune and death. (Screen shot from video game trailer)	168

CHAPTER 1

Introduction: "I Don't Want Batman as President"

Damien K. Picariello

It's natural to open up a collection like this and ask, somewhat skeptically, "What does Batman have to do with politics?"

The answer, as I hope you'll see as you begin to look over our chapters, is: A lot.

Consider Batman's origin story. The earliest depiction of this story has a young Bruce Wayne making a solemn vow following his parents' murder: "And I swear by the spirits of my parents to avenge their deaths by spending the rest of my life warring on all criminals."[1]

Where's the politics in that? Well, for starters, bringing criminals to justice is a job that we entrust to our governments. And it's a complicated job, so complicated, in fact, that it necessitates an entire criminal justice system, with layer upon layer of procedural rules for every step of the process, all of which are subject to public dispute and, if needed, revision.

Compare this to Bruce Wayne's pledge: He'll spend the rest of his life "warring on all criminals." How does this square with our societal commitment to criminal justice? What's the difference between this commitment and a war on crime of the sort to which Wayne dedicates himself?

D. K. Picariello (✉)
University of South Carolina Sumter, Sumter, SC, USA
e-mail: PICARIED@uscsumter.edu

D. K. Picariello (ed.), *Politics in Gotham*,
https://doi.org/10.1007/978-3-030-05776-3_1

Are the two compatible, and if so, in what sense? Or are the two opposed, and if so, is Batman's war on crime good or bad?

Asking this last question points us to the broader question of justice, perhaps the ultimate political question. Is Batman's war on crime just? If so, then what does this tell us about the relationship between justice and law? If not, then why do we celebrate his actions (at least, most of the time)? And what do we mean by "justice," anyway? How does the pursuit of justice fit with Batman's desire to "avenge" his parents' deaths? If we are committed to building a just society, does this society have a place in it for Batman?

That's a lot of political questions, and all we did was look at one line from one comic.

As we continue, it's worthwhile to quote, at length, from an interview with Frank Miller, the primary creative force behind the innovative and seminal *The Dark Knight Returns*. Miller says:

> When I create a story I take a very small thing and make it very big. It just happens to be the way I make my fiction. Someone mugs me and I make a Batman comic, to put it in the crudest possible terms. While there is room for political parody and while there is political meaning in all of this, presenting a hero is not presenting a case for political power. I don't want Batman as president, and I don't think the book says that at all. There's a tendency to see everything as a polemic, as a screed, when after all these are adventure stories. They can have a lot of ramifications, they can bring in an awful lot of other material, but anyone who really believes that a story about a guy who wears a cape and punches out criminals is a presentation of a political viewpoint, and a presentation of a program for how we should live our lives under a political system, is living in a dream world.[2]

It's important to recognize the ways in which Miller's words ring true, and remind us not to get ahead of ourselves. Miller's Batman is not going to tell us who to vote for, no matter how much we parse the text and subtext of *The Dark Knight Returns*. Christopher Nolan's *Dark Knight* trilogy, despite the mountain of politically charged interpretation and criticism focusing on the films, does not make a serious, intelligible case for a particular political party or program. As Miller says, "adventure stories" about "a guy who wears a cape and punches out criminals" are not arguments for "how we should live our lives under a political system…"

At the same time, Batman lives and acts within a political community, and he does things that we tend to think of as the exclusive province of our political authorities. Batman is inescapably political: He may not tell us how to vote, but he can certainly get us thinking about politics. In this sense, Miller is right if we're thinking about politics as who we should vote for and which policies we should support, but his warning seems a bit less urgent if we take a step back and consider some of the larger questions of politics, the fundamental or permanent questions, questions like those raised earlier, questions like: What is justice? What is a good political community? What is democracy (or liberty, or equality), and what does it require?

The chapters in this book don't provide definitive answers to these questions, but they do use Batman and the Batman universe as a provocative window through which to approach some of these questions with fresh eyes and to come away, perhaps, with fresh insights.

The chapters to follow explore the politics of Batman from a great many starting points, and they take their discussions in a great many different directions. Nevertheless, they have a couple of important things in common.

The first thing these chapters have in common is that they consider Batman (and, often, other characters in the Batman universe) not in isolation but rather in the context of a broader political community. After all, we can't talk about the politics of Batman without situating him within a community; politics is something that people do together, not alone. Some of these chapters consider the significance of Batman's work for the political community of Gotham City, and some of them consider the connections between politics in Gotham and politics in our own communities. Some of them do both. But all of them consider Batman and his allies and adversaries in the context of political community, asking what we might learn from such consideration.

The second thing these chapters have in common is that they all begin with the Batman universe and point outwards. They take an element of the Batman universe—usually, but not always, Batman—and use this as a starting point for a broader discussion of an issue or theme in politics and political thought. The Batman universe works in each of these chapters as a provocation, a spur, pointing us toward larger questions about politics and the political community. Other studies have sought primarily to understand Batman, his evolution, and his place in our culture; the chapters collected here use Batman and the Batman universe as a particularly interesting point of entry into broader conversations.[3] Our discussions start with Batman, but they don't end there.

Our first chapter, "Justice Unmasked" by Alan I. Bailey, begins by discussing the polarized and politically charged reactions to Christopher Nolan's *Dark Knight* trilogy. From here, Bailey introduces us to several of the concerns that will occupy much of our volume: The status of Batman as a citizen of Gotham; the differences between law, justice, and vengeance; and the question of Batman's impact on his political community. All of these themes appear repeatedly in subsequent chapters.

Our next several chapters focus on Christopher *Nolan's Dark Knight* trilogy, and they ask about the status of Nolan's Batman within Nolan's Gotham. Steven Johnston argues that Nolan's films raise interesting issues for democratic political communities but ultimately offer unsatisfying answers to these questions. Nolan's Batman, says Johnston, acts (and encourages others to act) in ways that ultimately undermine the democratic aspirations of his city. In my own chapter, "The Heroism of 'Sober Expectations,'" I take a different view, and I argue that in not expecting too much from his fellow citizens, Nolan's Batman has a great deal in common with America's founders. Finally, William J. Berger uses Nolan's films to discuss the legitimacy of Batman's actions and points out the unstable ground on which this legitimacy rests.

Our next few chapters situate Batman in the context of the history of political thought and use concepts drawn from this history to analyze the caped crusader. Ian J. Drake and Matthew B. Lloyd discuss Batman in the context of Plato's tripartite division of the human soul and ask about the consequences—for the city of Gotham and for Batman himself—of a soul governed by spiritedness rather than reason. Tony Spanakos puts Batman's actions in the context of Machiavelli's *Discourses on Livy* and suggests that Batman functions, in Gotham, as a particular kind of "republican prince," taking extraordinary action to correct imbalances in the city but never seizing political authority in perpetuity. Following on Spanakos's discussion of Machiavelli, Daniel J. Goff uses Machiavelli's *The Prince* to discuss Bruce Wayne's adoption of the bat as his animal trademark, as well as the significance of Batman's brand of theatrics for the city of Gotham.

In our next pair of chapters, our contributors discuss Batman's unique approach to crime and punishment. Mark D. White discusses Batman in the context of Gotham City's criminal justice system and asks about Batman's peculiar relationship to the city's law enforcement and legal institutions. In "The Retributive Night," Mohamad Al-Hakim explores Batman's treatment of criminals and tries to establish the Dark Knight's philosophy of punishment.

Each of our next three chapters tracks a particular development in American politics beyond the Batman universe and connects this to the development of a particular character or theme within the Batman universe. Christina M. Knopf tracks societal fears over time and connects this with representations of the Scarecrow; Salvatore James Russo examines the role of mass media in Gotham City and contrasts this with changing attitudes toward mass media among Americans; and Carolyn Cocca tracks changes in twentieth-century feminism and connects these to changes in the Batgirl character over time. All three of these chapters try to use the element of the Batman universe they discuss as a window into politics in the "real world."

Our final chapter follows on an observation that Geoff Klock makes about Frank Miller's *The Dark Knight Returns*: Miller's work is "not so much violent as it is more graphic and more realistic about the violence that *has always inhabited* superhero narratives."[4] Aidan Diamond extends this insight to *Batman v. Superman: Dawn of Justice*, asking us to consider the politics of Batman's violence within (and beyond) this notably violent film.

Nearly all of our contributors—and, yes, even our editor—are academics. But we hope that this collection is of interest to a wide variety of readers, both within the academy and beyond. We come from a variety of academic disciplines—political science, philosophy, communication studies, comparative media, and more—and when we all come together in a collection like this, we know we can't count on our fellow authors sharing our own academic backgrounds. So we've tried as best we can to write in a way that's both broadly accessible and intellectually rigorous: We've tried to write, in a sense, to each other.

Of course, we hope that our audience won't just be one another! We hope that you, dear reader—whether you're a professor, a student, a Batman fan, or just someone who liked the cover—will enjoy what we've put together and maybe even learn something from it. We invite you to join us as we explore politics and political thought through the lens of the Batman universe.

As editor of this volume, I'd like first and foremost to thank our contributors, who have put together what I think are an excellent group of chapters. I'm grateful for the support of my colleagues at the University of South Carolina Sumter and for funding facilitated by the USC Sumter Summer Stipend Committee and the USC Sumter Williams-Brice-Edwards Faculty and Staff Screening Committee; special thanks are due to

Mike Sonntag and Eric Reisenauer for their help and support in this regard. Thanks to Michelle Chen at Palgrave for her enthusiasm for this project and for tirelessly answering incessant questions and to John Stegner at Palgrave for his help in preparing the manuscript. I'm grateful to Joshua Raynor at DCComicsNews.com for helping us connect with folks in the comics world. This project would not have come to fruition were it not for the encouragement, help, and friendship of Andy Kunka, who knows everyone and everything, and is due tremendous thanks. Finally, I'm grateful to Lenny and Jil Picariello, Alex Picariello, and—as always, and deeply—Erin.

Notes

1. This account is informed by Will Brooker, *Batman Unmasked* (New York: Continuum, 2005), 53 and forward. Discussions of this same scene appear in several of the chapters to follow.
2. Christopher Sharrett, "Batman and the Twilight of the Idols: An Interview with Frank Miller," in *The Many Lives of the Batman: Critical Approaches to a Superhero and his Media*, eds. Roberta E. Pearson and William Uricchio (New York: Routledge, Chapman and Hall, 1991), 43.
3. For instance: Will Brooker, *Batman Unmasked* (New York: Continuum, 2005); Will Brooker, *Hunting the Dark Knight: Twenty-First Century Batman* (London: I.B. Tauris & Co., 2012); Roberta E. Pearson and William Uricchio, eds., *The Many Lives of the Batman: Critical Approaches to a Superhero and his Media* (New York: Routledge, Chapman and Hall, 1991).
4. Geoff Klock, "The Revisionary Superhero Narrative," in *The Superhero Reader*, ed. Charles Hatfield, Jeet Heer, and Kent Worcester (Jackson, MS: University Press of Mississippi, 2013), 119, emphasis mine.

CHAPTER 2

Justice Unmasked

Alan I. Baily

The Dark Knight Polarizes

Like many disputes in American politics, views of Christopher Nolan's *Dark Knight* trilogy run to extremes. Consider the following reactions to the trilogy's concluding film, *The Dark Knight Rises*: Conservative writer Bradley J. Birzer claims that *The Dark Knight Rises* "was not only the best of the three [*Batman* films directed by Nolan] but is arguably one of the finest films ever made." Even more strikingly, he continues, "[it] may also be the single most important defense of Western civilization ever to reach a Hollywood screen."[1]

Left-wing thinker and Occupy activist David Graeber disagrees on both points. He insists that "the film really is a piece of anti-occupy propaganda," not a spectacular vindication of Western civilization. Moreover, he judges it a poor spectacle on its own terms: "We went to the theater… in much the spirit of someone who was not a racist, or a Nazi, and would go to watch a screening of *Birth of a Nation* or *Triumph of the Will*. We expected the movie to be hostile, even offensive. But none of us expected it to be bad."[2]

A. I. Baily (✉)
Department of Government, Stephen F. Austin State University,
Nacogdoches, TX, USA
e-mail: bailyai@sfasu.edu

D. K. Picariello (ed.), *Politics in Gotham*,
https://doi.org/10.1007/978-3-030-05776-3_2

What Birzer sees as the movie's virtues Graeber views as vices. For Birzer, the merits of Nolan's *The Dark Knight* flow from two creative choices: "First, [Nolan] brought the characters into the realm of realism. They reside in the actual world, not a fantasy world… Second, Nolan fashioned his central character not from the pastel pages of a comic book but rather from America's western legend…"[3] In Birzer's view these choices result in a "powerful" cinematic narrative that speaks to a sense of national character which, like the "western legend, or myth, [is] larger than any single person, event or even culture."[4]

Graeber likewise emphasizes the movie's realism and its relationship to the western legend, yet he insists "that it's precisely the desire for relevance…which ruins the movie."[5] For Graeber, the effort to create a fictional world whose social and economic turmoil resembles the early twenty-first century (not just the French Revolution, as Nolan claims) results in a narrative that "stutters into incoherence." Graeber, too, sees a link between the Western civilization and Nolan's *The Dark Knight*,[6] but he highlights the protagonist's broody inwardness rather than the outward extension of Western, or any, civilization.

In a New Left twist on the classic psychoanalytic critique of comics, Graeber suggests that superheroes, like their adolescent male fans, "are purely reactionary. By this [he means] 'reactionary' in the literal sense: [as heroes] they simply react to things; they have no projects of their own."[7] The implicit political teaching of classic comic stories was Rightist in the sense that it offered "a warning about the dangers of human imagination."[8] Most comic books depict a *cosmos* where "God, or The People, simply doesn't exist," so, inevitably, the only catalyst for change is the nihilistic interplay of "shifting lines of force." Thus, the comic-book cosmos in extremis is "inherently fascist." And as comics have aspired to become politically serious and superheroes have developed "complex interiority," this Right-wing politics of imagination has come to the fore.[9]

From this perspective Graeber judges that Nolan's second film, *The Dark Knight*

> …began to fall flat the moment it touches on popular politics. The People make one lame attempt to intervene in the beginning…when copycat Batmen appear all over the city, inspired by the Dark Knight's example. Of course they all die horribly…From then on, they're put back in their place, as Audience, who like the mob in the Roman amphitheater exist only to judge the protagonists' performance …The end, when Bruce and

> Commissioner Gordon settle on the plan to scapegoat Batman and create a false myth around the martyrdom of Harvey Dent, is nothing short of a confession that politics is identical to the art of fiction.[10]

Back at the other ideological pole, Birzer expresses astonishment that "severe cultural liberals" did not bother to "rip to shreds" a spectacle that vindicates Western civilization so effectively. For Birzer, Nolan's *The Dark Knight* is in a class apart from other superhero stories and it is truer than other representations of Batman. After all, Batman was always more realistic than most superheroes. His "super" powers are merely human and technological, and Bruce Wayne's "complex interiority" seems inherent to his tragic origin story. Nolan's genius involved "tapping into" deep elements of Batman's character and *mythos* that have always been present "but not explicitly understood by the larger public." These include Bruce's namesake, "the Revolutionary War general, Mad Anthony Wayne," and the legendary King Arthur, whose retinue prefigures "Gotham Knights."[11]

As Birzer sees it, Nolan's *The Dark Knight* reveals Batman's descent from the deepest archetypes of heroism in the West:

> In Nolan's expert hands, Batman becomes what he always meant to be, an American Odysseus, an American Aeneas, an American Arthur, an American Beowulf, and an American Thomas More. Indeed, it would be hard to find another figure in popular and literary culture that more embodies the traditional heroism of the West more than in the figure of Bruce Wayne. He most closely resembles Aeneas, carrying on the culture of charity and sacrifice into the darkest and most savage parts of his world. Like St. Michael, he guards the weak, the poor, and the innocent. Like Socrates, he will die for Athens (Gotham) as it should be rather than as it is. Like Beowulf, he asks nothing for himself, merely the opportunity to wage the never-ending war against evil.[12]

Birzer belongs to the camp of Bat-fans for whom it is irreverent to treat the Dark Knight as anything less than a paragon of heroic virtue and moral seriousness. Indeed, he suggests, our very civilization hinges on how our artists and audiences comport with Batman. "If we treat him like a clown, as did the 1960s TV series, we do not know who he is—or who we are. If we treat him like a Gothic carnival freak, as did Tim Burton, same thing. If we treat him as the great American hero and symbol of an urban age, as did Nolan, we have a chance at survival."[13]

For Graeber, however, *The Dark Knight*'s only redeeming quality is to reveal the abjuration of political consciousness at the heart of the comic-book *mythos*. Thus, as realistic as the action was onscreen, Graeber is convinced that historical reality intervened

> quite decisively to point out just how wrong this vision is. The economy collapsed. Not because of the manipulations of some secret society of warrior monks, but because a bunch of financial managers who, living in Nolan's bubble world, shared his assumptions about the endlessness of popular manipulability, turned out to be wrong.[14]

Raising Comic Consciousness: *Superman* Versus *Batman*

In different ways, Birzer's and Graeber's visions of *The Dark Knight* are constrained by the lenses through which they see it. Birzer's image of "Western civilization" is an artifact of the Cold War era. He identifies our modern civilization too easily with those of Greece, Rome, and Europe's past, overlooking crucial differences. Graeber's emphasis on contemporary concerns about the power of ideology and spectacular media to exploit global audiences is apt. Yet, to accept Graeber's claim that "history" pierced the surface of "Nolan's bubble world," one must believe that history's signals are easy to decipher, that false consciousness is easy to diagnose, that illusory visions of history afflict mainly privileged people who dwell in "bubbles," and that an intellectual or social position beyond all "bubbles" is available. These assumptions, too, are beholden to Cold War-era intellectual movements, and their limits are increasingly apparent.

Rather than beginning with a particular vison of Western civilization or a general theory about comic-book consciousness, it is better to begin with the *Batman mythos* itself. What is it about *Batman* that appeals so strongly to twenty-first-century audiences? We can begin to answer this question by comparing Superman to Batman. Superman was a fitting icon for Cold War civilization, whose official ethos linked "truth, justice and the American way." Batman has been the most compelling superhero of the age of globalization—an age where the link between truth and justice seems more tenuous but in which the capacity to renegotiate that relationship through politics seems beyond reach. The Man of Steel is an assimilated alien. The Dark Knight is an alienated citizen.

"Alienation" has been associated with both adolescent and political longing, and in *Batman* these two senses of alienation—personal and political—are entwined. Part of Bruce Wayne's personality seems stuck in adolescence. As a result *Batman* constantly reminds its chiefly adolescent readers of the quixotic nature of comic-book heroism—its mixture of high seriousness and comic absurdity. What other superhero could receive interpretations as varied as the campy *Batman '66* and the brooding *Dark Knight*? Fans may reject one or another of these interpretations but both are genuine: The campy *Batman* reminds us that we're indulging in adolescent fantasy, while the gritty *Dark Knight* encourages serious reflection on the importance of heroes and symbols, as well as the power, and limits, of symbolic action to affect the world.

An erstwhile citizen, Bruce Wayne is alienated from Gotham—the city he seems to love but cannot trust. Umberto Eco wrote that Superman-in-Metropolis is "a perfect example of civic consciousness, completely split from political consciousness."[15] Alternatively, Batman-in-Gotham exemplifies civic consciousness struggling to articulate itself in the face of political failure. Batman is a character stuck in between the civic and the political. He is motivated by a personal cause and operates on the margins of legality but he crusades for the city, to enforce its law, albeit surreptitiously. He is a provisional vigilante sustained by the hope that Gotham will rise again, making his work unnecessary. Accordingly he refuses to exercise the ultimate state power—lethal force.

The Personal and the Political

Bruce Wayne (cum Batman) does have a project, both personal and political. He fashions his own freakish and idiosyncratic identity but does so for the city's sake, hoping to inspire it through its crisis and to terrorize those who would subvert it. Rooted in the injustice of his parents' murder, Wayne's dedication to becoming Batman is profoundly personal. But rather than seek vengeance upon the perpetrator, he seeks justice for the whole city. This crusade for justice is the political side of his project. Resisting the urge for revenge, Wayne commits himself to Gotham—swearing an oath "by the spirits of my parents, to avenge their deaths by spending the rest of my life warring on all criminals."[16]

Wayne's vow to battle crime converts the awful fact of his parents' mortality into an occasion for meaning-making and self-discipline. The experience of personal tragedy disabuses him of naïve faith in the justice of the world but he refuses to succumb to equally naïve cynicism about the pursuit of justice. At the heart of his political crusade for Gotham is a personal quest to redeem tragedy. These two aspects are united in a project of self-creation—becoming Batman.

Bruce's personal-political project is naïve but instructively so. To grasp the edifying absurdity of *Batman* we must consider it in light of problems inherent to political justice. How can we tell between a hunger for vengeance and a crusade for justice? Can a political crisis be so severe that individuals may take the law into their own hands? Are the obligations of citizenship wholly compatible with the prerogatives of selfhood? These questions may be answered in different ways, but it is only in political life that we ask them. And political questions such as these are more essential to *Batman*'s *mythos* than, say, *Superman*'s.

Political myths do not answer political questions but they can provoke us to consider them. To ask such questions is to pass beyond the horizons of a particular political community into a wider reflection on political justice itself. These vistas form the topography of philosophy and poetry. Batman's personal and political struggles in a corrupted Gotham City dramatize the questions of political justice for a modern urban audience.

Before further discussion of Bruce's personal project, then, we must distinguish a *political* conception of justice from other senses of "justice," of the sort we encounter in theology, ideology, or personal conviction. Theology may conceive of a just God, but even if God is lawful and reasonable, and the divine law is made available to God's people, this law still is not *public* in the sense of being endorsed and administered by a human political community. Should a community attempt to administer divine law or justice, it would still do so as a human, political, community. (Even churches are "political" institutions insofar as they are administered by flawed mortals.) In modern times, ideological conceptions of justice have also been influential. Ideologies tend to eschew theological claims in favor of rationalistic ones, but ideological "laws" are not lawful in the political sense of being recognized publically or chosen by a particular people. Regimes based solely upon ideology have been characterized by secrecy, repression, and distrust. In most cases they have ended in failure. Finally, we must differentiate political justice from personal judgment. This is a challenging task since public institutions must appeal to something more than abstract logic if they are to motivate personal allegiance. Still, the personal and political cannot be identical if only because the personal realm of conscience is "private" and opaque rather than "public" and transparent. Ultimately, it is not possible to translate a personal sense of "justice" into public codes, nor can political power force a change in a person's conscience or character rather than their behavior.

The problem of personal "justice" is central to *Batman*. There is always a tension between the personal and political, but in modern life it takes a different form than it did in ancient or medieval life. Those earlier orders relied on status systems that recognized hierarchical relations among public personages—like medieval feudalism with its kings, lords, knights, and serfs. Against this, modern democrats appealed to ancient models of political rule, especially democracy. Although ancient citizens, too, defined their freedom in terms of personal status (in opposition to enslaved persons, women, and noncitizens), the classical democratic *polis* introduced the principle of *isonomia*, which is similar to modern "equality under the law." This meant that in spite of kinship ties, political allegiances, or differences of wealth or capability, citizens were entitled to equal treatment before the public judge. In democratic Athens, citizens also could vote, serve in office, speak in the public forum, and initiate prosecution in the courts.

Modern democratic movements sought to eliminate status-based authority altogether, in favor of a more egalitarian regime made possible through an impersonal legal order. This meant reimagining civilization in terms of contractual ties formed by reasonable agreement among free and equal individuals. Rather than owing personal obedience to a lord, modern citizens are bound together through impersonal institutions that represent the whole "people." And, because offenses against the law are seen as violations not only of the victim but of the "people," a public advocate holds exclusive rights to prosecute alleged criminals in the courts. As a result, the institutionalized public prosecutor (such as the Attorney General or the District Attorney) is a unique feature of modern republics.

Because public prosecutors are elected officials, a tension exists in modern regimes between the political imperatives of partisan competition (i.e. electoral politics) and the official duty to uphold the law impartially. Modern political fiction, including *Batman*, exploits this tension to dramatic effect. The relationship between Batman and Harvey Dent is exemplary: An elected representative rather than a vigilante, Dent (cum Two-Face) is a sort of fun-house reflection of Batman. Like Batman, Dent has the medieval moniker of a "Knight"—the White Knight to Wayne's Dark. Dent rose to his station by securing the voters' allegiance.

Wayne rose to his by a vast personal inheritance. Dent seeks status through Gotham's politics but Wayne's social status compels him to hide from Gotham's gaze. Dent embodies faith in Gotham but his faith is weak. Wayne embodies doubt in Gotham but his loyalty is strong. When Dent's faith is shattered, he assumes an *alter ego* that signifies a schism between the personal and political sides of modern justice; his impersonal, amoral, coin-flips replace deliberate arbitration with blind arbitrariness. When Wayne's faith is shattered, he assumes an *alter ego* that signifies the blindness appropriate to political justice but not the public transparency of due process. Both are prosecutors, but one is silent. Finally, Dent's career in *The Dark Knight* exemplifies the tragic flaw of political mythmaking: To prevent Dent's fall from becoming Gotham's, too, Batman must supplement fiction with falsehood and confess to Two-Face's crimes.

The Inheritance

To elucidate more fully *Batman*'s personal-political *mythos*, we need to attend more closely to Bruce Wayne's inheritance and what he makes of it. Obviously Bruce's wealth adds to the realism of *Batman*. Without it, he could not dedicate himself to his heroic project. Aside from supplying necessary resources, the Wayne wealth and family name give Bruce a prominent status in the city. He uses his public status as a philanthropist and "playboy" to provide cover for his subterranean *alter ego*.

It is a mistake to exaggerate the importance of Wayne's money and status any further than this, because it overlooks Bruce's most important inheritance. That inheritance is the knowledge that some things, like life, are beyond all price. One needn't lose one's parents or loved ones in order to learn that life is priceless, but nothing teaches this more effectively. Bruce's true inheritance is knowledge beyond doubt of each life's infinite value.

What does it mean to say that life is "priceless"? Lives are assigned monetary value all the time in our civilization. Bruce Wayne has a high net worth, for example. Other examples of pricing life include the actuarial values assigned to lives by public and private bureaucracies. (Administrators and courts and insurance agencies routinely use such figures to denominate compensation or benefits or damages.) These life-prices are indispensable conventions of civilization as we know it. But in the end no amount of income or wealth truly can compensate for the loss of a life because each person is unique and irreplaceable. This is why death is also known as a great equalizer. Bruce's parents' death reveals his fundamental equality with the least fortunate mortals in Gotham. In this light, the vastness of Wayne's fortune only emphasizes the impotence of wealth to alter the ultimate truth.

Death may result from human violence or natural causes. When life is taken in a violent transaction between humans it seems as if a debt has been incurred against the transgressor, which must be repaid. Like financial debt, the victim's death imposes on the living an obligation to settle accounts. In the case of *Batman*, Bruce inherits an obligation to exact the debt of life from those responsible for his parents' untimely demise. For this reason it seems quite plausible that Bruce would make his life project to "avenge their deaths"—but why does he do so by "warring on all criminals" and commit to this "for the rest of [his] life" rather than making quick work of Thomas and Martha's assailants? The answer requires closer examination of the link between the logic of vengeance and political justice.

If we did not suffer injuries that provoke the desire for revenge, it is not likely that we would have a concept of "justice" at all, let alone attempt to realize it through political institutions.[17] But we live in a second-best world where such injuries occur. Revenge may seem like the appropriate reply to a murder, but the logic of pricelessness implies a continuous taking of life for life—an interminable feud. Political justice aims to transcend this cycle by putting the authority of impersonal public arbitration above that of personal vendetta.

Political justice in this sense begins with the Greek *polis* (especially democratic Athens) which supplanted the system of kinship rule with public arbitration. Under the kinship system, rule was not "political" but "personal," so to speak. Kinship groups entered into alliances through ceremonial exchanges of personally meaningful gifts among their "heroes." By the same token, mortal injuries were addressed through feuds or ritualized forms of vendetta that reflected the circular logic of repaying priceless debt with priceless debt. Alternatively, *political* justice relies on the notion "that there is a distinct form of 'civil' or 'political' authority which is wholly autonomous, which exists to regulate the public affairs of a political community, and which brooks no rivals as a source of coercive power within its own *civitas* or *respublica*."[18]

In practice, political justice operates on the pretext that when a lawful court renders its verdict, an injury is redressed once and for all. The establishment of political justice did not eliminate but "privatized" the social functions of personal statuses and relationships. In modern societies, in particular, "the state" claims monopolistic authority to use punishment as a means to establish order, deter crime, and redress injury on behalf of a political community. As Marcel Henaff summarizes it, "modern societies rely on the law for ensuring mutual public recognition, on the market for organizing subsistence, and on private gift relationships for generating a social bond. But without this social bond…this founding relationship and mutual recognition, in which each ventures something that is part of oneself into the space of the other, no community can exist."[19]

Bruce Wayne's commitment to make war on "all criminals" rather than exact revenge on his parents' murderers is a choice for political justice and against vengeance. The injustice he suffered did not compel him to reject the law's authority in principle, but he does reject the state's administrators in practice. That is to say, Batman defines criminality in the same way modern society does but he chooses to pay back his injury and serve Gotham in an unusual manner, by warring for the rest of his life instead of relying on the courts or running for office or just being a good citizen. Wayne's choice is a response to suffering a rupture in the "founding relationship" or social bond. Gotham failed to prevent his parents' violent death—a tragedy that should not have occurred in a well-ordered city—and this leaves him marooned in a dark alley with no one to trust. Having been orphaned by the society to which he still belongs, Wayne can venture into it again only on a pretext of apathy. Meanwhile, as Batman, he serves the city by venturing into Gotham's dark alleys under a mask of terror. Understood in this way, the Dark Knight is a sort of "shadow sovereign." He invokes not the corruptible will of the citizenry, or its flawed officials, but the incorruptible *persona* of Gotham itself.

The modern, sovereign, state is distinguished in principle from natural persons, either individually or collectively. As Thomas Hobbes defined it, the sovereign is an "artificial person" or "mortal god" created for the purpose of terrorizing corruptible mortals into obedience to the law. Modern citizens' legal obligations are understood in terms of allegiance or loyalty to that artificial person. Such a sovereign *persona* can be incorruptible only because it is artificial, unlike flawed humans or institutions. But according to Jean Jacques Rousseau's refinement of Hobbes's notion, this impersonal person is also "purely moral."

Thus, political justice in the modern sense involves a second way of conceptualizing public authority. In the civic conception, discussed earlier,

> rulers or magistrates [are] entrusted with the exercise of [political] powers for the time being. But we also distinguish [the *state*'s] authority from that of the whole society or community over which its powers are exercised… Rather the state must be acknowledged to be an entity with a life of its own…at once distinct from both rulers and ruled and…able in consequence to call upon the allegiance of both parties.[20]

Batman's mask symbolizes Gotham's sovereignty because it prevents Bruce Wayne's *persona* from being identified with the state's majesty. Batman's *persona* is magnificent and terrifying, as befits sovereignty, but it is displayed only under the cover of night rather than in the splendor of day. By concealing Wayne's face, the cowl affirms the distinction between Gotham's moral authority as an artificial person and Wayne's subservient status as its agent. But in choosing to serve as Gotham's shadow sovereign, Wayne cum Batman assumes the authority to use terror as a substitute for the social bonds that Gotham lacks. It is to the consequences of this decision that we must, finally, turn.

The Mask

Western civilization depicts justice as blind because equality under the law demands indifference to distinctions of reputation, wealth, or virtue. This sort of "blindness" is an essential feature of public or political justice, and this understanding of justice defines Bruce Wayne's crusade against "all criminals." But Batman's cowl adds the aspect of terror, rendering Wayne into an avatar of righteous or legitimate violence on behalf of the city in which he has lost faith. Like a bat, justice is blind, but her blindfold is not a mask meant to incite terror.

What justifies the Dark Knight's extraordinary claim to authority? The answer can be found in Bruce Wayne's oath, which invokes a *radical conception of politics* rather than a *political conception of justice* to authorize his personal war against crime and corruption. This self-authorizing logic permits the Dark Knight to employ terror in his crusade to restore order in Gotham. It also situates "the criminal" beyond the reach of ordinary political justice.

The idea of criminality Batman relies upon is *legal* but as a vigilante he, too, is a criminal in the legal sense, if not in a *moral* sense. Batman's vigilantism is not authorized by the state so in this sense it is *politically* illegitimate as well. In the radical sense of the word, however, to struggle for the people in the face of a corrupt regime is "political" action *par excellence*, but as seductive as a masked avenger of the righteous may seem, righteous terrorism finally fails to restore political justice in Gotham.

Batman's conception of the criminal (as opposed to crime) is made plain in the same famous scene from *Detective Comics*, when Bruce Wayne alights upon the bat-disguise as a means to "strike terror" into the hearts of criminals: "Criminals are a superstitious cowardly lot. So my disguise must be able to strike terror into their hearts. I must be a creature of the night, black, terrible."[21] Defined in this way, the criminal is outside of the political community and so, for the sake of the law, may be denied the citizenly status of equal recognition. Reducing "the criminal" to a psychologically and morally inferior type implies political exile—such a person must not be open to human reason or citizenly persuasion. By the same token, this logic authorizes Batman to execute Gotham's law in a hidden and surreptitious manner, rather than publicly and transparently as is proper among citizens.

Instead of attempting to persuade, Batman's terrifying cowl aims to manipulate the "superstitious" and "cowardly" by targeting their psychological and moral weaknesses. We, the audience, may admire Batman's criminal conduct only if we do not regard it as *morally* culpable. But if the good criminal is distinguished from the bad one in purely moral-psychological terms, no *political* principle can be invoked at all. In this light, the significance of the bat-mask is that it situates the Dark Knight on the same level as the criminal whose activity is essentially concealed from public view.

Political justice is essentially public, centered upon "obligations that are identical for all and defined based upon the acceptance of common rules and public statuses in a community of free and equal individuals."[22] Revolutionary activists and reactionary vigilantes share a disregard for the public and institutional (or conventional) aspects of political justice. Both reject "common rules and public statuses" in their respective quests for "a community of free and equal individuals," as they envision it. In this way, both are able to rationalize the use of terror in pursuit of their objectives. It is instructive to read the bat-mask's visual rhetoric of lawful terror in light of the rhetoric and logic of revolutionary justice articulated by Maximilien Robespierre, the French revolutionary leader. Defending the use of terror as a technique of revolutionary justice, Robespierre wrote: "If the mainspring of popular government in peacetime is virtue, the mainspring of popular government in revolution is virtue and terror both: virtue, without which terror is disastrous; terror, without which virtue is powerless."[23]

A revolutionary rather than reactionary, the historical Robespierre is a sort of photo-negative of Batman. Like Batman, Robespierre was famous for being principled—his nickname was "incorruptible." As a lawyer in pre-revolutionary France, he resigned from a judgeship because he did not condone the death penalty for murderers, even though the state did.[24] But Batman refuses on principle to kill criminals, precisely because that power belongs to the still-legitimate (if ineffectual) state. During the revolution Robespierre became a killer, presiding over the Reign of Terror. A middle-class man, Robespierre earned the trust of the poor and thereby received their support in popular uprisings. Bruce Wayne, a billionaire, pacifies the poor with philanthropy and supports his personal crusade with his own gifts, discipline, and tools. Robespierre wanted to raze a corrupt regime and till the human soil beneath it with terror, in the foolish faith that virtue would spring from the ruins. Batman wants to light up Gotham's dark alleys with terror to deter the vicious criminal element, in the foolish faith that this could not corrupt what remains of the city's goodness. Robespierre defines criminals as the "enemy of the people." Batman defines "the people" as the enemy of the criminal. Both are terrorists, but one is silent. Robespierre's career is an example in history of the tragedy of ideological violence. *The Dark Knight* is an example in fiction of the tragedy of conservative violence—in the end, Gotham is no better than when he started, but henceforth City Hall will always compete with an idealized shadow sovereign for the people's fidelity.

Justice Unmasked

The mask protects Batman from being detected by the Gotham City Police Department or other bystanders. It allows Bruce Wayne to maintain his aloof "playboy" image while furtively playing the role of Gotham's savior—to do good while no one is watching. These are typical functions of superheroes' masks, but there is a compelling case for viewing *The Dark Knight*'s cowl in specifically political terms. As Charlie Jane Anders has written, typical "superhero movies treat the mask as a simple method of concealing the hero's identity—or just as part of the image of the character that's going on lunchboxes... But the Nolan Batman movies are fairly unique in the amount of time they spend talking about the mask as symbol."[25]

Unlike the immortal Man of Steel, whose super-heroic vocation befell him when he fell to Earth, the mortal Crusader is not merely reactionary. Batman's mask symbolizes a project of self-development, at once personal and political, arising from his own tragic fate. Nolan's accomplishment is to show that however necessary this project may seem, personally, it ultimately fails politically. Anders sheds light on this by reading *The Dark Knight Rises* in light of the entire trilogy: "Back in *Batman Begins*," she writes, "Ra's Al-Ghul talks a lot about the difference between a man and a legend," but in *The Dark Knight*, Wayne's personal effort to burnish a legendary image is compromised by the need to prop up the city's brand. "Batman was a legend, but now Harvey Dent is propaganda. It's not just that Harvey's martyrdom is a lie—but also, his myth is used to prop up the social order. The powers that be in Gotham are all invested in the Harvey Dent story." Finally, in *The Dark Knight Rises*, Bane is "basically a pure propagandist" who fails or refuses to distinguish between killing and image-making. "Bane's superpower is getting his enemies to accept his frame on reality."[26]

Tracing a line of descent from legendary *persona* to political myth, and finally, to pure propaganda, the *Dark Knight* trilogy belongs to a tradition of speculation on the psyche, the city, and the imagination. It is too much to celebrate Nolan's *The Dark Knight* as the last link in an unbroken chain of legendary Western heroes. But it is too little to dismiss it as reactionary propaganda for the early twenty-first century. Rather, if the *Dark Knight* trilogy draws a moral from Batman's *mythos*, it is one fashioned for a culture that regards spectacle as a supplement for a flawed system of justice: Rejecting an imperfect political order is not enough, because the resulting vacuum is likely to be filled with personal legends or political myths that cannot satisfy the needs they arise to meet. Eventually Gotham will rise again, transfigured, or its very idea will perish. Should Gotham perish, it might yield a world like the one before cities existed—except terrifying spectacles would be fodder for combat among the new heroes. And on private platforms built on the ruins of public forums, audiences would wait passively in reserve to be enlisted for their next battle.

Notes

1. Bradley J. Birzer, "Heroism and Realism in Christopher Nolan's Batman," *The American Conservative*. January 8, 2018. https://www.theamerican-conservative.com/archive/januaryfebruary-2018/
2. David Graeber, *The Utopia of Rules: On Technology, Stupidity, and the Secret Joys of Bureaucracy*, (New York, Melville House, 2015), 207.

3. Birzer, "Heroism and Realism."
4. Ibid. Birzer continues: "And there were no antiheroes in that cultural fare, focused on the daunting challenge of extending the essence of Western civilization to those forbidding and often dangerous lands of the Rocky Mountains and beyond."
5. Graeber, *Utopia*, 211.
6. Herein, *The Dark Knight* refers to Christopher Nolan's cinematic rendition of *Batman*. When referring to a particular film in Christopher Nolan's *Dark Knight* trilogy, the full title is used. "*Batman*" refers to the fictional universe and *mythos* associated with the DC Comics franchise. "Batman" and "Dark Knight" refer interchangeably to the fictional character of Batman.
7. Ibid.
8. Ibid., 219. Graeber continues: "For the Left, imagination, creativity, by extension production, the power to bring new things and new social arrangements into being, is always to be celebrated. It is the source of all real value in the world. For the Right, it is dangerous; ultimately, evil. The urge to create is also a destructive urge. This kind of sensibility was rife in the popular Freudianism of the day: where the Id was the motor of the psyche, but also amoral; if really unleashed, it would lead to an orgy of destruction."
9. Ibid., 217.
10. Ibid., 222.
11. Birzer, "Heroism and Realism."
12. Ibid.
13. Ibid.
14. Graeber, *Utopia*, 223.
15. Umberto Eco, "The Myth of Superman," *Diacritics* 2, No. 1 (1972): 22.
16. Bill Finger, *Detective Comics*, No. 33, (New York, DC Comics, 1939), 2.
17. Here I refer to corrective justice rather than distributive justice.
18. Quentin Skinner, "The State," in *Contemporary Political Philosophy: An Anthology*, edited by Robert E. Goodin and Philip Pettit, (Malden, MA, Blackwell, 2006), 10.
19. Marcel Henaff, *The Price of Truth: Gift, Money and Philosophy*, trans. by Jean-Louis Morhange and Anne-Marie Feenberg-Dibon, (Stanford, CA, Stanford University Press, 2010), 154.
20. Skinner, "The State," 13.
21. Finger, *Detective Comics*, 2.
22. Henaff, *Price*, 240.
23. Maximilien Robespierre, "On the Principles of Political Morality that Should Guide the National Convention in the Domestic Administration of the Republic," in *Virtue and Terror*, ed. by Jean Ducange and trans. by John Howe (Brooklyn, NY, Verso, 2007), 115.

24. In France, judges assign penalties. In Anglo-American courts, juries assign penalties unless a defendant forgoes a jury trial.
25. Charlie Jane Anders, "Nolan's Batman Trilogy: A Unique Achievement in Myth-Making," *io9*, July 20, 2012. https://io9.gizmodo.com/5927630/nolans-batman-trilogy-a-unique-achievement-in-myth-making
26. Ibid.

CHAPTER 3

The Dark Knight: Toward a Democratic Tragedy

Steven Johnston

Many understand Christopher Nolan's Batman trilogy by placing it in contemporary historical context, rendering it a commentary on life in the post-September 11 world where terror is an ever-present possibility and security proves at best elusive. Life can end without warning, and democratic institutions find themselves at a disadvantage vis-à-vis fanatical adversaries that respect no rules or norms of any kind. Under such circumstances, what can—what must—a democratic society do to defend itself?

It is also possible to think of Nolan's Batman films along more philosophical and cultural lines. They raise profound social and political dilemmas, perhaps especially regarding the role of violence in democratic life that American films have engaged since their inception. Westerns, for example, have proven to be an invaluable source of insight and provocation, perhaps especially the films of John Ford. Many of his classics deal with themes of founding (and refounding) a community and the terrible price it incurs.[1] I think Nolan's films operate, knowingly, on this more esoteric plane. They call for a democratic polity, whether it likes it or not,

S. Johnston (✉)
University of Utah, Salt Lake City, UT, USA
e-mail: steven.johnston@utah.edu

D. K. Picariello (ed.), *Politics in Gotham*,
https://doi.org/10.1007/978-3-030-05776-3_3

to reflect back on itself and its way of life precisely because as a political form it experiences existential problems and difficulties unique to it.

In *The Dark Knight*, the second installment of Nolan's Batman trilogy, Gotham finds itself with more than an endemic crime problem. It is under siege (even more so than in *Batman Begins*). The city's criminal class has been waging war against it, co-opting much of the police force in the process, thereby neutralizing traditional means of combating it. For Gotham, this dire situation is more than a question of safe streets. It is a question of legitimacy—and thus existence. The institutions that constitute a democratic way of life do not seem to possess the resources required to sustain it. Into this aporia steps the figure of Batman.

This troubling force represents the possibility of not just security but also political renewal or rebirth. Gotham has suffered serious decline, but elements critical to the city refuse to consider it irreversible. They believe they can save Gotham; they believe it worth saving. Yet the price of this aspiration haunts them. Can democracy maintain its values and ideals when it faces an existential crisis? What happens when it turns to violence and abandons its commitments to the rule of law, due process, and basic individual rights in order to regenerate itself? How can dubious means used to achieve a good end not compromise it? In short, what might a democracy look like in the aftermath of an extralegal campaign undertaken in its name?

The Dark Knight raises (or evokes) many of these questions. Yet the ultimate superficiality of these engagements, which is not simply reducible to the commercial nature of Hollywood productions, reveals its largely sophistical character. That is, Nolan's Batman films flirt with a tragic conception of life and politics but retreat full bore from it when faced with its unhappy consequences. The Batman hopes the day comes when his contributions to Gotham will no longer be required. Thus, it's not that the film doesn't address the problematic character of Batman's role and the actions he takes. It's that the film assumes Batman's interventions, once completed, can be effectively absorbed: forgotten, ignored, denied, and mythologized. Accordingly, when Batman finally leaves Gotham at the trilogy's conclusion, Nolan largely disregards the city's democratic condition, namely, whether it has survived the Batman's usurpations. This is in keeping with the trilogy's failure to take seriously its own democratic context in which more than the elimination of an urgent threat is at stake. The film, as a result, rejects the very idea that the Batman's greatest success necessarily entails the city's greatest failure. For a thought-provoking film, then, *The Dark Knight*, in the end, is disappointingly unthinking. This means that we must think for it—to render it less reactionary and thus less dangerous to democracy, its moments of affective inspiration notwithstanding.

Origins Story

At the conclusion of *Batman Begins*, the first in Nolan's trio of films, Batman had awakened a city and put its enemies on the defensive. He had brought down one criminal empire, and Gotham seemed on the verge of a turnaround—though nothing was guaranteed. Lieutenant James Gordon, mildly alarmed, noted that Batman had "started something." And not all of it necessarily good. When Batman insisted, "Gotham will return to normal," Gordon cited the possibility of not just retaliation but escalation. Given the pressure Batman had brought to bear on Gotham's underworld, the city would soon suffer an unintended consequence: the criminal class counterattacking, as Gordon feared, in a war for survival.[2] Gordon also warned Batman of an ominous new menace to the city, someone who had already committed armed robbery and double murder and enjoys "a taste for theatrics, like you," namely, the Joker, then unknown. Batman promised he would look into it.

This development would turn out to be more than just another case of a criminal exploiting Gotham's vulnerabilities. Batman's anti-crime campaign engendered a particularly perverse reaction that no one seems to have anticipated: not one more gangster who can make a fabulous living flouting the law, but a public enemy who lives to deny law's meaningful reality. Manohla Dargis describes the Joker as "arriv[ing] in Gotham abruptly, as if he'd been hiding up someone's sleeve."[3] That sleeve, of course, belongs to Batman, whose very presence accounts for the emergence of his antithesis. The most chilling moment of the first film, then, might just be the appearance of its title before the credits roll. The very words *Batman Begins* promise that what the audience has just seen was little more than an opening skirmish. It suggests that things are going to get worse, much worse, before they (might) get better.

Batman, of course, wanted something more than the (mere) restoration of law and order. Through his example, he hoped to inspire people so Gotham would no longer have need of his extralegal services. Batman aspired, in short, to make himself unnecessary. He wanted an independent, self-sufficient city with autonomous citizens. His only sign of success would be his (ultimate) disappearance. While *The Dark Knight* reveals early on that Batman did engender a handful of copycat vigilantes, these would-be do-gooders dressed in homemade Batman costumes were comically inept, causing numerous problems but solving none. Batman treated them with utter disdain.

Nevertheless, Batman operated on the premise that if one person took a public stand against lawlessness, however morally and politically problematic, others would follow suit. This idea required more than well-meaning words. It called for action, violent action in particular. To overcome a sense of victimhood, Gotham desperately needed to convert people from passive subjects to active, engaged citizens. In the case of Bruce Wayne, in *Batman Begins*, he witnessed the gratuitous murder of his parents during a robbery when he was a small boy. Unlike his father, who committed money to Gotham but took no direct action himself, including during the robbery, Bruce Wayne would not make the same mistake. He refused to be his father's son. He would combine power with violence. He ostensibly dedicates his life to the rule of law, but his motivation stems in part from a desire for vengeance (denied him when his parents' killer is murdered before he has the chance to do it himself).

This background does not discredit Batman's crusade, but it indicates the complicated character of justice and civic virtue. If the Batman could become an exemplar for taking back the streets, the idea was that he would make it impossible for people to sit on the sidelines and watch what was being done to their city. They would have no more excuses revolving around the self-serving mantra that one person cannot make a difference. Instead, they would have to make public service, even sacrifice, their ethos. In this Batman did prove successful—to a degree. Batman's unilateral intervention produced one desired effect. In *The Dark Knight*, it led to the emergence of a committed, courageous public prosecutor ready to confront organized crime and devote all the resources of the state to its destruction. (This was no small thing given the murder of a like-minded prosecutor in *Batman Begins*.) At the same time, Batman possesses little more than a dim hope that exemplarity can eventually render his vigilante mission obsolete. This should come as no surprise. Among other things, what makes it possible in the first place is virtually unlimited inherited wealth that provides the resources that turn him into a one-man fighting machine. And even with all of the high-tech armament at his disposal, Batman barely holds his own against the criminal class, which is also well armed and well connected.

Batman, then, would not withdraw from Gotham with the first sign of success. His is a long-term project, which means he must monitor the situation and wait until Gotham is ready to fend for itself before abandoning his vigilantism. As mentioned, police corruption runs so deep that organized crime has an informal partner in the very institution designed to put it out of business. Still, Batman, to his democratic credit, presumed his obsolescence. He harbored no political ambitions. He did not plan to convert the gratitude he might win from the people into political office that he could then exploit for his own purposes Batman was a vigilante who deployed the power at his arbitrary disposal with ruthlessness, but he was not a would-be demagogue or dictator seeking to capture the state. He worked in public but did not seek the limelight for its own sake, its inevitability notwithstanding.

Power Elite

When Bruce Wayne, Rachel Dawes, and Harvey Dent (Gotham's wealthiest and most prominent private citizen and its top prosecutors) accidentally dine together early in *The Dark Knight*, the conversation inevitably turns to the Batman, whose extralegal activities have rejuvenated—and divided—the city. When Wayne, mischievously, objects to the self-assigned nature of Batman's mission in a democracy, where the people supposedly govern themselves, repeating the charge of lawlessness articulated in *Batman Begins*, Dent insists that the people of Gotham effectively elected him by their refusal to take responsibility for the well-being of their own city. Dent draws a historical parallel with ancient Rome, which would appoint a dictator—for a limited period—when faced with a crisis that normal institutions and standard procedures could not handle. "It wasn't considered an honor. It was considered public service." Rachel retorts that the last person, Caesar, so appointed never relinquished the position, thus defeating the purpose of his assignment. Dent's reply seems to suggest that an essentially tragic fate awaits those who would assume this (kind of) role. He (implicitly) invokes a limit that would-be political actors must observe insofar as doing what is (allegedly) necessary can shift from heroic rescue to predictable ruination. "You either die a hero or live long enough to see yourself become a villain." The larger concern appears to be that a polity can end up destroying itself through the very measures designed to protect and save it. The polity, in other words, can easily become its own worst enemy as the actions it takes to secure itself, however well intentioned, inflict damage that proves irreparable.

This conversation is revealing not just because of its philosophical bent. It occurs in a high-end restaurant where only the elite gather. Those who sit around well-appointed tables and wax political while enjoying the best food and wine money can buy are several steps removed from the realities they address. These movers and shakers make decisions for the people about what is best for their city—and for them. Gotham is a democracy in name alone. The people (might) enjoy (some of the) benefits of rule, but they will not directly participate in its exercise. Dent so impresses Bruce Wayne that Wayne decides on the spot to throw him a fundraiser, the significance of which initially escapes Dent. Wayne informs him that with his (and thus his friends') support, he will never need to hold another one. In Gotham, once the elite have given a politico their blessing, they have set him up for life. This is how the rich and powerful choose the people's (so-called) representatives for them—in behind-the-scenes gatherings in thinly veiled acts of noblesse oblige.

Bruce Wayne, then, is more than a cover for Batman. The two of them work together. As mentioned, Batman is a divisive figure. He may have the implicit approval of Gotham, given the results he produces, but the means he employs are still rooted in violence. He also deals extensively in the histrionic. Ironically, Batman learned and mastered his approach to social engineering from a murderous criminal gang (the self-styled League of Shadows) masquerading as agents of global civic virtue in *Batman Begins*. When he returns to Gotham in the first film, it is to save rather than destroy it. He employs the resources available to him through the family's business empire to launch his death-defying demarche. The tapered black costume that conceals his identity, designed to strike fear in his targets, puts to shame the body armor available to American military forces. And the combat vehicle he uses to patrol the city's streets reflects the militarization of American policing as it runs roughshod over the democracy it is allegedly meant to serve by transmuting the city into occupied territory and the people into a subject population that must bend to the Batman's will—though Batman effectively confines his use of the vehicle to the poor, decrepit parts of the city where crime is neatly segregated. What's more, thanks to Wayne Industries, Batman presides over a (personal) military-industrial complex that can develop new weapons and control systems, experimenting on Gotham to perfect them. The city becomes a de facto field laboratory, and the knowledge it generates is invaluable as Batman hones his law and order tactics and techniques.[4]

Gotham, however, does not descend into pure dystopian nightmare. To soften, if not erase, Batman's overbearing violence and implicate the audience in its exercise, Nolan deftly turns to children. In the first two installments, Batman enjoys brief moments of intimacy and solidarity with children, small boys, in particular, who do not fear him. They can believe unconditionally in Batman because they have not yet been corrupted, unlike their parents and elders. They know instinctively that Batman stands for what is good and right. This gives the audience permission to align themselves with Batman and scorn Gotham's citizens, who cannot sustain the political will necessary to fight the good fight and so cannot (be allowed to) stand in Batman's way. The best—because innocent—part of Gotham authorizes and legitimizes Batman.

The Dark Knight thus depicts a society that is not just ineffective or powerless but complicit in the lawlessness and corruption that bedevil it. These twin maladies stem from one source: organized crime. (The Joker, at first, appears merely to exacerbate an already intractable problem. He transcends criminality, however, as we see later.) Gotham's situation is worsened insofar as corporate America operates beyond the reach of law, which means Batman is partly responsible for the condition he would correct. While Wayne Enterprises comes across as a benevolent force as it enables Batman to perform his superheroics, it answers to no one but itself. Its abilities dwarf the state's power. The state cannot control crime, but not necessarily because the citizenry are cowardly. Entities such as Wayne Enterprises demand a minimal state apparatus so they can pursue their economic goals free from government regulation. A state apparatus strong enough to deal with organized crime might have sufficient power to deal with corporate America as well, another form of organized criminal activity.

Uncomfortable Truths

The Joker might seem like a ridiculous cartoon character given to fits of extreme, senseless violence, but he represents a much greater threat to society than organized crime. The Joker lives to expose hypocrisies, without which political communities appear to be incapable of functioning. Democracies claim to represent certain values, embody certain principles, and aspire to certain ideals, but the Joker deems this self-conception so much self-indulgent nonsense. Nothing and no one is immune from his scorn. People do not hold fast to their beliefs regardless of circumstances. According to the Joker, they are "only as good as the world allows them to be." Thus, when it is convenient, they will adhere to their commitments. When it becomes inconvenient, they will easily abandon them, and, when they abandon them, they will make allowances to justify it, as they do with Batman. When he no longer suits their purposes, they turn on him as well, as if he were nothing but a common criminal. The audience knows the Joker is not altogether wrong. Even Harvey Dent, who understands and acknowledges that the Batman is more or less the people's creation, insists that one day Batman will have to answer for his crimes. And these crimes are substantial. In *Batman Begins*, he resorted to torture to extract information from a corrupt cop. In *The Dark Knight*, to locate the Joker, Batman drops Sal Maroni, the mafia crime boss, from a fire escape several stories above street level to acquire information that he may or may not possess. These resorts to torture are more frightening than are any of the murders the Joker commits insofar as the audience cheers and applauds these signs of self-righteous self-assertion that the state cannot bring itself to perform.

Ironically, Batman cannot sustain the ruthlessness necessary to deal with the Joker. Locating the Joker before he can blow up two shiploads of people who refused to cooperate in his social experiment, Batman quickly incapacitates him, in part because the Joker is having too much fun with Batman to kill him. Yet Batman inexplicably saves the Joker from certain death, for which the Joker rightly mocks him. It's not as if Batman would have been held accountable for killing him. If anything, people enjoy the violence Batman dispenses, at least when it finds its intended criminal targets and does not produce unacceptable collateral damage. Batman does what the people themselves would do if they possessed the requisite power. Thus, they can identify with him: he stands in for a crippled state apparatus that cannot do its job.[5] This is what makes the action sequences in *Batman Begins* and *The Dark Knight* thrilling to watch. Not hampered by the limits that handcuff the police, Batman runs amok on the city's streets every bit as much as the criminal class he hunts. In one sequence in *Batman Begins*, in an effort to save Rachel's life, he races through the city to return to the Bat cave. Police pursue him. They have orders to arrest him on sight for his vigilantism. The automotive carnage mounts quickly, though Nolan's crash scenes deftly obscure the fact that human beings, police, are driving these vehicles. A claim made later in the film that no one has been killed borders on ludicrous. Batman was indifferent to human life (except Rachel's) as he fled Gotham.

Batman should have terminated the Joker, given the latter's crimes against Gotham. Despite his descent into the dark side to save the city, Batman allows its mortal enemy to live—to threaten it another day. As Dargis notes, the Joker is "a self-described agent of chaos....He isn't fighting for anything or anyone. He isn't a terrorist, just terrifying."[6] Batman's principled decision underestimates the Joker, a mistake made earlier in the film, when he was initially arrested, that cost many people their lives. The Joker, likewise, cannot kill Batman, but for a different reason. Batman "completes" him. In other words, the Joker understands the symbiotic nature of his identity—of their identities. While Batman precedes the Joker, the latter defines himself in opposition to Batman. If the Joker represents anarchy, Batman signifies order—his extralegal derring-do notwithstanding. The Joker knows that Batman, as he tries to re-impose order, will match every escalation of his nihilistic will-to-destruction. He needs someone to mimic him extremity for extremity. Just as he flaunts his contempt for law and order, Batman displays an equivalent disregard for it. And each must oppose and resist capture by the state in order to be.

Rachel Dawes may understand this dynamic duo better than any other character in the film. While she promised Bruce that she would wait for the day when Gotham no longer needed Batman, she comes to see, in *The Dark Knight*, that Bruce needs Batman as much as the city does—perhaps more. Maybe, but what matters here is that Gotham's need is by definition infinite. Crime will always outstrip the ability of the state to eliminate it. Whether it can reasonably contain and control it is a matter of judgment, but the state's ability to execute the tasks assigned it is always in some doubt, for some reason. Thus, its legitimacy is always in some doubt, if not actual crisis.

What kind of example, then, does Batman set for the city? Is it of selfless service despite the costs incurred? Is it for the untrammeled exercise of righteous violence ordinarily considered beyond the pale in a liberal political order of limited power and checks and balances? After all, a polity in crisis is always tempted to set aside constitutional "niceties" when it promises to bring about highly desired results. Gotham might conclude, in a moment of tragic insight, that Batman had the right idea. He was just the wrong agent to implement it.[7]

Against Evil

The Joker helps determine the Batman's example. Among other things, he is hell-bent on exposing Batman and rendering him impotent, thereby leaving the city open to its predators. After assassinating the police commissioner and an intrepid judge (Batman spoiled his effort to kill Harvey Dent), he promised to kill one citizen per day until Batman reveals himself to the world. Batman blinks and intends to surrender himself to authorities.

This is one of the more interesting moments in the film, not (so much) because Batman reaches the decision reluctantly but because he does so against the advice of his trusted butler and partner in criminal justice, Alfred. Alfred is the one who stakes out an explicitly Weberian perspective. When Bruce Wayne bemoans the impossible position in which he finds himself, fearing what he would have to do and become to stop the Joker, and asks Alfred what he is supposed to do, Alfred replies: “Endure.” “Take it.”

Alfred suffers from no illusions. If Wayne does not come forward, Batman will generate untold anger and resentment as the Joker makes good on his threats. People will hate him for his campaign, but that is precisely the point. Batman can make decisions that no one else is willing or able to make. He does what is best for the city knowing the cost—in this case lives lost—is undeniable and intolerable. Alfred bases his counsel, disconcertingly, on his mercenary experience in Burma when working for a “local government” that was trying to buy the loyalty of tribal leaders with invaluable gems. A bandit thwarted the scheme by hiding in the forest and stealing the stones before delivery. He did this just for the fun of it—and then gave them away. In order to capture the bandit, Alfred and his associates had to burn down the forest. There was no other way to stop him. He did not play by any known rules of any known game. So Alfred mimicked him. He remarks, more with the bandit than the Joker in mind: “Some men just want to watch the world burn.”

Alfred’s conception of the Batman figure entails refusing to accept the Joker’s assignation of responsibility for his crimes. If the Joker carries out his threat and kills people because Batman refuses to “out” himself, it is the Joker who is to blame, not Batman. Criminals do not get to make demands. Weber understood politics to be a tragic undertaking. Dirty hands are inevitable. This is especially true regarding the deployment of violence, which is anathema to a democracy, to its self-image and values. Weber assumed worthwhile ends might involve problematic means, but any good thereby achieved does not magically, retrospectively transform the actions taken on its behalf. Evil means remain evil despite any positive result secured, but they do not necessarily compromise the goal in whose pursuit they are deployed. The political actor, of course, cannot know what will happen in advance. That depends, in part, on what is done in the aftermath. Either way, Batman capitulates and only a clever ploy by Harvey Dent spares him from exposure, arrest, and civic irrelevance. Batman does not (fully) possess the tragic fortitude Weber claimed was indispensable to the practice of modern politics.[8]

This is not to say that Harvey Dent possesses it. He steps forward as Batman to stop the killings, but only to lay a trap for the Joker. Harvey knows the Joker will try to kill him, which will force Batman to capture the Joker to save Harvey—again. What Harvey did not understand is that the Joker wanted to be captured, which means that Harvey set into motion a sequence of events that produced consequences he could not abide. Harvey, in short, unwittingly became the agent of his own destruction.

Print the Legend

The Joker thinks he can expose Gotham's liberal pretensions by conducting a psychotic social experiment on (some of) the city's residents. As people flee the city on ferries, one boat contains prisoners under heavy guard and the other contains some of the city's finest denizens. The Joker has wired each boat with explosives and provided them with detonators—to the other boat. The Joker will destroy them both unless one of the boats sacrifices the other—to save itself. While it appears that Gotham's upper crust is ready to kill its criminal counterparts (who really deserve this kind of fate, anyway), in the end, each refuses to play the Joker's game.

In his final confrontation with the Joker, Batman hails the people's refusal to submit to terrorist pressure as a sign that the Joker did his worst for naught. The people proved they would not succumb to the dictates of self-preservation and commit preemptive murder. The Joker, however, like any good criminal, has a back-up plan. He has targeted the city's best and last hope for the future, Harvey Dent, for self- and civic destruction. As Batman and Commissioner Gordon note, they placed all their hopes and dreams for regeneration in Harvey and the city followed them. Untainted by the violence and illegality that marked Batman and Gordon, he was the best of the troika dedicated to saving the city. Harvey, however, when it turned personal, was unable to live with the consequences of the war that he and Batman initiated. In perhaps the film's tensest moments, the Joker murders Rachel Dawes. Though Batman did his best to save Rachel rather than Harvey, both of whom the police had kidnapped, the Joker lied about their respective locations.[9] Harvey, not knowing this, berates Batman for saving him instead of Rachel. Batman, of course, should have prioritized Harvey, given his importance to Gotham. Instead, he chose the personal over the political. In other words, the first time Batman was positioned to pay a real price for his commitment to Gotham, he refused it. Ironically, if he had tried to do the right thing and matched his words with deeds, he would have saved Rachel. More importantly, Rachel, also a Gotham prosecutor, would have rejected his decision. She would have insisted that Batman privilege Harvey's life over hers. Batman, however, did this for himself, not Rachel.

Following the Joker's gambit, Harvey sets out on a course of revenge against those he holds responsible for Rachel's death. He includes both Batman and Commissioner Gordon. Though Dent kills several police officers involved, Batman kills Dent before he can complete his vengeance against Gordon and himself. As the Joker assumed, Harvey buckled. He could not stomach the price commitment to his principles exacted. The city's new hero knowingly destroyed himself as he sacrificed his values for his bloodlust. It appears that the Joker wins and Gotham is doomed.

As Harvey lies dead at his feet, however, Batman tells Gordon they must conceal Harvey's fall from grace. The people cannot know their civic saint succumbed to base instincts and turned out to be little better than the Joker. Given the publicity surrounding Harvey's killing spree, it would be impossible to deny the deaths themselves—hence Batman's decision to take the blame for Harvey's rampage. With Batman as scapegoat, Harvey's legend can be born and sustain Gotham in its desperate hour of need. Gordon balks, at first anyway, but appreciates the civic logic of Batman's grand deception. The people need heroes, especially at delicate moments in history. If they lose their heroes, if they cannot believe that goodness can make a difference and prevail in the end, all hope—and thus Gotham—would be lost. Batman will be whatever Gotham needs him to be, and right now it needs a new villain to hunt, to sustain and complete its rebirth.

There is a disturbing similarity between the conclusions of Nolan's epic and *The Man Who Shot Liberty Valance*. Each film deems deceit essential for the greater good: the founding of a political community in *Valance*, and the rebirth of one in *The Dark Knight*. They assume people would become disillusioned and disaffected from the order if they learned the truth about its origins or its heroes, so they deliberately conceal the truth from them. They treat people like children who need fairy tales to secure their allegiance and affection. The truth concealed in *The Dark Knight* is more problematic than the truth buried in *Valance*, however, since Harvey Dent's murders were nihilistic acts of vengeance: self-indulgently pointless and, in the case of Gordon's son, utterly abhorrent. Liberty Valance, on the other hand, earned his lethal denouement. No one mourned for him. Ransom Stoddard bravely faced him in the street when no one else would defend the rule of law and protect Shinbone from Valance's reign of terror. Stoddard may not have fired the kill shot, but he forced the action that led Tom Doniphon to murder Valance and trigger rebirth. Harvey Dent, on the other hand, found himself broken by the Joker's games and knowingly succumbed to his worst instincts. He destroyed every principle in which he believed and for which he stood publicly. In the tragic aftermath, Dent merely added to the death and destruction already inflicted. He created nothing new. Ransom Stoddard, on the other hand, built a successful, even legendary, political career on a killing and a lie. He dedicated his life trying to become worthy of the founding crime that enabled it. He had injured the order to which he helped give birth and needed to see it repaired. Harvey Dent planned to kill himself after his murder spree with no thought for the good of Gotham. He descended into a narcissism rivaling the Joker's self-obsession.

Despite Batman's ostensibly noble gesture, there is every reason to believe that he and Gordon have weaned Gotham too early. Infantilized, there is no indication that the city is ready to go it alone. Yes, James Gordon has become Commissioner, but he always relied on Batman for anything beyond routine police assignments. And with Batman on the run, so to speak, what is to prevent the criminal underclass from reassembling itself and filling the void left by Batman's flight? After all, despite the (apparently) crippling setback delivered to organized crime in *Batman Begins*, it is alive and well in *The Dark Knight*, not despite but because of Batman's presence. Power begets resistance, Batman's unwelcome gift to the city.

Melodrama Not Tragedy

As *The Dark Knight* closes, Batman ostensibly sacrifices himself to save the city he loves. This also means he will not answer for the crimes he has committed on its behalf, as the city had insisted earlier. As a result, Gotham can now disavow and distance itself from Batman's law and order campaign, refusing any responsibility for it even though it was complicit in his endeavors. The film's presumption, reminiscent of *The Man Who Shot Liberty Valance*, is that the people of Gotham cannot face the truth of their political condition, namely, that those who act on behalf of the city are complicated, even compromised, figures who do not measure up to idealizations of them. Political orders (supposedly) need their villains and heroes in black and white if they are to flourish. This is what gives citizens the affective commitment and energy necessary to make the city a better place to live.

Is *The Dark Knight* the stuff of tragedy? Remarkably, Batman does not pay any actual price for his salvational crimes. James Gordon takes an axe to the Bat spotlight, a symbolic act of divorce by the city and its official repudiation of him. And while Batman rides off on his motorcycle as the police close in on his last known location (where he will be said to have murdered Harvey Dent), he is anything but a fugitive. Batman will not live a life on the run, despite what the closing shots suggest. Batman is a double. He can ride his motorcycle back to the caves beneath Wayne manor and return to his life of ease and luxury as Bruce Wayne, billionaire playboy. He has no fear that anyone will discover his identity. He can no longer play the Batman role, but this reversal hardly constitutes a sacrifice, let alone a tragedy. Taking the blame for Dent, he has willingly assumed responsibility for crimes he did not commit, but he suffers no harm from this ruse because his identity remains unknown and Batman's reputation was always beside the point.

The Dark Knight Rises concludes with a similar scenario, but with Batman playing the traditional superhero role where everyone knows his sacrifice. Thus, Nolan's films never hold Batman accountable for his lawlessness. Rather, he is presumed dead for having saved Gotham from a nuclear threat and is universally revered. He lives happily ever after in Florence with a new woman in his life. Batman lived long enough to both see himself become a villain and "die" to become a hero. The latter, what's more, erases the former. While *The Dark Knight* gestures toward a tragic perspective in which a figure sacrifices himself and his name for his home city and suffers vilification for it. *The Dark Knight Rises* shows this same savior figure treating his beloved Gotham with paternalistic disdain, letting its citizens believe, for their own good, that he saved them and died as a result, a sacrifice in which they take great pride. His heroic actions reflect well on them and they, in turn, salute him for it. For anyone knowingly and willingly to embrace death in such fashion renders the beneficiaries worthy of sacrificial death. It is an ancient Athenian dream. The great Pericles, in his funeral oration, argued that there was no greater honor than to die for Athens. It testified to the city's greatness. Parents should aspire to have more children with this ambition in mind. It would enable Athens to live forever—through death. According to this ethos, however, Batman's life is mere pretension. Not only did he not die. He was never at risk. Batman did not deserve, because he did not earn, the honors he received. He was a fraud. Now Lucius Fox keeps the official secret.

What of Harvey Dent? At the end of *The Dark Knight*, Commissioner Gordon presides over his funeral services. Gordon gives specificity to the script he and Batman outlined. He refers to Dent as "a hero. Not the hero we deserved—the hero we needed. Nothing less than a knight. Shining…" Gordon's noble-sounding eulogy suggests that Dent was better than Gotham, that the city had not earned, nor was it worthy of, Dent's sacrifice. It nevertheless received his beneficence, without which the city would have suffered immeasurably. When Gordon tells his disbelieving son that Gotham must hunt Batman even though he did nothing wrong, he reverses the funereal formulation, saying that Batman is "the hero Gotham deserves, but not the one it needs right now." What his son cannot fully understand is that Batman dedicated his life to Gotham, giving it the kind of devotion it warrants. He risked everything for the city he loved, but the people of Gotham need pampering and coddling. They need something other than Batman's tough truths and tougher measures. Gordon spins what he takes to be a noble lie, but it presumes a democratic people that will never be ready for the adult political world of truth-telling. The third and final installment solidifies this condescension.

How so? At the beginning of *The Dark Knight Rises*, it is eight years later, and the city enjoys hard-won security. On Harvey Dent Day, not the city's "oldest public holiday," but one of its "most important," Gordon considers revealing the truth about Dent (and thus Batman) but decides the time is not right, that the people are not ready for it. The time, of course, is never going to be right, and the people, of course, will never be ready. Gordon tells them only what they (allegedly) need to know, that Dent's death meant something. The truth eventually comes out anyway because Bane discovers Gordon's speech and reveals it for his own nefarious purposes. He makes a point of crediting his disclosure to Gordon, to make it believable. Regardless, since Batman ultimately saves the city and dies doing so, he will be absolved of his crimes without a word being said about them. They have already been effectively erased. The city will forget them. Gordon does not mention them at Bruce Wayne's funeral, where his identity remains a secret. Nor will Gordon mention them when a statue to Batman is unveiled in downtown Gotham to immortalize his self-sacrificing heroism. Gotham lives because of Batman. Gordon furthers another lie, only this time Batman has spared him complicity. Democracy lives, too, but only because it does not recognize its own death, at its own hands.

Notes

1. See Steven Johnston, *American Dionysia: Violence, Tragedy, and Democratic Politics* (Cambridge: Cambridge University Press, 2015), 41–53.
2. See David M. Halbfinger, "Batman's Burden: A Director Confronts Darkness and Death," *The New York Times*, March 9, 2008, http://www.nytimes.com/2008/03/09/movies/09halb.html
3. Manohla Dargis, "Showdown in Gotham Town," *The New York Times*, July 18, 2008, http://www.nytimes.com/2008/07/18/movies/18knig.html
4. In addition to the urban military hardware that Wayne Enterprises develops for Batman, Bruce Wayne engineers a totalitarian surveillance system enabling him to locate the Joker. He could pinpoint his (anyone's) whereabouts by turning his mobile phone against him. Lucius Fox destroys this system at the end of the film (after it has fulfilled its purpose), but the technology still exists.
5. See Elisabeth R. Anker, *Orgies of Feeling: Melodrama and the Politics of Freedom* (Durham: Duke University Press, 2014), chapter five.
6. Dargis, "Showdown in Gotham Town."
7. In the third installment, *The Dark Knight Rises*, the so-called Dent Act enhanced state power and was subsequently unleashed against organized crime, thereby eradicating it.
8. Max Weber, "Politics as a Vocation," *From Max Weber: Essays in Sociology*, eds. H.H. Gerth and C. Wright Mills (Oxford: Oxford University Press, 1958).
9. The Joker gave Batman a choice: save Harvey or save Rachel. He could not do both. Batman (thought he) chose Rachel, effectively condemning Harvey to death. Gordon was never going to make it to either destination in time, which Batman knew. The Joker's ruse saved Harvey, which was the Joker's plan all along, a prelude to his later destruction.

CHAPTER 4

The Heroism of *Sober Expectations*

Damien K. Picariello

"*Innocent* Is a Strong Word to Throw Around Gotham, Bruce"

When Miranda Tate tells Bruce Wayne that "*innocent* is a strong word to throw around Gotham," she means that in Gotham City, people often aren't as good as we'd like them to be.[1] She makes this comment in *The Dark Knight Rises*, the third film in Christopher Nolan's *Dark Knight* trilogy, but the description captures Gotham as it's depicted in all three films. Gotham, simply put, isn't a very nice place.

Miranda Tate isn't the only person to notice this. Discussing the politics of Nolan's trilogy, *New York Times* columnist Ross Douthat says that the difference between Batman and his adversaries "isn't a belief in Gotham's goodness; it's a belief that a compromised order can still be worth defending…"[2] Nolan's films, says Douthat, ask us both to acknowledge that Gotham City is deeply flawed, *and* root for a hero who defends the city from those who would destroy it because of its flaws.

Batman, in other words, does not expect too much of his city: he doesn't require that his city be perfect—or even, at times, that it be *good*—in order for it to be worth fighting for. Batman's willingness to tolerate

D. K. Picariello (✉)
University of South Carolina Sumter, Sumter, SC, USA
e-mail: PICARIED@uscsumter.edu

D. K. Picariello (ed.), *Politics in Gotham*,
https://doi.org/10.1007/978-3-030-05776-3_4

imperfection and injustice while still striving for improvement distinguishes him from the villains he battles over the course of the films, who insist that the city's imperfections render it, in one villain's words, "beyond saving." Batman, unlike his adversaries, doesn't expect the people of Gotham to be perfectly good, and he doesn't expect that the community they inhabit will be perfectly just. Batman's expectations for his city are modest: he knows it won't ever be perfect, but he still tries to make it better.

In this, Batman has something in common with the American founders, who coupled their desire for universal goods—liberty, justice, equality—with modest expectations about human beings and their capabilities. This chapter borrows its title from a 1973 lecture by political scientist Martin Diamond entitled "The Revolution of Sober Expectations," because the American founders, in Diamond's characterization, threaded the same needle in founding a new political community that Batman threads in attempting to better his city: they married the desire for universal goods with "sober expectations" about human beings and human nature, and thus proceeded "prudently" along dangerous and "uncharted paths," navigating between the extremes of demanding too much and settling for too little.[3]

Diamond contrasts the American Revolution with the "utopianly grandiloquent idea of revolution" that emerges from the French and Russian examples.[4] These revolutions were characterized by "the political pursuit of impossible dreams" like "utopian equality and fraternity" or "the transformation of the human condition itself," which "leads to terror and tyranny in the vain effort to actualize what cannot be."[5] The American founders avoided these "utopian expectations" and instead embraced the "sober and moderate" desire for "freedom under law," which "does not require terror and tyranny for its fulfillment."[6] The founders hoped to build a good society, but they had few illusions about human nature and its shortcomings—so they tempered their desire for "equal freedom" and "popular consent" with a "sober clarity regarding democracy," and designed a regime that would be "*decent even though democratic*," taking full account of the frailties of human nature without condemning human nature for being frail.[7]

To get a sense of the founders' ideas about human nature, we need look no further than the *Federalist Papers*, in which Alexander Hamilton, James Madison, and John Jay tell us exactly what they think about human beings. "[W]hat is government itself," asks Madison, "but the greatest of all reflections on human nature? If men were angels, no government would be necessary."[8] "Why has government been instituted at all?" asks Hamilton. "Because the passions of men will not conform to the dictates of reason and justice without constraint."[9] People can't be counted on to make good choices, or to do the right things: one of the main reasons we need government in the first place is to keep us in line, and protect us from the worst parts of ourselves. "A man must be far gone in Utopian speculations," Hamilton tells us, "to forget that men are ambitious vindictive, and rapacious."[10] In other words: the bad parts of human nature are so apparent that to overlook them would be to deny reality itself. And these bad qualities are shared by governed and governors alike: "Enlightened statesmen will not always be at the helm" of our governments, Madison assures us; even "a tolerable knowledge of human nature," says Hamilton, shows that people in power will often "sacrifice the national tranquility to personal advantage and personal gratification."[11]

But this doesn't mean that we should lose hope, either for human beings or for self-government—and it doesn't mean that we should stop pursuing justice, even in the face of the obstacles to its achievement. "Justice is the end of government," says Madison. "It is the end of civil society. It ever has been and ever will be pursued until it be obtained, or until liberty be lost in the pursuit."[12] Madison reminds us that human nature isn't all bad; rather, it's a mixed bag, in which good qualities coexist with less desirable ones. "As there is a degree of depravity in mankind which requires a certain degree of circumspection and distrust," he says, "so there are other qualities in human nature which justify a certain portion of esteem and confidence." And if we hope to govern ourselves, we need to place some measure of faith in these good qualities, even as we recognize the existence and persistence of the bad ones. "Republican government," says Madison, "presupposes the existence of these [good] qualities in a higher degree than any other form."[13]

What we can take from this is that the American founders thought of human nature as decidedly mixed—neither all good nor all bad—and that they tried to build a self-governing society that would pursue justice, working within the limitations set by imperfect human nature. In this sense, the founders—like Batman—struck a balance: they tried to make a good political community without either demanding that human beings become perfect, or condemning human beings for their imperfection, or insisting that human imperfection means that the pursuit of a better community should be abandoned.

Batman's heroism is therefore, like the founders' Revolution, a heroism of "sober expectations." In *The Dark Knight Rises*, the third film in Nolan's trilogy, one character accuses Batman of trying to "save the world"—but this isn't quite right. Batman doesn't want to save the world; he wants to prudently improve his corner of it, taking account of the limits imposed by human nature that make Gotham City (to say nothing of the world) both beyond saving and not in need of saving. Batman rejects the notion of saving of the world, and places himself instead squarely (as he tells Rā's al Ghūl) on the side of "the people of Gotham," working to make his political community better while accepting that it will never be perfect.

"This Is Not How Man Was Supposed to Live"

Our first introduction to Batman (in the person of his secret identity, Bruce Wayne) in *Batman Begins*, the first film in Christopher Nolan's *Dark Knight* trilogy, jumps between periods in his life. As we join the adult Bruce Wayne far from Gotham City in an Asian prison, we also observe some of the key events in Wayne's childhood that pushed him to this point. In this way, the movie shows us two things: first, it shows us that Bruce Wayne is a product of Gotham City—Gotham makes him who he is in an important way. Second, it shows us that Wayne has become dissatisfied with Gotham—so deeply dissatisfied that he would travel far from the city in an effort to find something better.

The film reviews for us some of the formative events in the young Bruce Wayne's life: he shares an affectionate relationship with a young Rachel Dawes, daughter of a household employee; he experiences human frailties like fear and bodily injury; he is educated and cared for by his father, who reminds him not to be discouraged by these frailties; he experiences loss and injustice when his parents are murdered; and he experiences compassion when James Gordon, a Gotham City policeman who shares nothing with Wayne other than citizenship in Gotham, comforts him after his parents are killed.

These formative experiences are interspersed with scenes from the adult Wayne's solitary life far from Gotham City, a life he has undertaken in order to understand desperation and crime and, ultimately, seek justice for his parents' murder. We get a better sense of why Wayne has left Gotham through another flashback, situated just before his departure. Here, Wayne is no longer a child and yet immature in other ways, back from college to testify at a hearing in which his parents' murderer will be released from prison. The murderer's release will be in exchange for testimony against Falcone, Gotham's crime boss. This bargain exemplifies the sort of justice available in Gotham, the sort that Rachel Dawes—Wayne's childhood friend, now working for the District Attorney—believes in and fights for. What the murderer did, says Rachel, is "unforgivable," and yet she's willing to release him from prison if it means that Falcone, who creates "new [murderers] every day," can be brought to justice. This exchange, Rachel knows, is imperfect, in that a murderer will have his punishment cut short, while the lives he took can never be restored. But Rachel implies that Bruce's parents—philanthropists deeply invested in their city—would have approved of the deal, since Falcone is "destroying everything they stood for" by perpetuating, and prospering from, the city's decay.

When Bruce reveals that he'd intended to kill his parents' murderer—as it happens, one of Falcone's hired guns does the job himself—Rachel says, "Your father would be *ashamed* of you," drawing a line between the kind of justice the young Bruce seeks—perfect, symmetrical, without compromise—and the kind of justice she believes in: imperfect, laden with compromises and sacrifices, sometimes fraught with choices between the lesser of several evils. Bruce finds this latter kind of justice deeply objectionable—he expects, and demands, more—and the unavailability of a purer kind of justice drives him from Gotham City.

This brings us to present day: Bruce Wayne finds himself very far from Gotham, imprisoned in an unnamed Asian country, searching for something different from what he found in Gotham. Here, Wayne meets Rā's al Ghūl, a member of an organization called the League of Shadows. Rā's al Ghūl presents to Wayne the alternative he's been looking for: a "path" for one who holds a "hatred of evil and wishes to serve true justice." Wayne joins Rā's al Ghūl and the League at an isolated, mountaintop monastery and begins his training in "the means to fight injustice." Rā's al Ghūl encourages Wayne to "devote [himself] to an ideal": the ideal of "true justice," without compromises, without choices between greater and lesser evils.

One sort of justice was available in Gotham; here, far from the city, is another sort. Wayne rejected the first sort of justice in favor of the second—but at the conclusion of Wayne's training with the League of Shadows, he's asked to execute a murderer. His response—"This man should be tried"—shows his enduring (perhaps unwitting) preference for the imperfect, corruptible, and sometimes corrupt form of justice available in Gotham City rather than the perfect, merciless justice meted out by Rā's al Ghūl and the League of Shadows. Bruce Wayne has removed himself from Gotham, but Gotham hasn't removed itself from Bruce Wayne. He may share Rā's al Ghūl's conviction that "criminals thrive on the indulgence of society's understanding," but he's willing to risk it: he sees the flaws in the kind of justice found in Gotham City, but he still prefers this kind of justice to the "true justice" offered by Rā's al Ghūl.

Then Rā's al Ghūl puts all of his cards on the table: Wayne is being trained by the League of Shadows so that he can return to Gotham and destroy the city, which has become irredeemably corrupt. Now Wayne turns conclusively against the League of Shadows, destroying their monastery—and saving Rā's al Ghūl's life—before returning to Gotham determined to do what he can to make his city better.

Bruce Wayne's encounter with, and ultimate rejection of, the League of Shadows frames his career as Batman over the course of the three *Dark Knight* films. Wayne had left Gotham in search of a kind of justice more satisfying than the sort found in the city, in which compromises are made, terrible crimes sometimes go unpunished or imperfectly punished, and qualities endemic to the human condition—mercy, greed, compassion, selfishness, poor judgment—complicate the perfect symmetry of Rā's al Ghūl's "true justice." He had found an alternative far from Gotham, where men of violence devote themselves to a perfect standard, an impersonal and impartial ideal of justice. But when faced with the consequences of this kind of justice, Wayne chooses to return to Gotham and work for its betterment despite its imperfections.

One way of thinking about this would be to say that in this first portion of *Batman Begins*, Bruce Wayne discovers what Aristotle calls "prudence," a virtue that Aristotle says is essential for political life. Prudence, for Aristotle, is "a virtue of…the part [of the soul] involved in the formation of opinions"; it equips one to "deliberate nobly" about "the human things," the "noble things and the just things," which things by their nature "admit of much dispute and variability."[14] Crucially, prudence is responsive to context, in the sense that prudence is concerned with action at a particular time and in a particular place, so that the prudent person must have both some sense of universal goods and some knowledge of the particular situation or community in which he hopes to act. Thus, for Aristotle, "prudence is not concerned with the universals alone but must also be acquainted with the particulars: it is bound up with action, and actions concerns the particulars."[15]

Bruce Wayne shares with Rā's al Ghūl the sense that Gotham should be doing better—that Gotham should be more just than it is—but he knows two things that Rā's al Ghūl doesn't. The first thing is that it doesn't make sense to take an ideal vision of "true justice" and apply it to Gotham City without an intimate understanding of the city, including those aspects of Gotham that might prevent it from becoming perfectly just. The second thing—and this is what Batman has in common with the American founders—is that human nature is a mixed bag. There are good parts, and these parts are why we shouldn't give up on Gotham City—but there are also bad parts, and an honest reckoning with these parts should make us moderate our expectations for the achievement of "true justice" in real life, among real human beings. If the desire for justice pushes Bruce Wayne to don his cape and mask, it is knowledge of—and citizenly attachment to—the people of Gotham City that provide him with the prudence needed to keep his desire for justice from becoming destructive.

Bruce Wayne's time with the League of Shadows is therefore a period of maturation, in more ways than one. Certainly, this is the period during which Wayne learns the crime-fighting skills that he employs as Batman. But he also sees the consequences of the League of Shadows' commitment to the "ideal" of "true justice," and he learns that he must temper his commitment to an "ideal" with prudence.[16] He must be modest in his goals: not to make Gotham *perfectly* just, but rather to make it *more* just, accepting that perfection will always be out of reach.

When Bruce Wayne returns to Gotham and begins his career as Batman, he has plenty of encounters with the bad side of human nature: criminals, crooked cops, deranged psychiatrists, and more. But the good side of human nature, and the good things that are possible when people form communities together, also features heavily. To start with, Gotham City has been good to Bruce Wayne, and this enables him to adopt the Batman persona. It's true that his training with the League of Shadows in "theatricality and deception" serves him well, but it's also true that the things that allow him to become Batman are largely inherited: his wealth, which allows him to buy the expensive things a crime-fighter needs; his company, Wayne Enterprises, which allows him access to exotic vehicles and equipment; his property, which allows him the space and secrecy to stage his adventures; even Alfred, his butler, who provides Batman with valuable assistance. All of these assets were developed by the Wayne family within the bosom of Gotham City. Unlike other popular heroes whose powers come from sources outside their communities—Superman is an alien, Spider-Man encounters a radioactive spider—Batman's abilities emerge almost entirely from his position *within* Gotham City.[17] As Rā's al Ghūl points out, Batman is just an "ordinary man in a cape."

It's also the case that Batman relies to a great extent not just on the tools that have passed to him by virtue of Gotham but also on the active cooperation of his fellow Gothamites. This becomes clear when he first contacts Detective James Gordon to enlist him in his crime-fighting project: when Gordon protests, "You're just one man," Batman responds: "Now we're two." Batman also relies on his childhood friend and off-and-on love interest Rachel Dawes to aide in investigating and prosecuting the criminals he apprehends. Batman can't do what he does alone: he needs help from good people who, like him, want to improve a not-so-good city.

When Rā's al Ghūl follows through with his plan to destroy Gotham, he shows up at Wayne Manor and has a tense exchange with his former student. "This is not how man was supposed to live," Rā's al Ghūl says, Gotham City, for him, falls irredeemably short of achieving "true justice." Then he tries to bring Bruce Wayne around: Wayne knows better than anyone how unjust Gotham is, so he should be at Rā's al Ghūl's side, "saving the world," not fighting against his former teacher. In response, Wayne says that he stands with the "people of Gotham." He doesn't buy Rā's al Ghūl's abstract notion of saving the world; instead, he's focused on protecting and improving his particular city, right here and now (Fig. 4.1).

Fig. 4.1 "This is not how man was supposed to live," Rā's al Ghūl tells Bruce Wayne

In this scene, Rā's al Ghūl, in a roundabout way, makes his best case against the people of Gotham. In the not-too-distant past, the League of Shadows had tried to destroy Gotham by fomenting economic catastrophe, which brought the nastier parts of human nature into sharp relief. "Create enough hunger," Rā's al Ghūl says, "and everyone becomes a criminal"; put enough pressure on people, and the bad side of human nature will rear its head. But as Rā's al Ghūl continues, he also shows us one of the reasons Bruce Wayne refuses to abandon Gotham: It was people like Wayne's parents, says Rā's al Ghūl, who foiled the League's plans by working for the betterment of their city, even when the odds looked slim.

Bruce Wayne doesn't expect everyone to be like his parents, nor does he expect everyone to be like James Gordon or Rachel Dawes. He knows his way around people generally and Gotham's people in particular, and he knows to keep his expectations modest. The fact that many of Gotham's citizens might turn to crime when faced with desperate circumstances doesn't shock him; rather, it pushes him to try and make the city's circumstances a little bit less desperate. Rā's al Ghūl would destroy the people of Gotham in the name of "man"; he would destroy Gotham City in the name of "the world." He is willing to annihilate particular human beings and cities for the sake of an ideal abstracted from particulars. Batman fights both to improve his city and to defend it against the destruction that emerges from this imprudent commitment to "true justice."

"They're Only as Good as the World Allows Them to Be"

Rā's al Ghūl's expectations for human beings in general, and for the people of Gotham in particular, had been too high. In *The Dark Knight*, Batman faces a villain who is quite different from Rā's al Ghūl and yet has something important in common with him. When the Joker tells Batman that the people of Gotham are "only as good as the world allows them to be," he's making the same point as Rā's al Ghūl, who'd said: "create enough hunger and everyone becomes a criminal." They're both saying: put enough pressure on people, and they'll do bad things. For Rā's al Ghūl, this had meant that "true justice" requires the destruction of Gotham. For the Joker, this means that the pursuit of justice itself should be abandoned.

Our introduction to the Joker comes as he's robbing a bank used to launder money by Gotham's crime organizations. The message here is clear: the Joker isn't an ordinary criminal; rather, his project, like Rā's al Ghūl's, is both larger and more destructive. His interactions with Gotham's criminals over the course of the film bear this out, as he by turns aids them, uses them, and discards them when they're no longer of use. As Alfred tells Bruce Wayne: "Some men aren't looking for anything logical, like money…Some men just want to watch the world burn."

We're also introduced early in *The Dark Knight* to Harvey Dent, Gotham's crusading District Attorney (and Rachel Dawes's boyfriend), who becomes an essential piece in the "battle for Gotham's soul" between Batman and the Joker. Bruce Wayne sees Harvey Dent as a reason to hope that one day, Gotham's elected officials will be brave enough to build a better city on their own: one day, Gotham may no longer need Batman. The Joker, on the other hand, sees Dent as a test case for his theory that anyone, given the right conditions, can be turned bad. If the Joker can turn Harvey Dent, he can demonstrate his point to the people of Gotham, proving once and for all that justice itself is a sham.

The Joker outlines this goal in one of *The Dark Knight*'s pivotal scenes: The Joker has allowed himself to be arrested, but his goons have kidnapped both Harvey Dent and Rachel Dawes. Jim Gordon's corrupt colleagues in the Gotham PD's Major Crimes Unit collaborated in the kidnappings, and the Joker uses this fact to try and undermine Gordon's resolve. "Does it depress you," he asks, "to know how alone you are? Does it make you feel responsible for Harvey Dent's current predicament?"

Gordon leaves the room, and Batman takes over the interrogation. Now the Joker outlines his critique of Gotham:

> Their morals, their code…it's a bad joke. Dropped at the first sign of trouble. They're only as good as the world allows them to be. You'll see. I'll show you. When the chips are down, these civilized people? They'll eat each other.

In other words: Placed in situations of stress—put under enough pressure—the "good" people of Gotham will abandon their goodness. The Joker's point here echoes Rā's al Ghūl's case against the city: "Create enough hunger and everyone becomes a criminal." The fact that Gotham's citizens are "only as good as the world allows them to be" shows that they're not good at all.

So here's where we are: Batman, Rā's al Ghūl, and the Joker all agree that Gotham is not as just as it should be, and its people aren't as good as they should be. For all three men, there are identifiable standards of justice and goodness, and Gotham doesn't measure up. For Batman, this is reason to strive for the improvement of his city within the bounds of the possible and the prudent; For Rā's al Ghūl, this was reason to destroy Gotham, which could never measure up to the standards of "true justice"; for the Joker, this shows that goodness and justice themselves are frauds, and that the quest for both should be abandoned. This is the point that the Joker intends to prove to the people of Gotham: "The only sensible way to live in this world," he tells Batman, "is *without* rules."

The Joker does manage to turn Harvey Dent, but he loses what he calls the "battle for Gotham's soul." This is so for a couple of reasons. The first is the failure of a grand social experiment he stages for the education of Gotham's citizens: He has two bombs placed on two ferries leaving the city, one carrying ordinary Gothamites and the other carrying inmates in Gotham's prisons—and each ferry's passengers hold the detonator for the other ferry's bomb. If the passengers on one of the two ferries don't decide to detonate the bomb on the other, the Joker will blow them both up. This elaborate piece of stagecraft is meant to demonstrate the Joker's point that when push comes to shove, moral codes go out the window, and ordinary people will unhesitatingly kill others to save their own skins, which point erases the difference between regular people and hardened criminals—and shows the foolhardiness of Batman's efforts on behalf of justice. But things don't go as planned: A prisoner throws one detonator overboard, showing his willingness to sacrifice himself to save innocent people, and the passengers on the other ferry can't bring themselves to blow up the boat full of prisoners. Human nature, it turns out, isn't quite as simple as the Joker had imagined.

The second reason that the Joker fails is more complicated than the first, and it leads into one of the plot points of the third film in the trilogy, *The Dark Knight Rises*. Reeling from the death of Rachel Dawes and having suffered disfiguring facial burns, Harvey Dent adopts the persona of Two-Face and goes on a crime spree, culminating in him threatening the life of James Gordon's child. Batman confronts Dent, and Dent responds with a version of the Joker's thesis: "You thought we could be decent men

Fig. 4.2 Harvey Dent tells Batman: "You thought we could be decent men in an indecent time. But you were wrong…the only morality in a cruel world is chance"

in an indecent time. But you were wrong…the only morality in a cruel world is chance" (Fig. 4.2).

Batman stops Dent, and Dent dies, but the choice Batman and Gordon make next shows that morality, for them, is more complicated than it is for Dent, the Joker, or Rā's al Ghūl: Batman elects to take the blame for Dent's crimes, reasoning as follows: "Sometimes the truth isn't good enough. Sometimes people deserve more. Sometimes people deserve to have their faith rewarded." Gordon and Batman will lie to the people of Gotham, so that they don't lose faith in human goodness—in just men like Harvey Dent, and in the pursuit of justice generally. With this lie, Batman and Gordon hope to keep the city's soul out of the hands of men like the Joker.

"I Hope You Have a Friend Like I Did"

The Dark Knight Rises begins with James Gordon (now Gotham's Police Commissioner) telling lies. He's speaking in honor of Harvey Dent, and he's perpetuating the lie that Dent was a hero and was murdered by Batman, in a continued effort to keep Gotham's citizens from losing faith in their elected officials and governing institutions—and in justice itself (Fig. 4.3).

If *Batman Begins* starts with Bruce Wayne's search for uncompromising justice, then it's notable that *The Dark Knight Rises* begins with a compromise: James Gordon does something bad that he understands as a

Fig. 4.3 A celebration to honor Harvey Dent and the Dent Act

contribution to a larger good, much as Rachel Dawes had supported the release of Bruce Wayne's parents' murderer in order to stop a more dangerous criminal. And there's reason to believe that Gordon's calculus is right: Gotham's criminal element has been suppressed using the Dent Act, a tough-on-crime law passed in honor of Harvey Dent, and the city is enjoying a new dawn of peace and—for some—prosperity.

At the same time, we're introduced to Bane, the masked, muscle-bound leader of a fanatical group of armed men. As with Rā's al Ghūl, we first meet Bane in an unspecified location far from Gotham, on a plane that takes off from an empty field. We soon learn that Bane, like Rā's al Ghūl, is devoted to an idea, a vision, rather than more concrete things like people or places: when asked his name, he says: "It doesn't matter who we are. What matters is our plan…Nobody cared who I was until I put on the mask." His henchmen take the same approach, sacrificing themselves willingly in the name of their goal. If Gordon prioritizes the well-being of Gotham and its people over the more abstract good of truth, Bane shows his commitment to his plan, his idea, through his willingness to sacrifice both people and personhood itself.

As the film continues, we get a look at the city that Batman continues to want to protect and Bane (it becomes clear) is committed to destroying, and it's obvious that the peaceful, prosperous Gotham of *The Dark Knight Rises* is just as imperfect as the violent, economically depressed Gotham of *Batman Begins* and the terror-stricken Gotham of *The Dark Knight*. Selena Kyle, a talented cat burglar looking to shed her criminal past, reminds Bruce Wayne of the economic inequality that characterizes his city, and the ominous consequences such inequality might produce: "There's a storm coming," she says. "[W]hen it hits you're all gonna wonder how you ever thought you could live so large and leave so little to the rest of us." A heist scene at the city's stock exchange showcases the shallow arrogance of Gotham's financial class—and it's worth noting that Bane's soldiers, carrying out the heist, pose as workers at the exchange: a messenger, a janitor, and so on, catering to the needs and whims of Gotham's overweening rich. We learn that impoverished youth have been taking to the sewers to work for Bane, since employment on the surface is—for them, at least—nowhere to be found.[18] When Alfred tells Bruce Wayne that he sees "the League of Shadows resurgent" in Bane's arrival, we have no need to wonder why the League still considers Gotham an unjust city.

And it's not just the League of Shadows who has little faith in Gotham's goodness. Bruce Wayne himself has grave doubts about the capacity of Gothamites—indeed, of human beings in general—to pursue good and resist bad. We learn near the start of the film that he's devoted a great deal of time and money to building a reactor that might allow Gotham to produce sustainable energy—but can also be turned into a nuclear weapon. Rather than trusting his fellow citizens and human beings to use the reactor only for good, he elects to conceal the project, hiding it from Gotham in a place where it can be easily flooded and destroyed if necessary. Miranda Tate, one of the other investors in the project, draws attention to Wayne's paradoxical position—he both loves and mistrusts his city—when she tells him: "Bruce, if you want to save the world, you have to start trusting it." But this misreads Wayne's purpose: he doesn't want to save the world—this is the kind of overreaching abstraction that the League of Shadows employs; rather, he wants to incrementally improve his city while exercising the kind of prudent caution that sometimes manifests in mistrust of his fellow citizens.

As the film moves forward, we learn that Bane has come to Gotham to complete the mission of Rā's al Ghūl and the League of Shadows. He is "Gotham's reckoning," the "necessary evil" that will destroy the city in the name of "true justice," and ultimately "for the sake of [the] children." In order to accomplish this, Bane injures Batman and then confines him in a strange prison far from Gotham. In Batman's absence, Bane and his men either destroy or block the bridges and tunnels connecting the city to the outside world, and then stage a scene at a football game—just after the singing of "The Star-Spangled Banner"—in which Bane addresses the people of Gotham, proclaiming their "liberation" and announcing his desire to "return control of this city to its people." The progression of these scenes suggests that Gotham is now both a country of its own and a stand-in for the American political community as a whole.[19]

Shortly after, Bane reveals to Gotham's citizens "the truth about Harvey Dent," to replace the lie that Gordon and Batman had advanced "[t]o stop you tearing down this corrupt city and rebuilding it the way it should have been rebuilt generations ago"—by which he means, presumably, on a foundation of unblemished truth and "true justice." Rejecting Gordon and Batman's compromise—advance a lie in order to improve the city—Bane insists that imperfect justice is no justice at all, and releases the prisoners held under the authority of the Dent Act, urging Gotham's citizens to support his remaking of the city.

It's at this point that James Gordon delivers the most explicit defense of the prudent pursuit of justice and the heroism of "sober expectations" found in the trilogy. Explaining the need for his lies to a young police officer named Blake, he says:

> There's a point. Far out there. When the structures fail you. When the rules aren't weapons anymore, they're shackles, letting the bad get ahead. Maybe one day you'll have such a moment of crisis. And in that moment, I hope you have a friend like I did. To plunge their hands into the filth so you can keep yours clean.

Gordon rejects the idea of a justice that is equally exacting at all times and in all places, a justice that requires the same simple and unchanging calculus in all circumstances; rather, he articulates a sense of justice that is situational, sensitive to ever-changing circumstances, and willing to tolerate dirty hands—imperfections, lies, the lesser of the available evils—in pursuit of a better community. In this sense, Gordon defends a prudent sort of justice, a desire to achieve as much good as possible keeping in mind the limitations of circumstance and human nature. Implied in Gordon's words and actions are his "sober expectations" about human capacities and needs—the need, for example, for people to be inspired by figures like Dent, even if such inspiration involves compromising with the truth. Gotham's citizens, Gordon and Batman believe, cannot be relied upon to act out of the rational desire for a more just city: they cannot be relied upon to make good choices all of the time, all on their own. They need help, and it falls to people like Batman and Gordon, with both faith (however limited) in their fellow citizens and a prudent appraisal of their capacities, to provide such help, even if it means dirtying their hands.

While Batman recuperates from his injuries and tries to free himself from the prison in which Bane has confined him, weeks and months go by with Gotham under Bane's control. Wealthy Gothamites are unceremoniously removed from their homes and their possessions expropriated; for Bane, destructively excessive economic inequalities call for violent redistribution, not delicate management. Revolutionary courts are established where guilt and innocence are decided before trial, and the only question is the sentence; for Bane, the question of justice is a simple one, and requires neither consideration of the particulars of each unique case nor the kind of deliberation in which juries engage.

The actions of Gotham's citizens during this period justify Gordon's (and Batman's) assessment of their capacities. Many of Gotham's police join in the fight against Bane—but many of Gotham's citizens enthusiastically ransack the homes of the city's elite and participate in Bane's revolutionary courts. Both Selena Kyle and Deputy Police Commissioner Foley are initially reluctant to aid in the fight against Bane, but ultimately make the right choice. All told, the people of Gotham merit a decidedly mixed verdict, which is perhaps why Gordon and Batman have faith in them even as they don't always trust them.

The film ends with the deaths of Bane and Miranda Tate (revealed to be Talia, Rā's al Ghūl's daughter and Bane's collaborator), and the apparent death of Batman, who seems to have sacrificed himself to save his city. It's revealed at the close of the film that Bruce Wayne has survived, and has found his way to a new life in Europe alongside Selena Kyle. Blake, having quit the police force, prepares to assume the Batman identity, and Gordon remains Police Commissioner. And Gotham remains safe from those who would destroy the city in the name of saving the world.

"A Portion of Virtue and Honor"

It's good that Batman and James Gordon are friends, but Batman doesn't rely only on friends like Gordon, Alfred, and Rachel Dawes for help in his struggle for a better city. Batman also relies upon the ordinary citizens of Gotham for assistance, which reliance is as often frustrated as rewarded. This, alongside Batman's prudent pursuit of justice in an imperfect city, is a recurring theme in the trilogy: the citizens of Gotham, like their city, are imperfect, and they let Batman down as often as they aid him. In *Batman*

Begins, maddened by drugs, they attack him; in *The Dark Knight*, they turn on him and reject his vigilantism, goaded by the Joker's threats; in *The Dark Knight Rises*, they collaborate with Bane in his faux-revolutionary project. But this is part and parcel of striving to better a flawed community. Batman does not let the fact that Gotham's citizens are sometimes bad stop him from trying to make the city good. He does not, as the League of Shadows suggests, reject humanity due to human frailty, nor does he embrace the Joker's suggestion that human frailty makes the pursuit of justice a laughable endeavor. Instead, like the American founders, he finds a middle path, maintaining "sober expectations" for his fellow Gothamites, accepting that human nature is a mixed bag, avoiding both the Joker's cynicism and the League of Shadows' disappointed idealism. In this sense, we can say that Batman's modest and moderate faith in his fellow citizens makes him a hero with particularly republican—perhaps particularly American—sensibilities. In the words of Alexander Hamilton:

> The supposition of universal venality in human nature is little less an error in political reasoning, than the supposition of universal rectitude. The institution of delegated power implies, that there is a portion of virtue and honor among mankind, which may be a reasonable foundation of confidence: and experience justifies the theory. It has been found to exist in the most corrupt periods of the most corrupt governments.[20]

And, we might add, in Gotham.

Notes

1. All quotations from the dark knight trilogy are drawn from the films themselves, as supplemented by *The Dark Knight Trilogy: The Complete Screenplays* (Tuxedo Park, NY: Opus Books, 2012). I'm grateful to the University of South Carolina Sumter for providing funding toward the completion of this manuscript. Great thanks are due to my fellow panel participants at the 2018 meeting of the Southern Political Science Association, and to my colleagues at USC Sumter for their helpful comments during and after my presentation at our faculty seminar series. For their willingness to talk (and listen to me talk) about this project, I'd like to thank: Tyler Brown, Josh Houben, Kyle Kelly, Andy Kunka, Matthew Morse, Jil and Lenny Picariello, Eric Reisenauer, and the students in my Film, Politics, and Social Change class. For listening to me go on long after

anyone else would have lost patience, I'm exceptionally grateful to Alex Picariello and—as always—Erin.

2. Ross Douthat, "The Politics of 'The Dark Knight Rises,'" *The New York Times*, July 23, 2012. https://douthat.blogs.nytimes.com/2012/07/23/the-politics-of-the-dark-knight-rises/
3. Martin Diamond, "The Revolution of Sober Expectations," in *As Far as Republican Principles Will Admit: Essays by Martin Diamond*, ed. William A. Schambra (Washington, DC: The AEI Press, 1992), 215.
4. Ibid.
5. Diamond, 217.
6. Ibid., 223; 217.
7. Diamond, 214, 221, 220.
8. "No. 51," in *The Federalist Papers*, ed. Clinton Rossiter (New York: Signet, 2003), 319.
9. Ibid., "No. 15," 106.
10. Ibid., "No. 6," 48.
11. Ibid., "No. 10," 75; "No. 6," 49–50.
12. Ibid., "No. 51," 321.
13. Ibid., "No. 55," 343.
14. *Aristotle's Nicomachean Ethics*, trans. Robert C. Bartlett and Susan D. Collins (Chicago: University of Chicago Press, 2011), Book 6, Chap. 5, 1140b25–7; 1140a26; 6, 7, 1141b8–9; 5, 6, 1141a1; 1, 3, 1094b15–16.
15. Ibid., 6, 7, 1141b15–17.
16. We might say that Wayne leaves his youth behind when he returns to Gotham. As Aristotle tells us, "a young person does not seem to be prudent. The cause is that prudence is also of particulars, which come to be known as a result of experience, but a young person is inexperienced: a long period of time creates experience" (6, 8, 1142a12–16).
17. Alan Baily makes a similar point in "Batman: America's Lockean Superhero," presented at the 2014 meeting of the Southern Political Science Association.
18. Douthat makes this point in "The Politics of 'The Dark Knight Rises.'"
19. This suggestion reappears later in the film, when the camera lingers on a pair of tattered American flags just before the climactic battle between Gotham's police and the League of Shadows.
20. "No. 76," in *The Federalist Papers*, 456–7.

CHAPTER 5

Deconstructing Batman's Legitimacy: The Radical Political Critique of Christopher Nolan's Batman Cycle

William J. Berger

Natascha (to Harvey Dent):	Gotham needs heroes like you, elected officials, not a man who thinks he's above the law.
Bruce Wayne:	Exactly. Who appointed the Batman?
Dent:	We did. All of us who stood by and let scum take control of our city.
Natascha:	But this is a democracy, Harvey.

Introduction

Though superhero myths commonly turn on an elision between goodness and legitimacy, giving us reason to endorse the actions of these individuals just in virtue of their goodness, the Nolan trilogy explicitly puts pressure on Batman's legitimacy deficit. Natascha, Wayne's romantic partner for an

W. J. Berger (✉)
University of Pennsylvania, Philadelphia, PA, USA
e-mail: zberger@sas.upenn.edu

D. K. Picariello (ed.), *Politics in Gotham*,
https://doi.org/10.1007/978-3-030-05776-3_5

evening in *The Dark Knight* film, expressly puts the question to Gotham City's District Attorney, Harvey Dent, who counters with an argument by fiat: Legitimacy is just good governance, and right now Batman is good governance. But Natascha presses the point: Oughtn't authority be structurally constituted by the people? The problem can't be waved away as lightly as Dent would dismiss it.

This is a central tension for Nolan, one important enough that it tracks the trajectory of the entire trilogy. The trilogy can be seen as an inquiry on the grounds of Batman's legitimacy, ultimately serving as a demonstration of its inversion on itself. Batman's legitimacy, Nolan argues, is unstable, and he uses the most compelling means at his disposal to sue the point: Insofar as our commitment and credulity to the Batman mythos is had through narrative, Nolan offers narrative to undo the conceit of his legitimacy.

It's just not a productive exercise to wrangle over whether Batman is a hero or anti-hero—it's not the probative dialectic. Batman is clearly a hero, saving Gotham from peril and catastrophe. Yet he does so extra-legally, without clear deputization, often violating law and virtue to effect justice (at least understood in some rough Manichean sense).

Batman comes to correct a corrupt world, one which, as Gotham's Assistant District Attorney Rachel Dawes puts it, "keeps the bad people rich and the good people scared."[1] And Bruce Wayne, due to both internal compulsion and systemic institutional failures, is moved to effect justice himself.[2] Beyond specifically democratic worries, we might look for any stable account of legitimacy aside from fiat. I understand legitimacy here as being more than Batman's license to act as he does. Rather I want to ask whether he plays a constitutive and fundamental role in Gotham's politics. This isn't some pedantic curiosity either, akin to demanding that X-Men's Cyclops consume sufficient daily calories to power his optical laser. Batman's standing as protagonist is predicated on him doing the right thing (and problematized precisely when this comes into doubt, as in the work of Frank Miller).[3] That is, even when Batman is in the wrong, it is relevant precisely because commonly he is (thought to be) in the right. But that rightness begs to be grounded by something. What Nolan demonstrates in his cycle, I argue, is that such an account proves self-defeating.

Without claiming that political theory is the dominant lens to evaluate the Nolan series, it is clearly a deeply probative one. The account offered here traces Hobbesian and Schmittian themes to argue for the critical intervention of the cycle, namely that Nolan challenges Batman's political legitimacy throughout the narrative arc of the films. While I don't mean to say that the films faithfully reconstruct the accounts of this or that political theorist, I do hope to mine the trilogy for its political theory using the work of Hobbes and Schmitt as set pieces to better access the resonance of the films and recover themes that have otherwise gone unrecognized. That being said the series, and the second film in particular, is so evocative of Hobbes' and Schmitt's work that it's hard not to wonder if Nolan did a read-through before authoring the screenplay.

Gotham's Corruption

Nolan's second installment in the series, and possibly its cinematic apex, *The Dark Knight*, begins with a bank heist. Heist movies have a long pedigree and commonly deploy a team of confederates collaborating to abscond with some treasure.[4] In order to work, however, the band of rogues needs to have trust among themselves. No one can effect the heist alone, so each must rely on the other to do their part. Ultimately each relies on the last in the chain to distribute the goods faithfully, else their efforts would have been for naught.

Of course the conceit assumes away the problem: How can there be trust among thieves? *The Dark Knight* does violence to the premise. In the film each member of the operation has been instructed by the boss—the Joker, we soon learn—to kill the member of the team that operates ahead of them, reducing the number of participants and marginally increasing their share of the windfall.[5] Audiences commonly overlook this inherent collective action problem, and it's this element that Nolan underscores in the film. The Joker consistently exploits exactly this kind of collective action problem—first here and again when he infiltrates Gambol's men, holding them hostage and instructing them to fight for the lone spot on his crew, and again when he incites vigilantism against Coleman Reese—the Wayne Enterprise accountant that stumbles on Batman's identity—for threatening to expose Wayne.

Collective action problems are an expansive mode of analysis, germane to almost any situation of conflict. The Joker brings to our attention that the fragility of Gotham is not the product of a criminal assault on the city, but the frayed civic fabric that stitches it together. Ordinarily, superhero narratives grapple with exogenous threats to civic stability, like the giant alien monsters of the *Avengers* series, rather than endogenous (and more ordinary) worries of civic decay. But it is this, in part, that makes Nolan's

Batman compelling—that the threat to Gotham is only personified and incited by the villains but ultimately located within the citizenry itself. Scarecrow, the Joker, and Bane all recruit the citizenry to effect violence against the city.

The Joker demonstrates the frailty of Gotham's political leadership by sowing chaos, illustrating the fragility of civic trust. To wit, the Joker consistently demands audiences with Batman, thus privileging his place in the city and highlighting this precarious legitimacy. But conferring Batman with such de facto legitimacy only serves to further rend the liberal norms of the city.

Midway through the film the Joker is taken into custody, thereby getting his meeting with Batman. Batman accuses the Joker of being a common criminal, but he retorts:

> Don't talk like one of them [i.e. the police]—you're not, even if you'd like to be. To them you're a freak like me… they just need you right now. But as soon as they don't, they'll cast you out like a leper. Their morals, their code… it's a bad joke. Dropped at the first sign of trouble. They're only as good as the world allows them to be. You'll see—I'll show you… when the chips are down, these civilized people… they'll eat each other. See, I'm not a monster… I'm just ahead of the curve.[6]

The Joker is explicit here that he aims (among other things) to show the inability of people to conform to rules. People's codes of conduct—the law, but more so, the social contract—rupture under stress. His point here isn't that people are evil by nature but that they don't have a settled nature. They are not committed to rules or order. And insofar as Batman's identity is constituted by an adherence to order (noted appropriately in repeated references to his serious and humorless demeanor), he doesn't represent the people whom he casts as good or at least "ready to believe in good" (Fig. 5.1).[6]

Furthermore, the Joker rightly points out that Batman is not obviously on the same side as law enforcement, let alone an officer of it. Gotham police are routinely corrupt, and in a way Batman refuses to be. Meanwhile, cops are on the take from the mob in *Batman Begins*, officers like Burke and Ramirez are corrupt and corruptible in *The Dark Knight*, and Commissioner Gordon is happily willing to lie, as when the body of Harvey Dent isn't located following the explosion at Gotham General Hospital. The police are mostly ineffective, where Batman is effective, and the police are divided, where Batman is devoted. Batman is beyond the

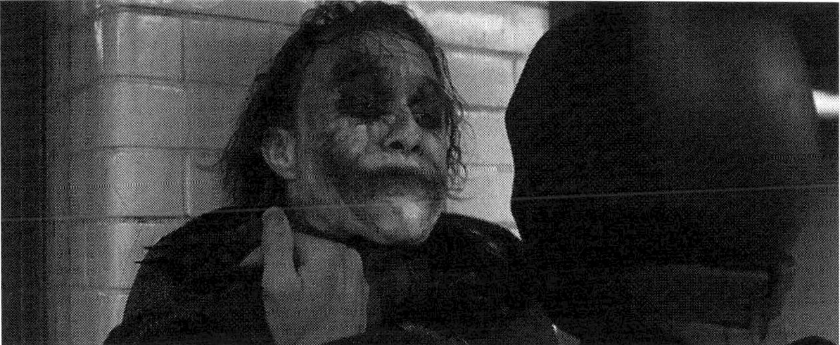

Fig. 5.1 The Joker confronts Batman. Screengrabs generated by Yosef Washington for the author

law, not merely distinct from it. Whereas Batman sees himself as an exemplar of the citizenry, the Joker casts him as aberrant and outside.

Batman seems reluctant to accept the Joker's gloss, but it's been constructed that way ab initio. The Nolan trilogy begins with a young Bruce Wayne falling down a boarded up well to be swarmed by bats. This is a flashback, a nightmare that visits an older Wayne while searching for some catharsis in the Orient. This episode is the genesis myth of Batman's character—he wants criminals to fear the law as he feared those bats. Upon returning to Gotham after his period in the wilderness, Wayne encounters a city that is enthralled by criminals, as Dawes decries:

> This city is rotting.... Corruption is killing Gotham ... [Falcone] carries on flooding our city with crime and drugs... Falcone may not have killed your parents, Bruce, but he's destroying everything they stood for... They all know where to find Falcone... But no one will touch him because he keeps the bad people rich and the good people scared.[1]

Fear is the undoing of Gotham, corrupting its police and political leadership, making its citizenry desperate. When Wayne meets Falcone he says as much. "Money isn't power down here—fear is."[1] Gotham faces a dual problem, then: People are in fear and there is no single body that commands it. Police, elected representatives, and criminals are all divided. Indeed, that is what Batman is instructed to combat. Ducard/Ra's al Ghul, Wayne's mentor, instructs him regarding his new persona, "To conquer fear, you must become fear... you must bask in the fear of other men."[1] Batman is to become the embodiment of fear, and it is that fear which is to push back on the criminal decay corrupting Gotham. But in doing so he positions himself outside of the demos.

The Hobbesian Take

The first film appears to be characterized by the instantiation and reification of fear. Al Ghul, Scarecrow, and even Batman himself repeatedly remind us what a scary world Gotham is, and it is through the vehicle of fear that Batman generates legitimacy (albeit an undemocratic sort).

Hobbes, of course, is the great theorist of fear. Throughout *Leviathan* he identifies how fear conditions our conduct and constructs the political state:

> [W]hat quality soever maketh a man beloved, or feared of many, or the reputation of such quality, is power, because it is a means to have the assistance, and service of many. Good success is power, because it maketh reputation of wisdom or good fortune, which makes men either fear him or rely on him.[7]

Fear is instrumental to the process of political consolidation and a tent-pole of power.

> The greatest of humane powers is that which is compounded of the powers of most men, united by consent in one person, natural or civil, that has the use of all their powers depending on his will, such as is the power of a commonwealth, or depending on the wills of each particular, such as is the power of a faction or of divers factions leagued. Therefore to have servants is power; to have friends is power; for they are strengths united.[8]

Fear shapes power, enabling the construction of the state from disorder. In nature no one has sufficient power to command all other agents, entailing a state of "continual fear, and danger of violent death."[9] At times some actors might have control over a group but never a sufficient number to be more than a gang. For Hobbes too, fear of the invisible is just as (if not more) effective than the thrall of an embodied threat,[10] and it is fear that directs people to consent to the social contract.[11]

When we meet Wayne in *Batman Begins* the city is fraying. Philanthropists like Wayne's father attempt to save the city but are ultimately unable to do anything more than hold the city in an equilibrium of turmoil. Philanthropists spend money on what they see as good, and the mob contests their efforts, using a gray-economy to promote evil. The scarcity in the city reinforces that equilibrium, and toward the end of the film, a veritable "war of all against all" ensues when a toxin is released, stirring the denizens of the Narrows[12] into a psychotic paranoid frenzy. Gotham is not a political whole, it is a mere aggregation of colocated groups and interests.

Batman seeks to put the criminals of the city under his thrall, aiding the police who are otherwise outmatched. By the beginning of *The Dark Knight*, Batman has got "criminals... running scared." That is, after all, how he thinks of himself. "I frighten criminals," he tells Ra's al Ghul. But al Ghul understands that he's meaningfully mistaken, "You frighten everybody," he retorts. The effect of Batman is to (albeit unwittingly) assume a kind of Hobbesian sovereignty. Batman seeks to be an intervention on the side of law, but as the Joker correctly notes, he's "not one of them" (i.e. the police)—he has become *political*. To become political, in this sense, is to take on a role that creates political order from the ground up. There are many political actors, of course, like mayors, senators, and police officers, who all have roles that are carved out in the legal documents of the state. I mean something different, though. To be political in the sense of Batman here is to be a part of or party to the foundation of that political order. The mayor occupies a role granted by the city's charter. Batman serves here to construct the very constitution of Gotham.[13]

Batman is the only symbol strong enough to enthrall the entire populous, good and evil. Batman sees himself as restoring order, but in fact he is the bringer of the law to Gotham, constructing the political where previously there was only cohabitation. Wayne understands that the true role of Batman is to serve as a symbol, and it is the efficacy of the symbolic that effects political order, similar to the way Carl Schmitt casts Hobbes' project.[14] This symbolic power runs at the core of Hobbes' project, according to Schmitt, whereby the image of the Leviathan is not mere abstraction but a representation and reconfiguration of the political order—one that rises from below rather than being ordained from above. Here too, Batman's efficacy results (and falters) from the symbolic traction of the myth he comes to signify. That is the apparent consequence of the emergence of Batman.

Hobbes Falters

Fear, however, is not a tidy or stable attitude upon which to rest politics, Nolan easily shows. This point isn't demonstrated with political theoretic argumentation or empirical evidence (though there is that, too[15]) but through the narrative. That is, the force of the political theoretic critique flows from the masterful composition of the second film.[16] Through the character of the Joker we see how fear is manipulable, mercurial, and ephemeral, effectively sublimating its efficacy, and with it the construction of Batman's Hobbesian authority. While there are 20 mentions of the word "fear" in the screenplay of *Batman Begins*, there are no mentions in *The Dark Knight*.

The Joker of the second installment insists on drawing attention to Batman's legitimacy deficit by repeatedly undermining his persona, identifying the similarities between himself and the hero. The Joker comes from outside the city to disrupt its civic norms, just as Batman comes to reconstitute them. Even though Wayne is very much a part of the city, it is only after returning from abroad in his new persona, Batman, that he is able to staunch Gotham's corrosion. While Batman is ultimately able to mitigate the damage of al Ghul, what is more consequential is the civic faith that appears to reemerge by the beginning of the second film. Wayne says as much in a fundraiser for Harvey Dent: "I believe in Harvey Dent. On his watch, Gotham can feel a little safer. A little more optimistic… To the face of Gotham's bright future—Harvey Dent." While ominously foreshadowing Dent's transformation into the character of Two-Face, the line signals civic optimism along with Wayne's aspiration that legitimate officers can relieve him of his executive capacity. Though he has precipitated a turn of tides against organized crime by the start of *The Dark Knight*, the larger accomplishment is that of fostering the rise of legitimate actors in Gotham, like Dent.

The transition, however, is aborted. The Joker exploits the psychological limitations of both Batman and Dent in order to turn Dent into a villain, ultimately leading Batman to kill Dent (thereby violating the sole self-imposed check on his power).

This is where the trilogy's political theoretic account gets interesting, however. By the beginning of the second film Batman has become a sovereign of sorts, inspiring good members of the city to stand up and leading criminals to retreat. But this proves of limited success. There is still criminality in Gotham. And as criminals aim to undermine Batman, it now constitutes a political, rather than merely legal, assault. This comes in stark contrast to the beginning of the third film, *The Dark Knight Rises*, where we are told of an intervening eight, largely quiet, years—years in which Batman has been absent from crime fighting. The mayor trumpets that the city is flourishing. "[Police Commissioner Gordon] can tell you about the bad old days, when the criminals and corrupt ran town with such a tight grasp that people put their faith in a murderous thug in a mask and a cape." But now, Gotham is florishing. Officer John Blake laments to Commissioner Gordon, "Sir, I've been a cop for a year and I've only logged half a dozen arrests. When you and Dent cleaned the streets, you cleaned 'em good. Pretty soon we'll be chasing overdue library books." The transition to a stable political order occurs *after* Batman exits, decidedly in his absence.[17]

The Dark Knight is plagued by the chaos that the Joker sows, exposing how "when the chips are down, these civilized people... they'll eat each other."

The morality of Gotham's citizenry still hinges on good and bad, as Hobbes would cast it, not justice and injustice. This distinction harkens to Hobbes' discussion of the natural condition of mankind (also known as the "state of nature"). There he argues that before political order is established every person has the prerogative to distinguish for themselves what is good and bad, and they do so according to what they like and dislike. It is not until the sovereign is authorized to rule that common categories of right and wrong—what we know as justice and injustice—are settled.

The Joker is able to contest the political by exposing this residual lack of accord, the lingering distinction between legal and political notions of justice and what people take to be the good given what they prize. He even successfully incorporates all criminal activity under his direction—ostensibly bringing greater order to the state—further illustrating the city's residual corruption. The Joker repeatedly shows the enforcement power of the city to be null and that even under the aegis of Batman, the city is still in a veritable natural state. Again and again, the bald collective action problems deployed in *The Dark Knight* demonstrate that fear has not been sufficient to construct a political order.

Schmitt Ascendant

In killing Two-Face (and violating his only self-imposed rule) Batman kills Gotham's "white knight," becoming "whatever Gotham needs [him] to be." When asked by his son why Batman flees, Commissioner Gordon responds, "he's the hero Gotham deserves… but not the one it needs right now. So we'll hunt him, because he can take it. Because he's not our hero he's a silent guardian, a watchful protector… a dark knight."[6] To preserve civic faith, Batman takes the blame for the death, rather than revealing Dent's criminal turn and shattering Gotham's feeble civic faith. In assuming this blame he comes to be understood differently by the citizens of Gotham. Instead of a vigilante acting outside the law, he comes to be seen as an enemy, attacking the very foundations of Gotham's political order. The end of the second film does not dislodge Batman from his key political capacity but only moves him to occupy a different, though every bit as critical, role.

Just as fear serves as a *political* role for Hobbes, as I explain earlier, the role of an enemy (not merely a criminal) serves as a *political* role in the theory of Carl Schmitt. Schmitt writes that "the political entity… is the decisive entity for the friend-or-enemy grouping; and in this… it is sovereign."[18] By this he understands politics to be constituted or founded by the opposition of forces that together protect and threaten the state. The juxtaposition of conflict mobilizes citizens to affiliate with the reigning political order and thus serves to ground political statehood.

What is striking here is that, more than taking the persona of the enemy in the Schmittian dialectic, Batman takes it upon himself to articulate the dialectic. He is its author and he dictates that he is to be the enemy, truly becoming "whatever Gotham needs [him] to be." It is this pivotal moment that constructs politics in Gotham and by the start of *The Dark Knight Rises* order in the city has been restored. Criminality—private corruption of the political ethos—has all but vanished. Batman's legitimacy comes by serving Gotham not as the friend but the enemy, the Dark Knight (Fig. 5.2).

Batman Begins grounds Batman's legitimacy in a kind of Hobbesian sovereignty, constructing the political domain through fear. As Schmitt notes of Hobbes' Leviathan, however, the symbol is not adequate to construct and cohere the political, and consequently Batman's regime fails to take hold.[19] The Joker is, again and again, able to undermine the resulting order, demonstrating that on Hobbesian terms (i.e. through collective action scenarios) the city is not in fact a political whole.

The killing of Dent acts as a point of inflection, whereby Batman becomes the enemy. Here we see the pivot of the political theory in the trilogy from the Hobbesian to the Schmittian. Gotham's nominal enemies remain fractured and of the private domain—Gambol, Maroni, the

Fig. 5.2 Batman becomes what Gotham needs him to be

Chechens. As such, they can't contribute to the Schmittian friend-enemy construction of a political space. Batman, as a public figure and purported political assailant, unites Gotham by assuming the mantle of enemy.

Batman has finally accreted stable political legitimacy in the move from hero as friend of Gotham to hero qua enemy. This is, to be clear, a true kind of legitimacy, where Batman chooses to occupy a role for the good of Gotham, even though it serves to his detriment. Wayne becomes a recluse and Wayne Enterprises falters in the intervening period, but Gotham, by contrast, steadies itself.

Bane and the Redundancy of the Schmittian Enemy

The vulnerability in such an arrangement is obvious, one that Schmitt himself attends to. As Gil Anidjar notes, facing multiple enemies at once "may constitute a serious, even dangerous problem" to the fabric of political order according to the philosophy of Schmitt.[20] Schmitt's *concept* turns on the binary friend-enemy dialectic, but what happens when enemies proliferate? How does the political react to a multiplicity of enemies?

Schmitt confronts this in "The Theory of the Partisan," writing, "Every two-front war poses the question of who the real enemy is. Is it not a sign of inner division to have more than one single real enemy?"[21]

Our age is not a series of global alliances partitioning Axis from Ally. The enemy of our era would seem to be the faceless outsider (likely from abroad) that threatens "our way of life."[22] Insofar as conventional conflict is moribund, our contemporary vulnerabilities have multiplied, from worries of electoral manipulation to cyber-espionage to international and domestic terrorism. What happens when the enemy multiplies in kind?

For what it's worth, Schmitt answers this by insisting on the original dialectic. He contends that a two-front partisan conflict will ultimately resolve into a conflict with the absolute enemy, where ostensibly one manifestation of the real enemy comes to be dominant. The stakes of such a conflict, he notes, are raised in the contemporary era given the persistent existential threat of nuclear attack.[23]

Nolan's filmic arc offers a different gloss on the two-fronted conflict, however. Nolan, of course, isn't directly concerned for the ontology of Schmitt's dialectic. Instead his work explores the dynamic of two antagonists, rupturing the city's political fabric in the process. Regardless of the eventual ends of that conflict (whether or not the enemy does indeed coalesce into a unitary subject), the third film looks at how that conflict, nuclear weapons and all, affects Gotham and ultimately the Batman mythos (Fig. 5.3).

Fig. 5.3 Bane as a populist rhetorician

Bane, the central antagonist of the last installment of the Nolan cycle, serves as such a redundant enemy. He feigns a rhetoric of the partisan, admonishing Gotham to "take control... take control of your city. Behold, the instrument of your liberation!" Instead of coalescing on one absolute enemy, Gotham dissolves in the process, expelling both Batman and Bane.

Bane is a mirror of Batman, accentuating the Schmittian problematic. The attack on Gotham is not merely brought by another in the litany of Arkham's villains but a student of al Ghul's, assuming the role of Commander of the League of Shadows (a role Wayne may have occupied but for his defection), matching Batman blow for blow in strength and acuity. And while Bane weaponizes the threat of nuclear attack on Gotham, the system is one developed by Wayne Enterprises, thus the product of Wayne himself.

If Batman's legitimacy is derived by serving Gotham in taking on the role of the enemy, that legitimacy is again undermined when Bane appears and obliterates the stabilizing effect of the designation. Just as the Joker provides a counterpoint to Batman's authoritarian streak by effecting chaos in the second film, Bane in the third film counterposes Batman as a carbon copy, puritanically fighting a crusade for no compensation, and funding the efforts through opaque channels, mirroring those of Wayne Enterprises. At least in Nolan's telling, the concept of the enemy ceases to play a constructive role in Gotham at the arrival of Bane, destabilizing the city's political dialectic.

Discussion

Where does this leave us? At the end of Nolan's project Gotham is splintered, bombed out, and anarchic following the mayor's death. While one might lay blame at Batman's feet for inviting this sort of Bedlam on Gotham, the films don't appear to give credibility to the charge. Ra's al Ghul begins the series by insisting on destroying Gotham, while Bane, with the aid of his daughter Talia al Ghul, returns to fulfill that ambition. So Wayne's narcissism isn't the cause of Gotham's assaults. But neither does he leave Gotham better off than when he began. The mob might have corrupted the city's institutions, but it didn't decimate them. Ultimately his ambitions of proving civic stability go unrealized, thereby adding scrutiny to his legitimacy deficit.

Beyond the dark, thoughtful, and nuanced characters that Nolan animates, as well as the Gotham he constructs around them, the films recruit heft by taking the political theory of the Batman universe seriously. Nolan isn't the only one to do this—Frank Miller certainly did too in the 1980s—but by taking on Batman's legitimacy deficit the films come to interrogate the character's very mythos. Indeed, at the time of their release there was robust discussion about the ways that the films tracked political headlines of the day including terrorism, executive power, and radical leftist politics.[24] With some distance I can't help but think that these critiques, while rightly attending to the political theoretical intervention of the films, lose the forest for the trees.

Instead, I see these films as offering a coherent narrative critique of Batman's legitimacy. Rather than construct Batman along the hero/anti-hero axis, Nolan levels a broadside at the foundational legitimacy of Batman's mythos. Bracketing specifically democratic commitments, Nolan is skeptical of any coherent account of legitimacy, one which cedes Batman the right to conduct himself as he does. In the absence of such an account, the character of Batman risks degenerating into a private actor, operating with no more license than any of his adversaries.[25]

In order to explore the matter, Nolan offers a cycle of three films that provide candidate accounts to ground Batman's legitimacy. The sentiment of fear, which runs through the Batman universe, is an obvious *prima facia* foundation for legitimacy. Mirroring Hobbes, Batman's authority derives from the terror he induces in both the city of Gotham and its (nominal) enemies. As such, he dons a mantle of Hobbesian sovereign. Fear, however, proves to be an unstable foundation for politics, as the Joker evidences. The Joker's chaos demonstrates how easily the cooperative equilibria of collective action scenarios can be ruptured. The Hobbesian fear that serves to cement the consent of the governed under the thrall of the Leviathan proves porous at the hands of the Joker's terrorism.[26] Instead, Batman must take on the role of the enemy in order to steady Gotham and wrest it from its assailants. Batman is ultimately more powerful as a symbol, but provocatively, a symbol of threat rather than a symbol of justice.

The final film in the cycle upends these Schmittian grounds of legitimacy by pitting Batman against Bane. While vying for control of a nuclear weapon that threatens the city's existence, they each present distinctive instantiations of the enemy, thereby throwing Gotham into chaos and again vitiating Batman of political legitimacy. Nolan's cycle, at least, provides no stable account of political legitimacy, with each attempt ultimately proving ephemeral.

Beyond political theoretical concerns, though, what of the use of medium and genre? Why ought we find Nolan's political critique of Batman, and the Batman universe more broadly, compelling or persuasive? And why present this critique as narrative? As I have said, these films are not, at least primarily, discourses on political theory. They don't advance an argument for how politics ought to function or what justifies political action. While the theory of Hobbes and Schmitt are certainly resonant with the film's narrative structure and dialogue, nowhere is their imprimatur invoked. (Nor are the films the least bit worse off for it.) There is certainly no substantive articulation of Batman's legitimacy deficit in the films, aside from the tangential comments referenced at the very beginning of this chapter. Rather, Nolan offers an endogenous critique of Batman, using the power and authority of the mythical narrative itself to level his critique. The world of superheroes is constantly being written and rewritten and is capable of being made consonant (or dissonant, for that matter) with any manner of normative theory. Whether the theoretical schema holds is not a matter of substance or cogency but of narrative—whether we as audience are taken and compelled by the character of Batman being depicted.

Nolan is working through a core problematic of Batman's legitimacy.[27] Since the narrative and mythos are decentralized and contested, there is no definitive way to establish Batman's legitimacy, however. Nolan's argument isn't a necessary entailment, that a Hobbesian authority of fear just does degenerate into a Schmittian friend-enemy dialectic, say. Instead, Nolan offers a riveting cycle of films, deeply rooted in the lore of the Batman universe, that struck a chord with both devoted and casual audiences. In providing a compelling narrative that persistently undermines possible political theoretic accounts to ground Batman's legitimacy, Nolan provides a kind of possibility claim: There is no sure way to guarantee Batman's legitimacy. It is through the film's narrative that Nolan problematizes Batman's mythology, casting the major normative axis not in terms of hero or anti-hero but as the possibility of legitimacy. Ultimately, through the crafting of a superb narrative, Nolan's cycle comes to articulate the paucity of such grounds of legitimacy.

* * *

The Nolan films are not political theory *simpliciter* but holistic works of their medium and genre. The characters, screenplay, plot, and cinematography together comprise a complete aesthetic narrative offering. But part of the depth of this cycle is the theoretical exploration that it takes on, beyond "just" telling a good story. It also comes to reflect on the political legitimacy of the Batman mythos more generally. Whether Nolan actually consulted the primary texts of Hobbes or Schmitt is entirely beside the point, of course. What is intriguing about the narrative arc of the films is how closely it tracks the major themes of these theorists, and how it puts them in dialogue with one another (a point which Schmitt took to be completely natural). As I have cast it, the cycle serves to problematize the politics of Batman, demonstrating the impossibility of guaranteeing his legitimacy. He is never officially deputized to assume his role in law enforcement, and aside from Dent's populist characterization of Batman's democratic grounding, there is no good reason to think that he serves in a particularly democratic capacity. Instead, Nolan looks more broadly for Batman's authority, first turning to Hobbesian fear and then to the Schmittian enemy, ultimately showing how his role as foe is destabilized by a multiplicity of threats. In Nolan's saga Batman and Bane obliterate one another, but the point serves to demonstrate that Batman's role qua heroic enemy is volatile in the presence of true existential threats. As such, he can no longer maintain his legitimacy as foe, devolving again to a hero without authority.

Nolan's films no doubt offer a critique of the proliferation of superhero blockbusters, each portending to save our way of life through sundry a-legitimate channels. I appreciate his pushback here. But the trilogy need not be a full rebuke of Batman, either. Rather it circumscribes Batman's authority to moments of peril that cannot be righted without coercive means. Batman's time is for those darkest of nights. But when the sun rises and order is restored, we need not place our faith in such problematic authorities.

Notes

1. *Batman Begins*. Directed by Christopher Nolan. Warner Bros. Pictures, 2005. The author would like to acknowledge Yosef Washington, graduate student in philosophy at the University of Pennsylvania, for tracking down the images in the chapter. He also wishes to thank his co-panelists and audience at the Southern Political Science Association (SPSA) conference for their thoughtful inputs and Damien Picariello, in particular, for his stewardship of the chapter and project in general.

2. While there are reasons to distinguish between the characters of Wayne and his alter-ego Batman, for the purposes of this chapter, I elide these subtleties and refer to the two almost interchangeably.
3. For example, *Batman: The Dark Knight Returns,* by Frank Miller. DC Comics, 1986.
4. For example, *The Bank Job* (2008), *The Italian Job* (2003), *Oceans 11* (1960), *Oceans 11* (2001), *Oceans 12* (2004), *Oceans 13* (2007), *Oceans 8* (2018), and *The Sting* (1973).
5. More precisely, by a factor of $\frac{1}{(n)(n-1)}$. For the nerds, you get this by asking how the payoff changes from having *n-1* people in the group rather than *n*. So $\frac{x}{n} - y = \frac{x}{n-1}$, where *x* is the value of the spoils and *n* is the total number of group members. A little arithmetic shows that the equation above solves for *y*.
6. *The Dark Knight.* Directed by Christopher Nolan. Warner Bros. Studios, 2008.
7. *Leviathan* by Thomas Hobbes. Indianapolis, IN, Hackett Press, (1994): 51.
8. Ibid, p. 50.
9. Ibid, p. 76.
10. Ibid, p. 64.
11. Ibid, p. 84.
12. Gotham's slum district.
13. Constitution qua "to constitute."
14. *The Leviathan in the state theory of Thomas Hobbes: meaning and failure of a political symbol.* By Schmitt, Carl. Chicago, IL. University of Chicago Press, 2008. Chap. 7.
15. "Scary warnings and rational precautions: A review of the psychology of fear appeals." Robert Ruiter, Charles Abraham, and Gerjo Kok. *Psychology and Health* 16, no. 6 (2001): 626.
16. Evidenced by *The New York Times*' "Critic's Pick," eight academy award nominations including Heath Ledger's posthumous win for best supporting actor and 94% positive rating from Rotten Tomatoes.
17. *The Dark Knight Rises.* Directed by Christopher Nolan. Warner Bros. Studios, 2012.
18. *The concept of the political: Expanded edition.* By Carl Schmitt. University of Chicago Press, (2008): 39.
19. Schmitt, *Leviathan* (2008): 80–81.
20. "Terror right." By Gil Anidjar. *CR: The New Centennial Review* 4, no. 3 (2004): p. 35.
21. *Theory of the Partisan: Intermediate Commentary on the Concept of the Political.* By Carl Schmitt. CR: The New Centennial Review, Vol. 4, No. 3, (2004): 60–61.

22. "The text of President Bush's address Tuesday night, after terrorist attacks on New York and Washington." By George W. Bush. http://edition.cnn.com/2001/US/09/11/bush.speech.text/ Accessed 09/03/18.
23. Schmitt, 2004, p. 66.
24. For example, "Batman Versus the Egalitarians." By Matthew Yglesias. http://www.slate.com/blogs/moneybox/2012/07/23/batman_versus_the_egalitarians.html

    "Dark Knight Politics." By Matthew Yglesias. https://www.theatlantic.com/politics/archive/2008/07/-em-dark-knight-em-politics/49451/

    "Political Superheroes." By Matthew Yglesias & Ross Douthat. https://www.youtube.com/watch?v=D8Pm1i6cEIk

    "The Dark Knight: Neither Superhero or Antihero." By Tim Delaney https://www.psychologytoday.com/us/blog/media-stew/200807/the-dark-knight-neither-superhero-or-antihero
25. I don't mean to say that Batman risks being *as bad as* his foes—that's likely a question of ethics as well as politics. But insofar as Batman takes on executive political capacities, his claim to authority is no greater than Bane's, say.
26. Not terrorism in the conventional sense, that is, deploying violence against civilian targets in order to exact political concessions, but rather terrorism in a Hobbesian sense, employing fear to challenge the foundations of politics.
27. Miller, 1986. "Dark Knight, White Knight, and the King of Anarchy." By Stephanie Carmichael. In *Riddle Me This, Batman!: Essays on the Universe of the Dark Knight* (2011): 54–69. "The Dark Knight Errant." By Christopher Bundrick. In *Riddle Me This, Batman!: Essays on the Universe of the Dark Knight* (2011): 24.

CHAPTER 6

Batman the Noble Dog: The Costs of Spiritedness for the Individual and Society

Ian J. Drake and Matthew B. Lloyd

Batman's self-imposed mission to rid Gotham City of its criminal element has always presented the problem of vigilantism. From the perspective of criminology, Batman's methods raise the problem of whether society can be governed, or govern itself, with extralegal law enforcement. The problem presented by Batman's behavior is often stated, as the ancient Roman satirist Juvenal famously put it, "*quis custodiet ipsos custodes?*" ("but who is going to guard the guards themselves?").[1] The threat posed by self-appointed guardians, such as Batman and other super heroes, has been frequently analyzed by scholars and fans alike. Yet, there is an additional, less frequently discussed, problem presented by Batman's behavior: what are the costs to Batman and the citizens of Gotham from a guard who refuses to govern? In this chapter, the authors discuss Plato's conception of spiritedness and analyze how Batman's behavior affects his soul and the souls of Gotham City's citizens. The authors suggest that the cost of moral

I. J. Drake (✉)
Montclair State University, Montclair, NJ, USA
e-mail: drakei@mail.montclair.edu

M. B. Lloyd
DCComicsnews.com, Greensboro, NC, USA

D. K. Picariello (ed.), *Politics in Gotham*,
https://doi.org/10.1007/978-3-030-05776-3_6

relativism in defining justice leads to a passion for revenge without the responsibility of leadership. The costs to the souls of Batman and Gothamites render all too willing to subordinate justice to revenge and be prisoners of their own sense of right and wrong.

Batman claims to abstain from governing Gotham, but he is part of the governance of the unruly city. He claims to be the enforcer of justice, doing what the public law enforcers refuse to or cannot do. Yet, in addition to the danger of an uncontrollable ("unwatched") vigilante, Batman—whether he admits it or not—governs Gotham through his vigilantism. As Nigel Lawson, a one-time Chancellor of the Exchequer of Britain, once said, "To govern is to choose." Batman chooses to enforce his own understanding of justice—sometimes in accord with the positive law, sometimes outside of it. But he thinks of himself as apart from the society, hovering above it in order to help redeem it. Yet, his behavior exacts costs which are more than theoretical. They are costs for himself, as a person and would-be member of a civil society. Also, there are costs for the citizens of Gotham, who see the example set by Batman and must live their lives under the regime he establishes. His methods are an example to the rest of Gotham's citizens, many of whom are victims of the criminal class and yearn for proper law enforcement and good governance. Batman may think he is not a ruler, but he rules nonetheless. In other words, he "chooses" and his choices have consequences for himself and Gotham's citizens. What are the costs? Are they worth it? Political theory, in particular ancient political philosophy, may provide a way of understanding the problems presented by Batman, super heroes, and the vigilantes of our real world.

Plato's *Republic* and the Noble Dogs of Ancient Athens

The ancient Athenian philosopher Plato's most famous work is *The Republic.* Written in approximately 380 BCE, it is concerned with the nature of the human soul, the structure of society, and the question of what role philosophy plays, or should play, in governance. Although Plato's world was vastly different from our own, he is still read today because he grapples with timeless questions regarding human nature and good government. The work has an alternate title or subtitle: "on the just." The Greek word for "justice" was "*dikē*" which has various, similar meanings, such as "justice," "order," and "all-in justice."[2] The Greek Goddess of justice was Dike, and her Roman name was Justitia. In God form, she represented order in nature and was originally one of the Greek seasons of the year.

Plato's *Republic* is concerned, in part, with the meaning and role justice plays or can play in a society. However, Plato does not conceive of justice as applicable only at the societal level. He also conceives of justice as applied to individuals. In fact, justice starts with individuals and the correct ordering of the individual soul. Plato contends that the human soul is composed of three essential parts: reason, spirit, and desires (*Republic* 443b–e).[3] Plato claims that justice is not limited to "someone's doing his own externally, but with what is inside him, with what is truly himself and his own" (443d). In order to be a just person, one must "harmonize[] the three parts of himself [i.e., reason, spirit, and desire] like three limiting notes on a musical scale—high, low, and middle" (443d). In short, justice starts with the individual and provides what Plato considers the pattern or model for justice in the wider society.

The just individual, or the justly, rightly ordered soul, possesses the three essential parts: reason (the ability to think dispassionately, with reference to facts and logical ordering of thought), desire (the passionate pursuit of bodily necessities, pleasures, and interests), and spirit (the motives for action, such as anger, ambition, pride, honor, loyalty). These are not abstractions. In fact, Plato thought each element had a particular location in the physical body: the gut held desires, spirit resided in the heart, and the head held the reasoning faculty.[4] In another of Plato's works, the *Phaedrus* (c. 370 BCE), he illustrates how the soul should function at its best by using an analogy of a chariot pulled by two horses. These three actors (one charioteer and two horses) represent the three parts of the soul, with the implication that one part of the soul will maintain control over the other two. The question is which part of the soul is in the driver's seat: reason, or spirit, or desire? Plato contends that the just, well-ordered soul puts reason in the charioteer's seat in control of the powerful horses of spirit and desire. All three parts of the soul are needed and, in fact, cannot not be eliminated. A complete, fully functioning soul must have desires and rationality. The question is what part governs?

The ill- or poorly ordered soul is one where, for example, desire is in the charioteer's seat. If reason and spirit are commanded by desire, then a person is ruled by their passions. A common example would be a person who uses reason to achieve their passions, such as consuming pornography or indulging in food and drink. The consequences of such pursuits are harmful to the body and soul. The desire-centered person is a kind of slave to their passions and their reasoning capabilities have been subordinated to serving base, low ends. One may retain a rationality capable of recognizing that excessive consumption of alcohol is or will be harmful. But if desires are driving the chariot, then the rational faculty is ignored or subordinated to the satisfaction of one's desire for the numbness of inebriation.

By contrast, the well-ordered and well-governed soul is the one with reason in the charioteer's seat. If reason controls desires and spiritedness, then one lives for well-considered purposes and uses reason to judge if and when to pursue a desire or to judiciously employ a motive, such as ambition, to reach a good end. With rationality in control, a person is able to govern their passions, check their emotions, and govern their motivations for acting.

But what of the person who puts spiritedness in the charioteer's seat? What kind of life does this individual lead? Spirit is a slippery concept for modern readers. (Reason and desire are familiar terms in our modern English lexicon, with largely the same meaning as they had in Plato's time. But spirit has multiple meanings today, with only oblique relevance to Plato's usage.) Spirit for Plato was concerned with motives for action and played the role in the soul of supporting the reasoning faculty in carrying out its decisions.[5] The Greek word for "spirit" is *thymos*, which is often associated with anger. For example, in *The Republic* the spirited part of the soul is associated with the angry reaction a person has when an injustice has been committed by another (439e–440d).

Plato takes the tripartite conception of the individual human soul and applies it to an imaginary city-state, the only kind of state known in the Greek world in Plato's time. The three parts of the soul—reason, spirit, and desire—are analogized to the three types of people (or three classes of citizens) in Plato's imaginary city-state—rulers, auxiliaries (soldiers), and the commercial class (441a). Just as the well-ordered individual soul places reason in command of spiritedness and desire, so too the well-ordered city-state puts rulers (who use reason) in command of auxiliaries (soldiers) and the "money-making" commercial class. The role of the rulers is to use reason to preserve the city-state. The role of the commercial class is to provide the material goods used and consumed by all within the city-state. The role of the auxiliaries (soldiers) is to defend the city against its enemies.

The auxiliaries must have righteous anger in order to take the rough action often needed to defend the city-state. They must use anger to motivate them, just as an individual uses their spiritedness to respond to an injustice. The soldiers are compared to "noble dogs" or "pedigreed dogs" in Plato's terminology (375e) since dogs are "courageous," possessing a "fearless and unconquerable" soul (375b).[6] Dogs are loyal to their owners and friendly toward those they know and hostile to strangers. This idea—doing good to one's friends and harm to one's enemies—is one the definitions of justice put forth in *The Republic* (332d).

Accordingly, the auxiliaries (soldiers) of the ideal city-state are like "noble dogs" who guard the city, showing hostility to its enemies and kindness to its friends. These soldiers play an essential role in the city-state. But soldiers are not placed at the apex of political power; only the rulers—who are associated with reason—retain the authority to rule. Again, the ideal city-state's power structure mirrors the ideal individual soul: reason (rulers) in the charioteer's seat, commanding desires (the commercial class), and spirit (soldiers). The spirited soldiers are associated with anger—albeit righteous anger—and must be watched, controlled, and subordinated to the rational decisions of the rulers.

This is the infrastructure of the well-ordered city-state. But what if spirit dominates reason? What if spirit—anger, even righteous, well-justified anger—is in the charioteer's seat? If so, reason is reduced to being merely a tool to achieve anger's ends. That is, the rational element no longer commands the spirit and desires. Plato understands this displacement of reason as a defect in the individual's soul. If reason is not in command, then the soul is ill ordered and "unjust." So too, does Plato consider the city-state to be unjust if ruled by the soldier class.

Batman, the Noble Dog

Batman might aptly be described as an auxiliary of Gotham: a defender of the city against its enemies. Like Plato's soldiers, Batman does not claim to rule. He displays righteous anger against the city's enemies, which, of course, include all criminals, from the petty thugs to the infamous arch-villains.

It is no secret to the denizens of Gotham City, especially the criminals, that Batman owns the night. He operates when the lights go out and the moon goes up in order to protect the city and its inhabitants from those who would do them harm. His commitment to his self-proclaimed mission was first shown in *Detective Comics* in 1939, a few days after his parents' death. Bruce, in a prayerful attitude, makes a solemn vow: "And I swear by the spirits of my parents to avenge their deaths by spending the rest of my life warring on all criminals."[7] However, his methods to achieve this goal are most unordinary. Instead of joining the police force, he chooses to dress up like a bat and prowl Gotham City by night. To confront criminals, Batman knowingly becomes a criminal. For example, in Frank Miller's *The Dark Knight Returns*, Batman's response to a US senator calling super heroes criminals is recalled: "Sure we're criminals. We've always been criminals. We have to be criminals."[8]

In Miller's *The Dark Knight Returns*, not only has Batman been missing for ten years, but in his absence, the office of mayor has fallen to a weak-willed politician who has ceded the office's power in Gotham. In the ensuing events, Commissioner Gordon kills a 17-year-old mutant gang member and is relieved of duty. The mayor is completely beside himself as he tries to determine whom to appoint as the new commissioner. The ensuing montage of news coverage asks the question: "Who will be the next Police Commissioner?" Miller's page layout and jump cut to the Batcave make it obvious that Bruce Wayne, Batman, is the only person truly capable of handling the issue. However, Batman is most effective outside of government, not in the politically legitimate context of a police commissioner.[9] Miller depicts Batman as the one individual who is capable of handling the chaos that is Gotham City. Yet, Batman explicitly rejects any legitimate political office. Accordingly, he fakes his own death at the end of the story, goes underground, and will ultimately save the city. At the moment that Gotham and the world were most vulnerable, he could have easily stepped forward after having saved the city and gained public acceptance. In this same volume, during Batman's absence from Gotham, a group of mutants arises and threatens the city. Yet, after Batman defeats their leader in single combat, the group switches their allegiance to Batman, renaming themselves the Sons of Batman. When Batman goes underground with his newest Robin and new allies, the Sons of Batman, he narrates:

> We have many years to train, years…to train study and plan … here, in the endless cave, far past the burnt remains of a crimefighter whose time has passed … [I]t begins here … an army … to bring sense to a world plagued by worse than thieves and murderers … this will be a good life.[10]

Batman chooses to remain a guardian of the city but will do so outside the boundaries of political legitimacy. An implicit question derived from Batman's status as a defender of the city is whether he possesses a well-ordered soul, at least in the Platonic sense. Batman is arguably what Socrates refers to as an "honor-loving" individual rather than a "wisdom-loving" individual (*Republic* 581c–d). Batman is motivated by righteous anger but untempered by wisdom. Although Batman may fulfill the role of a defender of the city, his personal soul is dominated by spiritedness at great personal cost and, perhaps, at a cost to the society of Gotham. He lives to achieve justice but must break the law—disregarding the rule of due process that restricts public law enforcement—to do so. Plato indicated that spiritedness controls desire, but it is also distinct from reason. In the individual soul the predominance of spiritedness results in an unjust soul, ill ordered, and often prideful and merely angry, emotional, and uncontrolled. Batman's sense of honor and righteous anger may save the city, but they do so at the cost of Bruce Wayne's soul.

Perhaps Bruce Wayne was destined from the beginning to lose himself to the tragedy that formed him. On that night in Crime Alley when Thomas and Martha Wayne were brutally gunned down by Joe Chill, Bruce Wayne lost any sense of innocence in his childhood. Bruce Wayne never fully recovers from his parents' murder. The death of his parents transformed Bruce Wayne into Batman. Wayne's promise to fight crime is born out of his anger and indignation at the impunity of his parents' murderer. Yet, Wayne never abandons his youthful pledge. As an individual governed by spiritedness, Wayne holds fast, training body and mind into his adulthood in order to keep his vow.

Wayne's promise alters his life inexorably. At the moment of the vow there is no longer a Bruce Wayne; although unnamed at this point in early comics, there is only Batman. Wayne's true self becomes "Batman," while his given name, "Bruce Wayne," becomes an identity that Batman uses to maintain the façade of an ordinary life. Unlike Superman, who seems to be able to juggle both his heroic identity and his Clark Kent persona with a knowing wink, Wayne turns over his daytime responsibilities to people like Lucius Fox at the Wayne Foundation, first introduced in 1979.[11] Wayne is happy to leave the important decisions to Lucius. Wayne's night-time activities as Batman have precluded him from making his commercial business a priority. In the introductory scene, Lucius Fox questions Wayne on what else could be more important than the Wayne Foundation. The answer, of course, is Batman and his single-minded crusade against crime.

Wayne's love life is also sacrificed to his guardian's pledge. Wayne accumulates a long list of failed romances that usually end with Batman being the stumbling block either because the playboy façade of Bruce Wayne is intolerable for the woman involved or because Batman is too great a burden. True love will mean finding someone with a lifestyle that is compatible with Batman, not Bruce Wayne. For example, Julie Madison first appears in 1939 as Bruce Wayne's fiancé.[12] With no inkling of Bruce's real identity, she is saved by Batman on an early case. Julie is around for a year and a half until she breaks off the engagement in 1941, proclaiming, "If you'd only find yourself a career instead of being the public's number one playboy… I'm sorry Bruce, until you decide to make something of yourself, I'm afraid our engagement is off."[13] Clearly, Batman is Bruce's priority and the prospect of a wife is not enough for Wayne to reveal himself. After being saved by Batman and Robin in 1940, Julie comments that Batman and Robin "are real heroes…, if only Bruce was so dashing!"[14]

In the 1970s, Bruce develops a relationship with Silver St. Cloud, a young woman with a career as a convention organizer. Wayne laments his doomed relationship with St. Cloud, noting:

> She doesn't know the real me, not inside! There's a part of me she can't ever know! Always the same problem ever since the first girl I loved, Julie Madison! They love Bruce Wayne … but Bruce Wayne has become a daytime mask for the Batman! The problem is … would I have it any other way?[15]

When St. Cloud by chance discovers Wayne's identity as Batman, she tells him she could never adjust to the danger to which he exposes himself each night: "I couldn't live with that! Never knowing what each night would bring!"[16]

Is there no one that is capable of loving Bruce Wayne and able to accept his identity as Batman? Batman's pledge has cost him love and companionship. Over the years, Catwoman has become more of an anti-hero than an outright villain because the romantic attraction for this pair has always generated interest among readers. Catwoman has "gone straight" a few times over the years in accordance with a relationship with either Bruce Wayne or Batman. Over the course of the first 50 issues of *Batman* Volume 3 (2016–present), writer Tom King depicts a long courtship between Batman and Catwoman, with a marriage proposal to culminate in a wedding in issue #50. Unfortunately, for Batman, Catwoman (whose real identity is Selina Kyle) has second thoughts. Catwoman does not question the love between them but rather how making Batman happy would impact his ability to fight crime. Catwoman sees that righteous anger is the most important factor in Batman's effectiveness. She refuses to take Batman away from Gotham City. She writes to him, "If I help that lonely boy, with the lonely eyes, I kill that engine. I kill Batman. I kill the person who saves everyone."[17] The implication is that Batman has become so important for Gotham City's security that Batman must sacrifice his happiness. Bruce asks his confidant and butler, Alfred Pennyworth, "Alfred, can I be happy?"[18] Batman's *thymos* is all consuming and prevents him from achieving happiness. From the Platonic perspective, Batman's soul is ill ordered and yields an ill-ordered life.

The Spirited Gothamites: The Costs Batman Exacts on Gotham

Just as Batman's behavior exacts costs on his personal soul, so too does his anger threaten the souls of Gothamites. Those of the populace who admire Batman may become lovers of spiritedness at the cost of ignoring the virtues of wisdom. Many citizens of Gotham praise Batman for the crimes he commits in the name of justice. Indignation, felt by both Batman and the citizens of Gotham, can lead to acts of justice but also to acts of injustice, which are endorsed by the populace. This is not merely speculation. A historical example, that occurred during Plato's lifetime and almost certainly known to him, demonstrates the costs to wise governance of spirit-ruled citizens.

In 406 BCE, during the Peloponnesian War between the city-states of Athens (Plato's home city) and Sparta, a fabled naval battle occurred. The Athenians had sent a large fleet of ships to relieve a besieged fleet at Arginusae on the island of Lesbos, located off the west coast of modern Turkey. The fleet was hastily assembled and had an unusual command structure: eight generals combined to command the fleet. The Athenian fleet won a resounding victory by using the innovative tactics of a double line of ships (a front line and back line) and dividing the fleet into eight separately commanded divisions. After the battle, the eight Athenian commanders decided to divide the surviving fleet, allocating a large number of ships to relieve a besieged fellow fleet, while leaving a smaller contingent to rescue survivors of the Arginusae battle. Unfortunately, a storm prevented rescuing all of the survivors and many drowned as a result. Additionally, the victorious generals failed to take the time to recover the bodies of the Athenian dead in order to bury them according to the proper funeral rights.[19]

These failures, both to rescue all survivors and to recover the fallen, were so culturally and politically important in the Athens of the time that they overwhelmed the Athenian populace's joy regarding the important naval victory. In fact, when the populace learned of the generals' failures after the battle, the democratic (citizen-run) government in Athens put the generals on trial as a group. This was not only unusual in Athens, it was illegal to not try an accused individually. (By chance, the great philosopher Socrates was sitting, for the one time in his life, on the council that decided the fate of the generals. He was chairman of the government assembly on the day the motion against the generals was presented and he refused to submit the motion to the assembly. He was later overruled.) As a result of the populace's anger the eight generals were condemned to death.[20] This incident is cited by Allan Bloom as an example of the "moral indignation" that Plato so condemned and feared in *The Republic*. It was an example, on a societal scale, of spiritedness (an angry sense of honor) triumphing over reason, which would have grasped the reasons for failing to rescue all survivors and recover the dead.[21] The Athenians were dominated by their prideful adherence to traditional notions of valor and reverent treatment of the dead, which produced the loss of several otherwise victorious and valuable military leaders. In short, spiritedness triumphed over reason and cost the society dearly.

Similarly, Batman's actions have taken a toll on the society of Gotham. In a future Gotham City in which Batman has retired and attempted to leave crimefighting in his past, an older Bruce Wayne must come to grips with an unintended legacy of his days as Batman. This is the setting of Frank Miller's seminal and celebrated *The Dark Knight Returns*. One of the themes that Miller explores is the effect of Batman on the city. In mock late-night talk show format, the guests argue over Batman's effect. Dr. Wolper, a psychologist, argues that Batman himself is the cause of the criminals he fights; he likens it to a membrane that bounces back harder than it is struck.[22] Dr. Wolper contends that because Batman dresses in costume and acts with dramatic flair, he generates an equally dramatic response from the opposite side of the law. Furthermore, it is argued that Batman inspires other vigilantes, creating an even more dangerous environment for the citizens of Gotham. A series of vignettes demonstrates how Batman's unintended acolytes cause havoc with their frequently failed efforts to fight crime or quell vice: a psychopath shoots up an adult cinema, a misguided Batman impersonator gets himself shot, and a store owner successfully defends a customer from a mugging.[23]

The toll Batman's methods take is clearly shown in the advent of a gang of mutants, which adopts the nom de guerre "Sons of Batman" and proceeds to prey upon the criminals of Gotham. The Sons of Batman lack the real Batman's discipline or moral compass. For example, they apprehend a shoplifter and instead of making the punishment fit the crime, they chop off the shoplifter's hands.[24] Gotham's media turn against Batman and claim that Batman is responsible for the creation of the Joker as a response to his own actions. Additionally, the media suggest that Batman's failure to quash the Sons of Batman shows that Batman may condone their excesses.[25]

In a more recent series, as mentioned earlier, Catwoman becomes a possible long-term love interest for Batman. Yet, after Catwoman breaks her engagement with Batman, he lets his bitterness influence him, causing him to act more aggressively against Gotham's criminals.[26] Emotionally devastated by Catwoman abandoning him at the altar, Batman apprehends and abuses one of his recurrent nemeses, Mr. Freeze, for a series of murders. Afterward, Batman realizes he was emotionally distraught when he confronted Mr. Freeze and imagines the possibility that Freeze might not be the real murderer. Wayne's sense of guilt at the abuse of Freeze allows him to convince himself that Freeze is innocent of this particular crime. When Freeze is put on trial, Bruce Wayne manages to get on the jury in order to convince the jury to acquit Freeze. Wayne urges the jurors to acquit based on the possible fallibility of Batman, claiming reasonable doubt exists. In the midst of serving on the jury, Wayne gains insight into average Gothamites' views of Batman and his methods. They see Batman as nearly infallible. One of the jurors says, "Batman has saved me, you, everyone here."[27] Wayne argues passionately:

> You say guilty, you put the Bat into that same cold cage. You all raised your hands. You all said he saved you. So do what you would do for any other man who'd done that. What you would never do for God. Save him.[28]

Wayne's point is that Batman is not God; he is not omnipotent nor entitled to decide who lives or dies. Wayne succeeds in convincing the jury that Batman might have made a mistake in identifying Freeze as a murderer and persuades the jury to acquit Mr. Freeze.

The trial of Mr. Freeze illustrates the average Gothamites' willingness to condone Batman's vigilante methods, disregarding the very rights that a jury trial is meant to protect: due process, the scrutiny of evidence, and the prosecution's burden of proving guilt beyond a reasonable doubt. Fortunately for Gotham, Batman possesses sufficient self-awareness that he prevents this potential instance of injustice in the trial of Mr. Freeze. Yet, the trial demonstrates to readers and Bruce Wayne that Batman has become more than a symbol; he has become many Gothamites' preferred form of justice. Batman's spirit-guided actions have unintentionally resulted in a citizenry willing to abandon the exacting scrutiny required for a criminal trial. (Wayne only barely convinces the jurors that Batman could have been mistaken regarding Mr. Freeze.) But for Wayne's integrity and diligence in correcting a possible error, the citizens would have embraced Batman's vigilantism and abandoned solemnity of the jury process. Although prevented in this instance, this is an example of the costs Batman's spirit-driven acts have had on the people of Gotham.

Conclusion

The Dark Knight's methods are a product of righteous indignation at the existence of a criminal class that acts with impunity and a political class that seems weak willed and indifferent, both of which make Gotham an almost ungovernable city. Yet, Batman's methods are also a threat to peace and good governance in their own right. Batman does not intend to be a leader for Gotham. In fact, at one point he expressly eschews any political role by his rejection of a veritably assured term as a US senator, proclaiming that being a senator is "a job I couldn't do without Batman."[29] Nevertheless, Batman leads—and influences—by example, which is driven by his emotional sense of justice. Plato was scornful of the dangers of the spirit-driven soul: it is excessively proud, driven by emotion, ungoverned, or restrained by reason. Spirit—a sense of indignation and a desire for moral rectitude—can guard the city, but it cannot govern it. Batman finds he must be as wary of his supporters as of the city's criminals. The Sons of Batman and vengeful jurors are both products of Batman's extralegal methods. Like the Athenians who were angry at the generals of Arginusae and gleefully supported their execution, the Sons of Batman and jurors of Gotham exact emotion-driven, indignant justice against the criminals of Gotham. Yet, these efforts result in injustice; these are the legacies of Batman's *thymos*-driven war against crime: the abuse of the accused, the conviction of the innocent, and the perversion of injustice into justice.

In Plato's *Republic* Socrates asks several of his interlocutors for their various definitions of justice. One interlocutor, an old father and authority figure, Cephalus, claims justice is rendering what is owed, while his son, Polemarchus, claims justice is doing good to one's friends and harm to one's enemies. Socrates does not reject these conventional definitions outright but rather suggests that they are insufficient. He notes that rendering what is owed cannot be an iron law because it could lead to harmful effects. For example, one who borrows a knife will need to return it to the owner. But what if the owner in the meantime has gone insane? Would it be just to return a knife to an insane man? The danger of harm to the lender, borrower, and others is obvious and suggests that justice must be contextual. Similarly, the claim that justice is helping one's friends and harming one's enemies is doubtful when one considers who is a friend. Socrates points out that friends seek to benefit one another, but such efforts are biased, interested, and not objective. If justice is helping friends, then it is an unbalanced, often idiosyncratic effort, and often inconsistent.

Cephalus and Polemarchus's definitions of justice are conventional but problematic, as Socrates' objections demonstrate. Yet, the most problematic definition is provided by a third interlocutor, a young angry man named Thrasymachus. Young Thrasymachus voices frustration with these definitions of justice and Socrates' confounding objections. Thrasymachus has an altogether different and radical definition of justice: it is the rule of the strong. He claims that the city is a composite of opposing groups and interests and that only the rule of the strong can preserve the city. He contends that the character of the rulers is key and Socrates agrees on this point. Yet, Thrasymachus concludes that results are what matter and the only good results are those that benefit oneself. On an individual level, this means moral relativism; one's personal preferences are all that matter and satisfying those preferences are and should be one's objective in life. On a societal level, this means that the preferences of the rulers are the only ones that matter politically. Those out of power are subservient to the rulers' choices. Thrasymachus concludes that what is thought of as injustice is actually justice because it profits people more than it usually would, acting in a conventionally just manner (343b–344c). This moral relativism, if implemented on a society-wide basis, would justify any regime that seeks to protect the rulers, even at the cost of the citizenry.

Batman's villains display Thrasymachus's relativism: whatever benefits them is "just." Yet the citizens of Gotham, like Thrasymachus, also would be frustrated at Socrates' objections to the conventional notions of justice. They want to be rid of crime and, in light of their corrupt and often inept city police officials, they are willing to embrace Batman's extralegal methods. Yet the citizens' demands for security may yield injustice: Batman's excesses go unchallenged, vigilante imitators are inspired, and wisdom in the meting out of justice is sacrificed in pursuit of punishing enemies and rewarding friends.

Additionally, what if Batman were a person of lesser character? This question has been addressed periodically, most notably in the early 1990s as part of the *Knightfall* series, with the character Jean-Paul Valley. Valley briefly became Batman at Bruce Wayne's request, while Wayne recovered from an injury. Valley was a trained assassin, but he lacked the moral character of Bruce Wayne. His methods quickly departed from the original Batman's and degenerated into vicious revenge. Wayne felt compelled to relieve Valley of his duties.[30] Valley is an example of the morally relativistic approach that a Thrasymachus-like Batman might take. This is the ever-present danger presented by any super hero: the might-makes-right approach might be tempting to a superior being. A spirited-led guardian may devolve into a desires-led soul, seeking only his or her own pleasure.

Batman is a "noble dog," guarding the city through the leadership and courage his spiritedness allows. Yet, his spirited soul exacts costs on his happiness and produces a man unwilling to lead his fellow citizens. His fellow Gothamites also change the character of the city's society: they embrace vigilantism and a definition of justice that renders what is owed but even at the risk of giving an insane person a tool that injures them all. At worst, some—the Sons of Batman—embrace Thrasymachus's moral relativism and serve their own ends, calling it justice. These are the cumulative harmful consequences of Batman's spirit-dominated soul. The tragic irony is that Batman has always wanted to serve Gotham, even if it cost him personally. But his spirit-driven crimefighting has harmed the very people he has sought to save.

Notes

1. Juvenal, *Satire VI*, trans. G.G. Ramsay (Internet Ancient History Sourcebook, 1999), https://sourcebooks.fordham.edu/ancient/juvenal-satvi.asp (accessed August 30, 2018), 6.O29–34.
2. Rachel Barney, "Callicles and Thrasymachus," *The Stanford Encyclopedia of Philosophy* (Fall 2017 Edition), ed. Edward N. Zalta, https://plato.stanford.edu/archives/fall2017/entries/callicles-thrasymachus (accessed August 30, 2018).
3. Citations to *The Republic* are to Plato, *The Republic*, trans. G.M.A. Grube, revised by C.D.C. Reeve (Indianapolis: Hackett, 1992).

4. Josh Wilburn, "The Spirited Part of the Soul in Plato's Timaeus," *Journal of the History of Philosophy* 52, no. 4 (2014): 627.
5. Ibid.
6. Grube translates the term as "pedigreed dog," whereas Allan Bloom translates it as "noble dogs." Plato, *The Republic of Plato*, Second ed., trans. Allan Bloom (New York: BasicBooks, 1991).
7. Bill Finger, Bob Kane, Sheldon Moldoff, *Detective Comics* 1 #33 (New York: DC Comics, 1939), 2.
8. Frank Miller, Klaus Janson, Lynn Varley, *Batman: The Dark Knight Returns*, 4 vols. (New York: DC Comics, 1986), 3:31.
9. Miller, Janson, Varley, 2:16.
10. Miller, Janson, Varley, 4:47.
11. Len Wein, John Calnan, Dick Giordano, Glynis Oliver, *Batman* 1 #307 (New York: DC Comics, 1979), 3.
12. Gardner Fox, Bob Kane, Sheldon Moldoff, *Detective Comics* 1 #31 (New York: DC Comics, 1939).
13. Bill Finger, Bob Kane, Jerry Robinson, George Roussos, *Detective Comics* 1 #49 (New York: DC Comics, 1941), 2.
14. Bill Finger, Bob Kane, Jerry Robinson, *Detective Comics* 1 #40 (New York: DC Comics, 1940), 12.
15. Steve Englehart, Marshall Rogers, Terry Austin, Jerry Serpe, *Detective Comics* 1 #474 (New York: DC Comics, 1978), 8.
16. Steve Englehart, Marshall Rogers, Terry Austin, Glynis Oliver, *Detective Comics* 1 #476 (New York: DC Comics, 1978), 15.
17. Tom King, Lee Weeks, Bettie Breitweiser, *Batman* 3 #50 (New York: DC Comics, 2018), 35.
18. Ibid., 33.
19. Donald Kagan, *The Peloponnesian War* (New York: Penguin, 2003), 459–60.
20. Anthony Everitt, *The Rise of Athens: The Story of the World's Greatest Civilization* (New York: Random House, 2016): 370–71.
21. Bloom, "Interpretive Essay," in Plato, *The Republic of Plato*, Second ed., trans. Allan Bloom (New York: BasicBooks, 1991): 377.
22. Miller, Janson, Varley, 2:9.
23. Miller, Janson, Varley, 2:33–34.
24. Miller, Janson, Varley, 3:28.
25. Miller, Janson, Varley, 3:36–42.
26. Tom King, Lee Weeks, Bettie Breitweiser, *Batman* 3 #50 (New York: DC Comics, 2018).
27. Tom King, Lee Weeks, Bettie Breitweiser, *Batman* 3 #52 (New York: DC Comics, 2018), 8.

28. Tom King, Lee Weeks, Bettie Breitweiser, *Batman* 3 #53 (New York: DC Comics, 2018), 18.
29. Bob Haney, Neal Adams, Dick Giordano, *The Brave and the Bold* #85 (DC Comics, 1969).
30. Doug Moench, Mike Manley, Joe Rubinstein, Adrienne Roy, *Batman* 1 #508 (New York: DC Comics, 1994).

CHAPTER 7

The Dark Prince of the Republic: Machiavelli, Batman, and Gotham City

Anthony Petros Spanakos

Gotham is a fallen city.[1] The city is not only violent but criminality is so entrenched that Gotham's problems are political, not simply criminal. In the 80 years since Bob Kane's creation of Batman, Gotham has not improved. No matter how many times Batman upends a criminal enterprise, interrupts a one-off act of violence, or defeats super-villains bent on world domination, Gotham does not change. So how effective is Batman, really? Why does Batman limit himself to stopping crime, rather than seizing the state and running it properly (a la Lenin)? Curiously enough, Niccolò Machiavelli, often caricatured as a theorist of the unethical use of violence, can help explain this.

Batman fans would see a lot of Gotham in Machiavelli's depiction of Florence. Florence, for Machiavelli, was fallen, corrupt, and in need of liberation. At the end of *The Prince* Machiavelli makes an emotional plea for a prince to come and save Italy.[2] It is easy to see Batman, the city's constant savior, as such a figure. But, while Batman does indeed play an important role in arresting corruption in and restoring glory to Gotham, he does so as a *republican* prince, a figure that is described in Machiavelli's

A. P. Spanakos (✉)
Department of Political Science and Law, Montclair State University, Montclair, NJ, USA

D. K. Picariello (ed.), *Politics in Gotham*,
https://doi.org/10.1007/978-3-030-05776-3_7

Discourses.[3] In this work, Machiavelli encourages the emergence of multiple princes (as opposed to a single one) whose contributions to the vitality of the republic are not limited to the occupation of office. Such leaders attack the heart of corruption, often with crushing violence, with the chief aim of wresting power from a group that has taken power at the expense of the rest of society.

Although Batman's task is usually set in terms of fighting crime, it is really a battle against a fallen city, a political challenge. This is most clearly visible in Miller and Mazzucchelli's *Batman: Year One (BYO)*, where Bruce Wayne finds his political identity not as a member of the elite class (the *grandi*, Machiavelli's term for the "notables") nor as an ordinary citizen (part of the people) but as a vigilante who strikes at the class which controls the city.[4] In so doing, he not only uses extra-legal violence but also avails himself of other such leaders working within the state apparatus (notably, police Lieutenant James Gordon and District Attorney Harvey Dent). His goal, not to replace or transform but to restore Gotham, is consistent with the Machiavellian republican prince who counters violence against the republican constitution—even with dictatorial power—in order to restore it. An out-of-retirement Batman in *The Dark Knight Returns (DKR)* follows a similar Machiavellian path although in that story arc Batman faces a city that is essentially not being governed.[5]

Machiavelli's Republican Princes

Machiavelli's counsel has the aim of arresting and reversing the corruption in a polity. Corruption is the result of either the imbalance of competing factions (the *grandi* or notables and the people) or because the absence of strong rule opens the polity to internal chaos or invasion from without.[6] The two factions which he believes are present in every society inevitably enter into conflict because the people "do not want to be dominated or oppressed by the nobles, and the nobles want to dominate and oppress the people."[7] Machiavelli is clinically skeptical of both factions and advises the prince to balance these two "humors," though he argues that it is better to err on the side of the people. Such a balance is only possible when there is a prince (in a principality) or a governing body (in a republic) with *virtù*.[8]

Unlike classical theorists, Machiavelli saw the conflict between competing factions as having positive effects on the polity as a whole. Unlike many modern libertarians he insisted on the necessity of a strong Governor.

The recourse to the use of force to maintain balance and order appears in his writings on principalities and republics. Indeed, in *Discourses*, Machiavelli clearly warns that "where the material is so corrupt, laws do not suffice to keep it in hand; it is necessary to have, besides laws, a superior force, such as appertains to a monarch, who has such absolute and overwhelming power that he can restrain excesses due to ambition and the corrupt practices of the powerful."[9]

In case a reader may have thought Machiavelli was not serious in his insistence on the use of "superior force" even in a republic, Machiavelli praises the ancient Roman republican office of the dictator as well as ancient Greek tyrants who brought about republican conditions. The former involves senators selecting a leader who can operate outside of the law so as to restore good order in a time of crisis.[10] The latter involves usurpation of authority by someone who effects changes Machiavelli considers necessary (such as the elimination of elites and distribution of their wealth, among others) once in office.[11] Neither of these leaders is a prince of a principality but someone who takes princely authority in a republic. Importantly, the acquisition of such authority—which may not result from senatorial or even popular consent[12]—is deemed necessary for countering deep-seated corruption in a republic.[13] On this reading, a republic can, and at least from time to time must, have a prince of sorts. But, Machiavelli suggests that there should not only be a single prince but multiple princes.[14]

In describing a republic that is not corrupt, Machiavelli writes that the population grows because marriage and children are more desirable, property rights are protected, and children will "not only … be born free.... but.... if they have virtue, they will have a chance of becoming rulers [*principi*]."[15] The chance for the free—but not necessarily high-born men—to become a prince is not unique to a republic. Machiavelli was well aware of low-born men taking on the purple as a result of military success. But the rulers to which Machiavelli refers in this passage seek neither imperial office nor is it clear that they seek to be the only ruler. It would make little sense that a well-functioning republic would breed virtuous men who would seek to eliminate the republic and establish a principality. Similarly, a well-ordered republic could hardly expect to produce only one such person in a generation but is more likely to produce several (or even a class of) would-be virtuous rulers. At the same time, Machiavelli refers to these civically engaged virtuous men as rulers and not merely citizens. The expectation is that they take a greater role in rule and its consequences than is typically found in citizens. The republican prince is more than a citizen but less than a typical prince in that he is not a *mono-arxos* (sole ruler). He is a republican prince because of his activity, not by virtue of any office. As there is no need to hold a formal office (including that of a dictator or tyrant) there can be more than one. Additionally, given the weight that Machiavelli gives to checking the actions of different groups, having only one such prince over time could itself be very dangerous for the republic. A Peisistratus may be essential for re-founding the republic but the republic would not likely endure if he continued in perpetuity as a tyrant.[16] The single founder needs to be followed by multiple leaders and good laws.

This may be one of the principal differences between *The Prince* and *Discourses*. The former is dedicated to a single member of the Medici family and the text calls for a single ruler to (re-)found Italy. The latter—which contains "all I know and have learnt from a long experience of, and from constantly reading about, political affairs"—is dedicated to two people, Zanobi Buondelmonti and Cosimo Rucellai. They were selected "on account of their innumerable good qualities" and therefore "deserve to be" princes.[17] These two are, obviously, princes without a principality. Even if they held the office of prince, since they are both Florentines, they would both hold the same position in the same principality. Given Machiavelli's trenchant and recurring depiction of humans being motivated by envy and his ultimate rejection of the Spartan model (the most successful case of diarchy), Machiavelli must be thinking of a republic in which there are princes who through *virtù* challenge the *grandi*, lead the multitude, and contribute to the preservation of the republic's life and liberty.[18] Further, it is likely that his advice is also directed not only to these two well-born citizens (and perhaps not to them at all) but to any who choose to follow his lessons.[19]

The prince who re-founds a republic is remarkably similar to a prince in a principality, in that authority should be concentrated and there is considerable leeway in terms of the morality of the means used to re-establish rule. Re-founding involves much more institutional flexibility than restoring the republic. The former might involve destroying a particular class or massive appropriation and redistribution of assets.[20] The latter is more conservative, even in a case of deep corruption, as it involves bringing the various competing political groups into a proper balance. Moreover, the prince at a re-founding operates in an expansive moment whereas princes who aim to restore the republic operate in and over time; theirs is not a one-off action. Batman does not seek to re-found Gotham (having vanquished villain A, he does not seize power and lay down a new law). Rather, he aims to rid Gotham of the activity that leads to the perversion of its republican form.

Princes in a republic should restrain a faction that has been able to severely dominate the other faction and re-instill authoritative rule to prevent anarchy and invasion. The inability of the system to remain in healthy balance and its propensity to lurch toward decisively and dangerously disordered situations constitute corruption for Machiavelli. Such corruption is evident in Gotham in two ways. *BYO* has a Gotham in which the *grandi* rule over the people and have fundamentally corrupted the institutions of government. Non-corrupt "states... do not permit any of their citizens to live after the fashion of gentry. On the contrary, they maintain there perfect equality, and to lord and gentry residing that province are extremely hostile."[21] Gotham is the antithesis of this presentation. Batman, therefore, must strike at the class that has taken the privileges of gentry and remove the oligarchic de facto rulers of the city. In *DKR*, rule has been essentially abdicated by politicians and increasingly seized by nefarious gangs. This corruption also requires the strong-hand of a republican prince and Batman must confront the gang that the government mollycoddles so as to save the city. In each case the cause and resolution of corruption are different, but in both cases Batman (with others) acts as a republican prince, willing to use violence not bounded by law in order to restore a republic (founded on law).

Batman: Year One's Republican Prince/s

Frank Miller introduces Bruce Wayne's class identity early in *BYO*. His home, "Wayne Manor... [was b]uilt as a fortress generations past, to protect a fading line of royalty from an age of Equals."[22] The Waynes were famous for their philanthropy; nevertheless, they were still apart from the people: spatially, they lived in Wayne Manor, and socio-economically, they maintained a staff, including a butler. Following the deaths of his parents, Bruce studied in boarding schools, traveled overseas, and participated in international secret societies.[23] He was not the boy next door.

His high birth is introduced in *BYO* via a contrast of his return to and James Gordon's arrival in Gotham. The former is by plane, the latter by train. The trip by plane makes Gotham look more beautiful than Bruce thinks it is. The trip by train shows the worst of it, leading an anxious

Gordon to insist his wife arrive by plane. That Gotham seems beautiful and terrifying depending on the vantage point of the observer is consistent with the reality of Gotham City: its people live distinct lives and perambulate in different Gothams. Poverty/wealth, crime/safety, and misery/flourishing are characteristics of different zip codes.

James Gordon's entry into Gotham does not get better as he quickly learns that the police and city are in the pockets of the wealthy. His partner, Sergeant Flass, and other police officers, assault Gordon when it is clear that Gordon will not play the game of the others. His response is to deliver a private beating to sergeant Flass as a warning. The warning seems to work with Flass but not for the corrupted class, and in the final pages of the Fourth Book police officers kidnap Gordon's daughter (who is saved by Batman).[24]

Not only are the police working on behalf of one segment of society, they also engage in counter-productive policies. When one mentally ill man holds three children hostage, the city's first response is to send in a SWAT team whose tactics Gordon compares to "war."[25] Gordon walks in, disarms, and then punches out the man. Although he threatened to bring Branden (the leader of SWAT) up on charges if he pursued a recklessly violent rescue, Gordon's effort is not entirely by the book nor does it eschew violence.

Gordon is realistic. He sees his role as enforcing law and order not in a Platonic sense (where there is a grand and identifiable notion of what order is at all times) but as contextually driven (more in line with a Machiavellian realism). His focus on what is before him (with all its deviations from what should be) allows him to contemplate working against fellow officers and the Mayor and with a vigilante. At the end of the Third Book he thinks Batman's "…a criminal. I'm a cop. It's that simple. But-but I'm a cop in a city where the mayor and the commissioner of police use cops as hired killers…."[26] Were the world or Gotham different, Gordon could work with internal affairs and an anti-corruption wing of the Mayor's office to try to weed out a small group of corrupt colleagues. But Gordon realizes that Gotham is so fundamentally fallen that he must work outside of the law in order to preserve the law.

Bruce knows Gotham better and faces fewer moral quandaries. He is fully aware that one part of the city rules others and benefits itself in so doing. Although the Mayor was amused by Batman's early appearances, as they were non-threatening and dealt with petty crime, his attitude changes markedly in the Second Book. There Batman crashes a sumptuous dinner held at the Mayor's mansion and declares: "Ladies. Gentlemen. You have eaten well. You've eaten Gotham's wealth. Its spirit. Your feast is nearly over. From this moment on—none of you are safe."[27] This enrages the Mayor and his cabal and they begin an aggressive assault against Batman.

Batman's dinner appearance allowed the reader to see into the private space in which oligarchies are formed and reinforced. His intervention is not a typically political one and it is not one that follows the rule of law associated with the republican government. He enters by subterfuge and breaking the law. He threatens people having no public authorization and without recognition of any innocence prior to legal establishment of guilt. He pledges to pursue justice without being concerned about the constraints of the law or the political system. And, of course, he has no legal right to pursue justice.

Yet Batman's respect for the law and political system is sincere and immense. In Book Two, Gordon meets with a young District Attorney, Harvey Dent, and shares his frustration with the "system."[28] He knows that Dent was pursuing one criminal for many years but he was unable to put him behind bars because "witnesses change their **testimony**. The rest **vanish**..."[29] At this point he has not yet made the decision to go outside the law and to support Batman's extra-legal activities.

Unbeknownst to Gordon, Batman is hiding under Dent's desk. He had already begun to work with Dent (as he soon would with Gordon) in an attempt to root out the city's corruption. Seeking out Dent (and later Gordon) is important as it shows that Batman is aware that the system is not entirely corrupt and restoration of the city could not come solely via the force of an external agent, a vigilante. This is evident when Batman reveals, "I need an ally—an inside man. I need Jim Gordon. On my side."[30]

Importantly, neither Gordon nor Dent are able to make progress until Batman gets a drug dealer, Skeevers, to roll on Flass on the subject of drugs and then Flass turns on Commissioner Loeb.[31] The *status quo* of the corrupt polity was simply that powerful, that ingrained, that no change could come except from someone outside the system. Indeed, prior to Batman's arrival, mobsters laughed at Dent in arraignments and Gordon was, basically, fighting for his life and dignity. Yet the existence of Gordon and Dent shows that the system's institutions are not beyond saving, that they could be restored. However much the man in the Bat-suit attracts attention, the judiciary becomes one of the principal ways of ameliorating corruption in Gotham City and the courts play a fundamental role in the resolution of the conflict in the Fourth Book. They by no means "save"

Gotham, as evidenced by a reference to a new threat, the Joker, at the very end of the story.[32] Nevertheless, the Batman has helped create conditions in which the courts (and the police) can effectively do their jobs.

The republican prince is republican not because he believes that a republic is perfect nor because of his strict use of republican tactics, laws, and institutions. Quite the contrary is the case as Machiavelli happily cites ancient Greek tyrants as examples of how republics were rescued from corruption. These tyrants used considerable and, for many observers, excessive force upon taking power. Importantly, however, their actions were not motivated by their own glory; rather, they were a form of re-balancing between competing groups within the polity. And while upon seizing rule they held considerable power, they did not dominate as tyrants but governed as republicans.

Batman does one better. He understands that there are other republican princes out there. While they are not a wholly coordinated party, their interests and motivations overlap in such a way where each can individually and all (Batman, Gordon, Dent) can collectively contribute to reversing republican corruption. None of them do so by *strictu* sensu following the law. Rather all engage in or deliberately turn a blind eye toward extra-legal activities including the unauthorized use of coercion.[33] Batman does not follow the law, Gordon does not arrest Batman, and Dent does not bring charges against Batman or Gordon. But operating outside and beyond their roles as citizens and officers of the law (in the cases of Gordon and Dent), they are able to restore the polity so that the police and the courts adjudicate without being controlled by one particularly entrenched group.

The Dark Knight Returns to Restore a Corrupt City

Gotham continues to be a moral cesspool in *DKR*.[34] Unlike *BYO*, where Gotham is controlled by a particular political-economic clique (the Mayor, police commissioner, their wealthy backers, their police enforcers), Gotham in *DKR* is effectively not governed at all. The Mayor constantly prevaricates and expects others to make decisions. The President and Governor do likewise. The absence of leadership at a moment of high tensions with the Soviet government because of the Corto Maltese crisis[35] contributes to an atmosphere of extreme moral permissiveness (an actress known for her work in pornographic films takes on the role of Snow White and says, "I'm doing it for the kids"),[36] an absence of law enforcement, a prevailing apocalyptic narrative among the people in the street, and opportunistic vigilantism. In this environment, a new and particularly vicious group, the Mutants, emerges to wreak havoc upon the city.

DKR features an aged Bruce Wayne who put away his Batman uniform years ago and, of course, is struggling in his retirement. The book opens with him almost dying in a high-speed car race—an obvious challenge he imposes on himself in a late-middle age crisis. It is not "a flaming coffin for **Bruce Wayne**," but Wayne is already half-dead.[37] Without his Batman identity, he is literally half a man. The retiring Commissioner Gordon has just had a death threat posted on his office door and as Bruce walks the streets at night he finds he is "learning to **hate** the city that's given up…."[38] Gotham has always been unlivable but people somehow lived lives and, however psychologically stunted Bruce's own life was, he helped them resist wicked conditions in their quotidian lives.[39] Regular television dialogues in *DKR* have Lana Lang, his Chief Public Advocate, refer to Batman's importance as dual: first, actually fighting crime and second, being a symbol of resistance to raise the hearts of the people whose backs have been broken by life in Gotham.[40] Lang explains:

> We live in the **shadow** of crime, with the unspoken understanding that we are **victims**—of **fear, of violence,** of social **impotence.** A **man** has risen to show us that the power **is**, and always has been in **our** hands. We are under **siege**—he's showing us that we can **resist**.[41]

The extent to which the city is fallen is evident in the new threat, the Mutants. Without police patrolling the streets, the Mutants linger looking for potential victims to "slice and dice."[42] A few catch Bruce Wayne on an aimless walk which eventually takes him to Crime Alley.[43] He looks like a great target—old, fragile, vulnerable—but the Mutants pull back from assaulting him because he seems "into it." They kill for fun and because they can. They only hold back so as to deny someone else the pleasure, not because of any morally justifiable position.

The Mutants hold no political office but their prowling the streets at night gives them greater control over the city than the government which seems unwilling to rule. The Mutants grow as a group and acquire a massive cache of weapons ("You could overthrow a small **government** with this much firepower").[44] The Mutant leader inspires his members (and cows the citizens), saying: "We have the strength—we have the will—and now we have the funds. Gotham City belongs to the mutants!"[45] They thus move from contributing to a problem of criminality toward one of governance.

Unlike *BYO*'s Gotham, where there is an elite cabal that governs behind the scene, no one governs here. Leaders are neither opportunists nor puppets. They deliberately avoid any decision. This is most evident with the news coverage on how to handle the Batman situation (whether he should be permitted to act or arrested for doing so). While public figures make arguments in favor of and against his vigilantism, the President defers to the Governor who defers to the Mayor who defers to the police commissioner. When Gordon is Police Commissioner, an advisor convinces the Mayor that Batman is a negative social force. But the Mayor does not fire Gordon (who refuses to issue a warrant for Batman's arrest), nor does he force him to apprehend Batman. Instead, the Mayor has a one-on-one meeting with the leader of the Mutants in jail, which, predictably, ends in the murder of the Mayor. The next Mayor indicates a similar interest in negotiating with the Mutants, and the first act of a new police commissioner is to issue a warrant for the arrest of Batman.

In *BYO*, there is the possibility of removing the evil at the head of the government and its agencies to make way for a rejuvenated and more virtuous city. In *DKR* there is little such hope. Batman does not need to rebalance forces in such a way where the *grandi* do not dominate the people (*BYO)* but must essentially eliminate the threat of a native rebellious group. As was the case in *BYO*, his actions in *DKR* are especially Machiavellian.

Putting aside his first highly unsuccessful melee with the leader of the Mutants, the second battle between Batman and the Mutant leader is paradigmatic of the republican prince. Here it is worth noting Machiavelli's resuscitation of the historico-literary figure of the Roman dictator, chosen by the Senate to protect the republic. Batman, without a formal election but certainly with the ascent of the people, is a modern-day Cincinnatus. He literally leaves retirement to solve a crisis of the republic through a personal assault against the republic's enemies. Gordon's last act as Commissioner is to give Batman access to the Mutant leader who is in his prison cell. Batman takes the Mutant leader out of jail and fights with him in a mud-pit in front of the entire Mutant community. The Mutant leader exclaims: "I kill you. I show you who rules Gotham City."[46] This statement suggests that Batman is challenging the Mutant leadership's rule over Gotham, as though this rule were already recognized as fact. The Mutant leader, however, is utterly humiliated and beaten before all of his followers. Two pages later, one ex-Mutant, proclaiming the era of the "Sons of Batman," declares: "The mutants are **dead**. The mutants are **history**. **This** is the mark of the **future**. **Gotham City** belongs to the **Batman**."[47] But if the city belongs to Batman, if Batman takes ownership of Gotham, he nonetheless refuses to rule.

The defeat of the Mutant leader displays many of the criticisms that Batman's critics highlight. A tele-journalist lists some of these when asking Lana Lang about her defense of Batman. "How can you condone behavior that's so blatantly **illegal**? What about **due process—civil rights**?"[48] Batman's list of crimes increases considerably with this battle. But in Batman's use of extra-constitutional force as a private citizen, he defenestrated the primary force dominating and undermining the republic. And he did so with highly efficient use of force—single combat, an essential duel, with the victor taking the city. Unlike the prince of *The Prince*, the Batman's success in defeating the most viable contender does not lead to his seizure of power because, like a republican prince, Batman's interest is not taking power for himself but in constraining the power of others.

The Sons of Batman, inspired by Batman's use of violence to punish crime, use force that Machiavelli would see as excessive both as a means and an end. To the former point, they use a grenade to stop a robbery. To the latter, they are rather pedestrian in that they seek to stop single crimes rather than to contribute to a restoration of order. With the defeat of the Mutant leader, the Sons of Batman see an opportunity to expand their activities, to basically fill the void left by the Mutants. But when their leader exclaims, "Gotham City is helpless. This is our **chance** to **raze** Gotham—to **purge** Gotham—" a clear "No" is heard from Batman. "Tonight **we** are the law. **I** am the law," he tells them.[49] But making sure that this "I am the law" is not misunderstood, he warns them that any misbehavior under his watch will be punished. He stops the Mutants who broke out of jail and gets them to join in the nocturnal effort to rescue the city from the post-nuclear anxiety which created a violently anarchic condition. Alongside Gordon and regular citizens, they ride to the defense of a city which was in an autophagial state made possible by the state's lack of good laws and good law enforcement.[50] Batman offers both law and force, like the legendary re-founders of republics that Machiavelli cites, including Agathocles, Cleomenis, Hiero, and Clearchus.[51]

Then, having saved the city through extra-legal activities and violence, breathing life into the fighting spirit of an "impotent" Gotham citizenry, and reengaging Superman, a more moral and by-the-book guardian,

Batman fakes his own death and withdraws into the underground to take responsibility for training a generation who, prior to coming under his tutelage, were wild and hopeless. Unlike Peisistratus, who took power and redistributed wealth away from elites, or Cincinnatus, who succeeded in battle and returned to his farm, Batman takes the path of Machiavelli: that of the teacher who sees no shame in dirty hands for the sake of his *patria*.[52]

Conclusion

Machiavelli lauded men of *virtù*, unencumbered by moral quibbling when swift and decisive action would bring about the public good and restore a polity. His advice in *The Prince* is generally understood as being applied to an occupant or pretender to royal office, but his *Discourses* give advice to, and exhorts the emergence of, republican princes. He grants such republican princes considerable tactical latitude for the purpose of restoring vitality and balance to a republic that has fallen to severe corruption. While James Gordon and Harvey Dent resemble republican princes in part, it is Batman who exemplifies this character most fully. Batman's relationship to a fallen Gotham in *BYO* and *DKR* demonstrates the core of a Machiavellian republican prince.

Thinking of Batman in this way may also help resolve what might otherwise be a curious and disturbing issue. If Gotham is such a consistent mess—its police force cannot police, its government is (almost) always corrupt, and its people are downtrodden and oppressed—why does Batman not simply govern? Why does he not respond to Machiavelli's exhortation in *The Prince* but instead respond to the more implicit exhortation in the dedication in *Discourses*?

Batman is no revolutionary. He emerges as a response to a system that is out of balance and his efforts are to restore rather than transform the city (and political system) that produced him. The prince who transforms a principality does so in a singular moment that not only requires means that exceed the generally accepted norms of behavior but encourages the near monopolization of power in the hands of the ruler. Restoration of a republic requires different and better distribution of power. Certainly one or more princes will need to use apparently excessive and, at times, extra-legal means, but they do so in order to re-equilibrate power and wealth in society. They want to reinvigorate institutions and the law. They want citizens to move from timorous to vigorous. They do not want to act alone; they want to enable both citizens and institutions to emerge and challenge their power, so that no one dominates and the republic is at peace.

Notes

1. The author thanks Damien Picariello, Ian Drake, and Mishella Romo for comments on an earlier version of this chapter.
2. The edition cited in this text is Niccolò Machiavelli, *The Prince: Cambridge Texts in the History of Political Thought* (Cambridge: Cambridge University Press, 1988). Edited by Quentin Skinner and Russell Price. Translated by Russell Price. Henceforth *P* (chapter and page).
3. The edition cited in this text is Niccolò Machiavelli, 1970, *The Discourses*, (New York: Penguin Books, 1970). Edited with an introduction by Bernard Crick, using the translation by Leslie J. Walker S.J., with revisions by Brian Richardson. Henceforth *D* (chapter and page).
4. Frank Miller and David Mazucchelli, with Richmond Lewis and Todd Klein, *Batman: Year One* (New York: DC Comics, 2005). Henceforth *BYO*.
5. Frank Miller, with Klaus Jansen and Lynn Varley, *Batman: The Dark Knight Returns* (New York: DC Comics, 1997). Henceforth *DKR*.
6. This competition is expressed in a number of places notably *P* IX, 34. Unlike most of his predecessors in Christian Europe, Machiavelli casts corruption as a degradation of the political system's effectiveness rather than its moral character.
7. (*P* IX, 34, see also *D* I. 4, 113).
8. *Virtù* for Machiavelli is not quite "virtue." It is the ability to achieve political goals, particularly by demonstrating a martial and/or manly spirit.
9. (D I. 55, 246).
10. For a discussion on the office of the dictator, see Carl Schmitt, *Dictatorship* (Malden MA: Polity, 2014). Translated by Michael Hoelzl and Graham Ward.
11. John P. McCormick, "Of Tribunes and Tyrants: Machiavelli's Legal and Extra-Legal Modes for Controlling Elites," *Ratio Juris: An International Journal of Jurisprudence and Philosophy of Law* 28, no. 2, (2015): 252–66.
12. Machiavelli's choice of examples, however, suggests that popular support is the result of popular observation of what the usurping ruler does once in office (not the acquisition of office).
13. McCormick (2015) argues that a moderately corrupt republic can be improved through republican institutions which enhance the power of the people vis-à-vis the *grandi*. But, in cases of extreme corruption, more radical and tyrannical responses are necessary.

14. Importantly, not when rule is founded (D. I, 25, 26).
15. (*D* II, 2, 280).
16. Peisistratos was an Athenian who ruled Athens as a tyrant for much of the years between 561 and 527 BC. Though he came to power by violence and deceit, he fought against oligarchs, confiscated their property, and redistributed them to the poor. Machiavelli, who was less concerned about how one attained office than what one did in office, sees Peisistratos as a good tyrant because he attacked the oligarchs who had too much control over Athens *vis-à-vis* the poor.
17. (*D*, Dedication, 92, 93). See also Catherine Zuckert, *Machiavelli's Politics* (Chicago: University of Chicago Press, 2017) for a similar reading.
18. (*D*, I, 2–3).
19. Zuckert (2017, 298) suggests that Machiavelli's dedication in *The Art of War* is evidence that he did not believe they learned the appropriate lessons.
20. McCormick (2015) examines this at length.
21. (*D* I, 55, 245).
22. (BYO 1, 13).
23. See *Batman Begins* (2005). Directed by Christopher Nolan. Screenplay by Christopher Nolan and David S. Goyer.
24. (BYO I, 26–29 and IV).
25. (*BYO* II, 37).
26. (*BYO* III, 80).
27. (*BYO* II, 48).
28. Harvey Dent eventually becomes the villain Two-Face.
29. (*BYO* II, 50).
30. (*BYO* III, 76).
31. (*BYO* IV).
32. (*BYO* IV, 106); see Picariello's chapter in this collection.
33. A very good question to be asked is whether the actions committed by Batman and Gordon are "extra-legal" (beyond the authority of the law) or "illegal" (explicitly proscribed by the law) or perhaps both. The author is grateful to Mishella Romo for raising this issue.
34. *DKR* was published before *BYO* but the story is set decades later.
35. *Corto Maltese* was a character/comic series created by Hugo Pratt.
36. (*DKR* II, 27).
37. (*DKR* I, 2).
38. (*DKR* I, 3, 4).
39. The trilogy of Christopher Nolan films highlight how Bruce Wayne struggles to lead a normal life. (Nolan 2005, Dark Knight 2008, Dark Knight Rises 2012). *Dark Knight* 2008. Directed by Christopher Nolan. Screenplay by Christopher Nolan and Jonathan Nolan. *Dark Knight Rises.*

2012. Directed by Christopher Nolan. Screenplay by Jonathan Nolan and Christopher Nolan.

40. See Giorgio Agamben, *Homo Sacer: Sovereign Power and Bare Life* (Stanford: Stanford University Press, 1998). Translated by Daniel Heller-Roazen.
41. (*DKR* II, 10). Lang raises an interesting issue: that Batman's impact is not simply negative (restraining the power of others) but may be positive as well (empowering those who have been cowed by crime). Machiavelli certainly advocates on behalf of protecting and creating institutional spaces to empower the people (McCormick 2015), but he is also highly critical of the people as political actors acting *on their own*. Lukes' analysis of Machiavelli's distinction between the "palazzo" (palace) and "piazza" (plaza, forum) explicates this clearly. Timothy J. Lukes, Timothy "Descending to the Particulars: The Palazzo, The Piazza, and Machiavelli's Republic Modes and Orders," *Journal of Politics* 71, no. 2, (2009); 520–532. On the distinction between power as positive (transformative, as in the progressive and Marxist traditions) or negative (in conservative and liberal traditions), Machiavelli's position is contextual and realistic, rather than ideological. During extraordinary moments of (re-)founding, his sense of power is more positive than at moments which are more oriented toward restoration. Although both forms are found in both *The Prince* and *Discourses*, the former gives more emphasis to power as positive and the latter as negative.
42. (*DKR* I, 5–6).
43. Crime Alley is the location in Gotham City where Bruce Wayne's parents were murdered before young Bruce Wayne's eyes.
44. (*DKR* II, 15). There is an irony here since the island of Corto Maltese's sovereignty is threatened by dueling Cold War antagonists, while one of those countries—the USA—allows its own sovereignty in Gotham to be compromised by heavily armed criminal enterprises.
45. (*DKR* 17).
46. (*DKR* II, 43).
47. (*DKR* II, 45).
48. (*DKR* II, 10).
49. (*DKR* III, 19, 21).
50. (*P* 12, 42–43, *D* I, 4, 113).
51. See McCormick 2015.
52. (*P*, XVII). See the discussion of the Exhortation in Maurizio, Viroli, *Redeeming* The Prince*: The Meaning of Machiavelli's Masterpiece*, (Princeton: Princeton University Press, 2014).

CHAPTER 8

The Lion, the Fox, and the Bat: The Animal Nature of Machiavelli's *The Prince* and Batman

Daniel V. Goff

At the time of its publication in 1532, Machiavelli's *The Prince* was met with great controversy and was banned by the Catholic Church.[1] *The Prince* was an innovative work because it served as a veritable "how-to" book for rulers to negotiate the tumultuous era in which Italian city-states warred against each other, the Pope, and nations such as France, Spain, and the Holy Roman Empire. The message of *The Prince* was also novel and blasphemous—men are evil, greedy, and untrustworthy and most controversial, rulers should act immorally for the good of the state. It is worth noting that Machiavelli wrote *The Prince* for Lorenzo de' Medici "The Magnificent" who was the son of the powerful Piero de' Medici and the nephew of Giovanni de' Medici (Pope Leo X).[2] *The Prince* was ideally suited as a guide for the ruling Medici family who had taken over Florence in 1512 and actually arrested, imprisoned, tortured, and exiled Machiavelli to his country home during the transition of power. In this way *The Prince* can be viewed rather cynically as an attempt by Machiavelli to regain influence over the ruling powers of his beloved Florence.

D. V. Goff (✉)
Strategic Initiatives Group, USMC, Washington, D.C., USA

PhD Student, Salve Regina University, Newport, RI, USA

D. K. Picariello (ed.), *Politics in Gotham*,
https://doi.org/10.1007/978-3-030-05776-3_8

Machiavelli and Batman have two compelling connections that are explored throughout this chapter. First, Machiavelli explains that the prince must have the qualities of a lion and a fox. A prince needs to have the animal nature of a lion to scare away the wolves and the animal nature of a fox to stay out of traps.[3] The use of animals as symbols bears a striking resemblance to Bruce Wayne's choice to adopt the bat as his symbol. What animal nature is inherent in the bat which gives Batman the power to fight crime in Gotham? Second, Machiavelli notes in *The Prince* that the murder of Remirro de' Orco by Cesare Borgia left the citizens of Romagna "satisfied and stupefied."[4] Batman similarly "satisfies and stupefies" Gotham but in a much different manner than Cesare Borgia. Throughout this chapter prominent Batman comic books are employed to make connections between Batman's and Machiavelli's utilization of animal nature and the latter's observations considering the satisfying and stupefying murder of Remirro de' Orco. This is done with the purpose of demonstrating that Batman is Machiavellian in nature while also adopting a moral code that goes beyond the mere safety of the state advocated by Machiavelli.[5]

Machiavelli's Lion and Fox

Machiavelli addresses the importance of animal nature in chapter 18 of *The Prince*: "How princes should honor their word." Machiavelli starts this chapter with the observation that many crafty men have used their cunning nature to overcome opponents who abide by honor and principle. This observation is further developed by noting that there are "two ways of fighting: by law and by force."[6] Fighting by and through the law is natural to men, but force is natural for animals. However, fighting using the law is not always adequate and a prince must know how to use the nature of the beast to ensure his survival. Following this point Machiavelli notes that the ancient heroes of Greece were trained by the centaur Chiron, which serves as an allegory instructing men to act as both men and beasts and to recognize when the situation calls for each. Lacking the ability to act as a man and as a beast when needed is a cause of ruin according to Machiavelli.

Although Chiron is mentioned only in passing, it is worthwhile to examine his importance in further detail. According to ancient Greek mythology, centaurs were by nature wild, heavy drinkers, prone to violence, and generally uncivilized. Chiron by contrast was cultured and educated due to the influences of his foster father Apollo and his fellow

God and sister, Artemis. From these Gods Chiron learned many skills including medicine, archery, prophecy, music, hunting, and the ability to teach and mentor humans. Chiron was also physically distinguished from his fellow centaurs as he was typically depicted with human front legs and often wore human clothing. The front legs also signified his noble birth as he was the son of the Titan Cronos and the nymph Philiyra. According to Greek mythology, when Chronos was with Philiyra he was discovered by his wife Rhea and transformed himself into a horse to escape. As a result, Chiron was a centaur with distinct human features signifying his unique and special origin. Chiron's major contribution to Greek mythology was his ability to train heroes in preparation for their trials and quests. The list of heroes mentored by Chiron includes Achilles, Jason, Ajax, Aeneas, Perseus, Theseus, Acteon, and Heracles. By mentioning Chiron, Machiavelli subtlety implies that a prince who endeavors to master his human and animal nature in the ways instructed by the ancient Chiron embodies the attributes of heroes passed down by ancient Greek mythology.[7]

For Machiavelli, the two most important animals to emulate were the lion and the fox. The lion and the fox were well-understood metaphors during Machiavelli's time as they appeared in many works including *Aesop's Fables* and ancient Hebrew proverbs.[8] What is unique about Machiavelli's use of the lion and the fox is they are presented as complementary and necessary for the survival and success of a prince. For Machiavelli the weakness and strength of each animal can be summarized as, "the lion is defenseless against traps and the fox is defenseless against wolves. Therefore, one must be a fox in order to recognize traps, and a lion to frighten off wolves."[9]

To act solely as a lion is foolish according to Machiavelli. From this premise Machiavelli makes the claim that a wise prince must not honor his word when it places him at a disadvantage and when the context within which the promise was made no longer exists. The justification for such dishonesty according to Machiavelli is that men are "wretched creatures" who will not keep their word, therefore neither should a prince.[10] Through historical and personal examples Machiavelli concludes that those princes who know when to act like a fox and employ a cunning nature and deceit fare best. However, a prince must appear kind, compassionate, and devout—but only insomuch as others believe him to be kind, compassionate, and devout. The appearance of goodness will allow the prince to deceive men because there are always those willing to be deceived.

Machiavelli uses the example of Pope Alexander VI: "he never did anything, or thought anything, other than deceiving men; and he always found victims for his deceptions."[11] Machiavelli further justifies deception by stating a prince cannot observe the virtues of faith, charity, kindness, and religion because he will be forced to defy those virtues to keep his state in order. Therefore, failing to employ deception for the benefit of the state is a greater evil than to act deceitfully. At this point in the chapter, Machiavelli makes a veiled reference to Ferdinand of Aragon when he states that he "never preaches anything except peace and good faith; and he is the enemy of both one and the other, and if he had ever honored either of them he would have lost either his standing or his state many times over."[12] This contemporary case is used to illustrate his point: Aragon is a modern, successful example of a prince and ruler.

An aspect of the animal nature of the lion, the ability to cause fear, is important to note. This concept is articulated in chapter 17: "Cruelty and compassion; and whether it is better to be loved than feared, or the reverse." A prince should have a reputation for compassion rather than cruelty but must be careful not to rely on compassion alone. Here Machiavelli uses the example of Cesare Borgia as a prince who used cruelty to better maintain his state. It was through Cesare Borgia's cruelty that Romagna was reformed and order restored.[13] To Machiavelli, Cesare Borgia displayed more compassion through his cruelty than the Florentine people who let Pistoria be destroyed for fear of being labeled cruel.[14] The lesson to be learned from this example is that a prince can safely incur the charge of cruelty so long as the people of the realm are "united and loyal."[15] A prince could even execute individuals so long as he is not hated. This cruelty to individuals is preferable to those who are compassionate and allow disorder to reign which invariably leads to further disorder. To further illustrate this point, Machiavelli quotes Virgil's Dido: "harsh necessity, and the newness of my kingdom, force me to do such things and to guard my frontiers everywhere."[16]

Machiavelli then asks his famous question, "whether it is better to be loved than feared, or the reverse."[17] Of course Machiavelli states that it is best and preferable to have both qualities but if you must choose only one, because it is difficult to have both, then it is best to be feared. Friendship is even discarded by Machiavelli who states friendship is bought with money and not with nobility because a man will worry less about doing harm to a man who is loved compared to a man who is hated. It is the fear of punishment which drives men, and this can be exploited by a prince who chooses to use fear wisely. However, a prince must avoid being so cruel that his citizens hate him, and this can be avoided if the prince does not take the property or women of his subjects. Machiavelli cites the famous Carthaginian General Hannibal as an example of a leader who used the instrument of fear effectively. He goes on the explain that even though Hannibal's enormous army conducted difficult foreign campaigns and was composed of many different races there was never any tension among the troops or animosity toward the general and that was due to Hannibal's "inhuman cruelty."[18] In contrast to Hannibal, Machiavelli offers Scipio as a leader who was too lenient which led his army to mutiny against him in Spain and his officers to loot Locri against his orders. Machiavelli concludes this chapter with the observation that men "love as they please and fear as the prince pleases"; thus, a wise prince should rely on what he can control—fear—so long as he avoids hatred.[19]

The Origins of The Bat

Batman's animal nature cannot be examined without first detailing his origin because the two are inexorably linked. Batman first appeared in *Detective 27*, which was published in May 1939 and featured Batman swinging on a cable with a criminal in his clutches as two other men look on helplessly.[20] Batman was clad in black and gray which contrasted with his bright yellow utility belt. Batman's cape resembled an enormous dark winged creature and his black cowl had two prominent black ears which were evocative of a bat. From his first image it was clear that Batman was very different from Superman who was presented in bright colors with his face plainly visible. It was not until *Detective 33*, which appeared in November 1939, that Batman's origin was explained. Young Bruce Wayne was made an orphan when a gunman killed his parents as they strolled the streets of Gotham after watching a movie. As young Bruce kneeled sobbing in the candlelight next to his bed with his hands clasped together as if in prayer, he swore an oath to avenge his parents' death and to protect the people of Gotham.[21] From there the story moves forward and explains that Bruce learned how to be a scientist and to condition his body physically. After his extensive training, Bruce returned to his family's estate a wealthy young man, but he required a disguise to fight Gotham's criminals and corrupt officials. Batman's origin is explained when Bruce proclaims his plan as a bat flies in through a window giving him a spark of inspiration:

> Criminals are a superstitious cowardly lot. So my disguise must be able to strike terror into their hearts. I must be a creature of the night, black, terrible... a . a... a bat! That's it! It's an omen. I shall become a bat![22]

This origin was only a small portion of *Detective 33* as the "The Batman Wars Against the Dirigible of Doom" storyline served as the major focus of the issue. However, this initial explanation of Batman's origin has stayed largely intact for over 75 years.

Frank Miller's *The Dark Knight Returns*, published in 1986, adds to the Batman origin story by showing that a young Bruce Wayne fell into a cave at Wayne Manner and the bats which filled the cave had a profound and frightening impact on young Bruce. This retelling is presented as a sequence of flashbacks and *The Dark Knight Returns* origin story was largely used in Christopher Nolan's Batman movie trilogy.

In 1987, Frank Miller and David Mazzucchelli revisited Batman's origin in the *Batman: Year One* story arc which ran from *Batman 404–407*. In this story Miller and Mazzucchelli elaborated on Batman's origin and offered a new take in which they portrayed Bruce bleeding in his father's study after his first attempt to patrol the streets of Gotham without a terrifying disguise left him stabbed, shot, and nearly arrested. As Bruce sits slumped near death, a bat crashes through the window and perches himself in front of Bruce:

> Without warning it comes...crashing through the window of your study... and mine...I have seen it before...somewhere...it frightened me as a boy... frightened me...yes Father...I shall become a bat.[23]

Miller and Mazzucchelli transform the symbolism of the bat as an object of fear to criminals into an object of fear to a young Bruce Wayne. In both examples the Batman disguise is designed to induce fear in those who oppose Batman by leveraging the form of a bat-like creature that may not be human and may even be otherworldly. The bat symbology as an element of terror is consistent with Machiavelli's concept of fear embodied in the animal nature of the lion but in a different form. The bat is not diminished in its power compared to the lion but targeted and appropriate for the environment of Gotham City. Gothic Gotham with its slums and dark alleys is the perfect environment to be inhabited by a menacing bat-like creature of the night.

The fear aspect of the bat symbol is further explored by Miller and Mazzucchelli when Batman unleashes a wave a violence against Gotham's criminals. As police Lieutenant James Gordon briefs a room of fellow policemen three large posters are situated on the wall behind him, meant to be artist renditions of the mysterious Batman. One poster can be best described as a bat demon, the other two are closer to the common depiction of Batman but the images help create the implication that Batman may not be human. Gordon goes on the explain:

> If we can all stop being hysterical for a moment, gentlemen. Our vigilante—or Batman, as he's called, has apparently committed seventy-eight acts of assault in the past five weeks. During this time, certain patterns of timing and method have emerged. It is clear that he possesses extraordinary physical skill…

At which point Detective Flass interrupts, "Not he. It."[24] Later in the same issue Batman cuts the power and crashes the dinner party of prominent Gotham City officials and underworld bosses and proclaims, "Ladies. Gentlemen. You have eaten well. You've eaten Gotham's wealth. Its spirit. Your feast is nearly over. From this moment on—none of you are safe."[25] This moment signifies that Batman is not the object of terror for low-level criminals solely but for the city's criminal masterminds and corrupt elites as well. Gotham's underworld has been put on notice and it is not the law that will bring them to justice, it is the vengeance of the bat that will bring peace to Gotham.

The bat not only serves as a symbol of fear but also incorporates the fox's cunning nature as well. In many ways, the bat incorporates the strengths of the lion and the fox but without their weaknesses. The bat symbology does not embody the fox outwardly, but its "nature" is ingrained in Bruce Wayne through training and experience. There is a period between the death of Bruce's parents and his becoming Batman where Bruce trained in many different disciplines in preparation for his war on crime. This training is very similar to the training of heroes at the hands of Chiron noted by Machiavelli in chapter 18 of *The Prince*. It is too simplistic to claim that Alfred Pennyworth, the Wayne family butler and long-time caretaker of Bruce, is Batman's Chiron. However, Alfred was trained as a combat medic and he has theatrical skills which he developed in his youth.

Bruce's years away from Alfred and Gotham included formal education in Europe as well as intensive training in a variety of more specialized skills. Bruce trained as a magician under the great John Zatara, his martial arts skills were honed by David Cain and a host of various masters, he learned demolitions, criminology, race car driving, ventriloquism, detective work, and even Eastern philosophy and meditation techniques. In addition, Batman can speak almost every language and fight in any style. Batman, driven by his personal war against crime, is the culmination of unbound will for self-improvement reinforced by unlimited opportunity facilitated by his extraordinary wealth. Batman uses all these skills in a manner consistent with the deceptive "skills" of the fox because his mask is Bruce Wayne: a billionaire, socialite, and playboy. Underneath this façade Batman has unfettered access and connections to Gotham's elite facilitated by Bruce Wayne.

Batman also employs another cunning disguise rarely noted in the Batman mythos, that of "Matches" Malone. Malone presents himself as a low-level criminal for hire but actually is a disguise for Batman utilized to penetrate the seedy underworld of Gotham City. Usually, Malone can be found in bars or working jobs in Gotham City's underworld, but these activities are another means for Batman to gather intelligence against criminals. Often portrayed with sunglasses, a fine mustache, and a cheap suit, Malone is described as having "a perfect North Jersey accent. Flat and nasal."[26] Malone first appeared in *Batman 242,* published in June 1972, and ever since has been Batman's outlet to gather information that would be otherwise unavailable to Bruce Wayne or Batman. Malone is pure deception and thus embodies Machiavelli's nature of the fox. Behind all the physical training and technological wizardry that money can buy, it is Batman's mind that makes him a formidable opponent not only for the underworld of Gotham but for otherworldly supervillains as well. In his ability to adapt and leverage people through fear or deception, Batman is surely a prince in the tradition of Machiavelli.

Satisfied and Stupefied

The description and explanation of Remirro de' Orco's murder takes place in chapter 7 of *The Prince*: "New principalities acquired with the help of fortune and foreign armies." A civilian who becomes a prince through good fortune with little effort will find it difficult to maintain his position because good fortune is fickle and inherently unstable. Additionally,

Machiavelli notes that even a talented citizen with many skills will be unable to command because he does not have loyal troops of his own. Conversely, princes like Francesco Sforza, the Duke of Milan, labored through many struggles to gain power but, once attained, found it easy to maintain.

This takes us back to a man who Machiavelli respected, Cesare Borgia. Borgia, also known as "Duke Valentino," acquired his state through good fortune when his father became Pope Alexander VI. However, Borgia inherited an army with questionable loyalty and Colonna and Orsini factions vied for power, which made his position precarious. Borgia plied the Orsini and Colonna factions with gifts and titles to win them over to his camp. However, the Orsini eventually realized that Borgia was moving to undermine them and instigated a revolt which was put down with the help of the French. Borgia found himself alone and in control of the Romagna, but he soon realized that the region had a history of weak rulers and was prone to disorder. To restore order in the Romagna, Borgia tasked Remirro de' Orco to pacify and unify the region. A "cruel and efficient man," Remirro de' Orco soon brought the region in line through violence and the region began to show signs of prosperity under Borgia's rule.[27] Fearing resentment for the heavy-handed tactics employed by Remirro de' Orco, civil tribunals and city representatives were established to give the citizens a greater influence in civil and governmental affairs.[28] Recognizing an opportunity to win over his subjects completely, Borgia had Remirro de' Orco cut in two and displayed in the piazza of Cesena with a block of wood and bloody knife next to the body.[29]

The mention of the block of wood is curious. The piece of wood was not described as a cross but what else could it be and why mention the block of wood otherwise?[30] If the block of wood was indeed a cross, it appears that Borgia signified that the murder of the tormentor of Romagna was sanctified by God. This religiously ordained use of violence on behalf of the citizens of Romagna must have been a compelling endorsement for Borgia's rule and methods. Machiavelli said that this act alone left the people of Romagna "satisfied and stupefied."[31] To the people of Romagna, Borgia was the source of their persecutor Remirro de' Orco, but he was also their savior through his murder. The religious contextualization of Remirro de' Orco's murder is especially compelling considering that Cesare Borgia's father, Rodrigo Borgia, was Pope Alexander VI at the time.

Even though Borgia was successful in solidifying his power over Romagna through the staged and symbolized murder of Remirro de' Orco, it was not long lived. Pope Alexander VI fell ill and died and Borgia himself became very ill as well. In a weakened state Borgia failed to ensure that a similarly pliant Pope was chosen; instead, Julius II was made Pontiff, and he held no affection for Borgia. Even though Borgia was cunning, feared, and maintained unified and prosperous landholdings, his rule over Romagna did not last because he rose to power through the influence of his father. Machiavelli holds Borgia in high regard as a prince and ruler but notes that the error which caused his downfall was his inability to get a sympathetic Spaniard chosen as Pope which would have let Borgia continue to rule Romagna.[32]

Like Cesare Borgia, Batman regularly leaves the citizens of Gotham "satisfied and stupefied" through his magnificent and terrible displays of vengeance against the criminals of Gotham. The "satisfaction and stupefaction" of Gotham which Batman orchestrates has many unique characteristics, but the outcome is similar to that which occurred in Cesena when Remirro de' Orco's body was left on display in the city's main square. The theatricality of displaying Remirro de' Orco's body cannot be understated. Cesare Borgia wanted the people of Cesena and Romagna to know that he had taken their tormenter away. It was a public display lacking any shame and full of temerity. Likewise, Batman incorporates a similar theatrical flair in the way he brings criminals to justice. He often leaves them at the Gotham City Police Department's door or hung from a light pole in the street usually beaten or incapacitated. He wants to publicly proclaim his commitment against crime in Gotham City, not only to law-abiding citizens but also to criminals and those contemplating crime. Batman shuns public attention and prefers to hide in the shadows, only stepping out into the light when he has the advantage, but he seeks out attention and notoriety with his public displays of the consequences of crime.

Batman "stupefies" the citizens of Gotham in many ways. He occupies the minds of Gotham's citizens as someone whose status is somewhere between a man and a beast. He is an urban myth to many, a savior to some, but also a judge and jury to Gotham's criminals. To aid him in this stupefaction is his mastery of technology: Batman employs almost every form of transportation from a plane to a submarine. He shows up where he wants, when he wants, and employs military-grade equipment to leverage his mobility and access. Batman may not often be seen in person, but his widely evocative vehicles are often seen patrolling Gotham's cityscape. This ability to field high-tech equipment stems from his supreme scientific and engineering intellect but also benefits from access to the resources of his multi-national company, Wayne Enterprises. The Bat-Plane and Bat-Submarine aside, Batman's bodysuit is often portrayed as a technological marvel which incorporates armor, weapons, communications gear, and forensic equipment. However, Batman's utility belt is his most well-known piece of technology. In his utility belt Batman has planned and prepared for all contingencies. At his disposal he has a range of objects from the simple batarang to a Kryptonite ring in case he must battle Superman. Part of the wonder of Batman is that he is always prepared and uses unique technology to overcome his enemies. Machiavelli was also a proponent of preparedness and versatility: "all wise princes…not only have to have regard for present troubles but also for future ones, and they avoid these with all their industry."[33]

Batman "satisfies" Gotham because he is a savior of a city in need of saving. Unlike Metropolis, Gotham is besieged by criminals and the Gotham City Police Department relies on Batman to help keep the peace. This relationship has been strained over the years. During *Batman: Year One* and *The Dark Knight Returns* story arcs, the Gotham City Police Department tries to arrest and alternatively kill Batman. However, most of Batman's story arcs have a continuity which sees him aligned with the Gotham City Police Department and especially its Commissioner, James Gordon. The Bat Signal on top of police headquarters is proof that Batman is a reluctantly accepted agent for peace and justice, even though he operates outside the law and almost exclusively through Commissioner Gordon. As the Bat Signal shines over Gotham like a beacon, the people of Gotham know that Batman is somewhere in the night protecting them. Not only does the police department approve of Batman, albeit grudgingly, so do the citizens of Gotham. This "satisfies" the people because it frees them from the threat of harm, much like when Cesare Borgia removed Remirro de' Orco from Romagna.

Unlike Cesare Borgia, Batman operates with a strict moral code which is chiefly oriented around a conviction not to kill. Of course, Batman has no issue with beating confessions out of criminals, hanging them from buildings, threatening them with broken legs or arms, and generally pummeling any criminal he runs across. However, for all his brutality and violence, Batman will not kill, even his arch nemesis the Joker, who he well knows will do harm to the people of Gotham if and when he escapes custody. The furthest Batman has gone to subdue the Joker was to break his neck in *The Dark Knight Returns*. However, the Joker, in a final act of will, wrenched his neck further, killing himself in the process. Batman's vow not to kill distinguishes himself from the criminals plaguing Gotham. In return for this the citizens of Gotham sanction Batman's actions and are "satisfied" with his techniques and results. If Batman were to resort to murder, he would run the risk of being hated and upset the delicate balance that sets the conditions for Gotham City's support for Batman. In *Batman: Cold Days* (*Batman 51–53*) story arc by Tom King and Lee Weeks, Gotham City's Machiavellian "satisfaction" is explored in a unique manner. As the story unfolds we learn that Bruce Wayne is serving on jury duty for the murder trial of Mr. Freeze, who is accused of killing three young women. As the jury deliberates, Bruce Wayne is the only juror to voice doubt about Batman's role in the case, and he claims to believe that Mr. Freeze could be innocent. Bruce Wayne explains that Batman conducted the autopsy, gained access to police information, and apprehended Mr. Freeze all illegally. As Bruce Wayne continues he concludes that if Batman is not God and capable of making errors then there is "reasonable doubt" and Mr. Freeze should be acquitted.[34] This story demonstrates the level to which Gotham trusts Batman, and this tremendous trust is a direct result of their satisfaction with his methods, his mission, and morality.

The concept of Batman as an accepted vigilante was explored in Sean Gordon Murphy's *Batman: White Knight, a* story in which Batman was nearly rejected by the Gotham City Police Department and the citizens of Gotham because he had become reckless and began to be viewed as a cause of violence rather than a cure. The story begins with Batman driving a Bat-Tank wildly through Gotham in pursuit of the Joker. During the course of this chase Batman injures construction workers and causes a great deal of damage. When he finally corners the Joker, he is videotaped beating the Joker savagely and forcing pills down his throat. These pills are actually an experimental medicine to cure Jack Napier of his insanity and rid him of his alter ego, the Joker. As Jack Napier recovers, he resorts to the law to challenge Batman's privileged position by proclaiming:

> Batman endangered innocent civilians by driving an unlicensed weaponized tank over rooftops…he assaulted me as I was trying to surrender…you and a dozen officers stood by while he forced unknown medication down my throat until I stopped breathing. Add that all up and what do we have? Reckless endangerment, destruction of public and private property, a dozen different traffic violations, assault and attempted murder by lethal dosage. If you don't arrest Batman, then I have no choice but to file suit against the GCPD to answer for his crimes.[35]

During the litigation and subsequent struggle, Batman is incarcerated, and it is revealed that there is a multi-billion-dollar fund secretly hidden in Gotham's natural disaster account to pay for all the damage Batman causes during his suppression of crime. Instead of a savior, Batman is identified as a corrupting influence over Gotham that masks basic inadequacies in governance and community policing. Batman regains civil acceptance only when Jack Napier reverts to being the Joker and Gotham is again overrun by criminals. Later, it is disclosed that the Batman destruction fund is financed by Wayne Enterprises and its subsidiaries and that the whole sequence of events had been instigated by Harley Quinn as a way to rid Gotham City of Batman.

The Bat as Lion and Fox

While Batman comic books and Machiavelli's *The Prince* seem like unlikely works for comparison, the similarities between the use of "animal natures" and the ways in which a prince or someone in power "satisfies and stupefies" his realm are significant. Batman's bat symbology, born from his childhood terror, is turned against the criminals of Gotham like a psychological weapon similar to the fear caused by Machiavelli's lion. Batman also has the characteristics of Machiavelli's fox by employing deception and intelligence-gathering not only in the form of his playboy Bruce Wayne persona but most creatively as "Matches" Malone. Batman's mental agility and extreme skill in inductive logic, characterized by his moniker, "The Detective," also demonstrate a likeness to the fox. This attribute, more than his physicality, adheres to Machiavelli's description of a successful prince.

Batman's ability to "satisfy and stupefy" Gotham City resembles Cesare Borgia's influence over Romagna, but it also has some very distinct features. Gotham is dark, dirty, crime ridden, and in need of a hero compatible with the city's image and character. Batman fills that role and leverages his theatrics, technology, and violence to prosecute a very personal war against crime while also protecting the citizen of his native city. However, this vigilantism comes with a set of moral restraints and rules; Batman will not kill and takes measures not to harm innocent civilians. This notion has been tested in different Batman comic book story arcs and demonstrates the level to which the citizens of Gotham trust and are satisfied with Batman even though it is difficult for Batman to maintain an equilibrium. Machiavelli would take issue with Batman's morality, as he would find it self-limiting and argue that it is not compatible with the overall well-being of the state because villains, who obey no such restrictions, always return to harm Gotham's helpless citizens. It is reasonable to conclude that Machiavelli would advocate the killing of such villains as the Joker, Bane, Mr. Freeze, Killer Croc, the Riddler, the Penguin, Two-Face, Ras al Ghul, and the like to ensure that they can never again perpetrate cruelty toward the people of Gotham.

In this way Machiavelli would rather endorse the anti-hero which became popular in the 1980s such as Marvel Comics' Punisher or Alan Moore's character Rorschach from *Watchmen*. However, it is Batman's code and methods which allow him to maintain the trust and confidence of Gotham City. Indeed, this concept will be explored further when Brian Azzarello and Lee Bermejo release *Batman: Damned* under DC Comics' new Black Label imprint, a series intended for mature readers. In this "out of continuity" story the main question to be explored is: what would happen if Batman finally killed the Joker? Barring any changes to Batman's moral code that the authors may introduce, the key aspect to understand regarding Batman's similarity to Machiavelli's ideal prince is the service rendered to the state and the concomitant personal requirement that one must master one's own mental capabilities to maximize survival and success. No comic book character fits that description better than Batman.[36]

Notes

1. Niccolò Machiavelli, *The Prince* (New York: Penguin Classics, 1961).
2. Ibid., 29.
3. Ibid., 99.
4. Ibid., 58.
5. Ibid.
6. Ibid.
7. *CHIRON—Elder Centaur of Greek Mythology*. http://www.theoi.com/Georgikos/KentaurosKheiron.html (Accessed on August 27, 2018).
8. Revital Refael-Vivante, "Of Lions and Foxes: Power and Rule in Hebrew Medieval Fables," *revista paz y los conflictos*, no. 2 (2009): 24–43.
9. Ibid., 99.
10. Ibid., 100.
11. Ibid.
12. Ibid., 102.
13. Ibid., 95. Romagna was a historical region that roughly corresponds to present-day Emila-Romagna. The region was bounded by the Apennines

to the southwest, the Reno river to the north, the Sillaro river to the west, and the Adriatic to the east. Cities in the region included Cesena, Forli, Imola, Ravenna, Rimini, and San Marino. Ibid.

14. Pistoria was a client-city of Florence which broke into conflict between two factions in 1501–1502. Order was finally restored only through the use of force.
15. Ibid.
16. Ibid., 96.
17. Ibid.
18. Ibid., 97.
19. Ibid., 98.
20. Kane, Bob. *Detective #27*, New York: DC Comics, 1939.
21. Kane, Bob. *Detective #33*, New York: DC Comics, 1939.
22. Ibid.
23. Miller, F. and Mazzucchelli, D. *Batman #404*, New York: DC Comics, 1987.
24. Miller, F. and Mazzucchelli, D. *Batman #405*, New York: DC Comics, 1987.
25. Ibid., 16.
26. Dixon, C. and McDaniel, S. *Nightwing #14*, New York: DC Comics, 1998.
27. Niccolò Machiavelli, *The Prince*, 57.
28. Ibid., 58.
29. Ibid.
30. Dr. Jeff Black, Distinguished Visiting Professor of Political Science at the US Air Force Academy, conversation with the author, July 22, 2018.
31. Niccolò Machiavelli, *The Prince*, 58.
32. Ibid., 61.
33. Ibid., 40.
34. King, Tom and Weeks, Lee. *Batman #53*, New York: DC Comics, 2018.
35. Murphy, Sean Gordon. *Batman: White Knight #1*, New York: DC Comics, 2018.
36. I would like to express my sincere gratitude to Dr. Shaun Baker of the US Naval Academy and Dr. Jeff Black of the US Air Force Academy for editorial support and encouragement. Any errors or deficiencies in this chapter are solely my own. I would also like to thank my family for allowing me to take over the end of the family dinner table and cover it with comic books.

CHAPTER 9

Criminal Justice in Gotham: The Role of the Dark Knight

Mark D. White

Of all the facets of the Dark Knight's life and career as the protector of Gotham City, none is more interesting than his relationship with the police department and how he conducts himself alongside and in contrast to his official counterparts. In his more rational moments, Batman's description of his role resembles police officers or detectives, limiting himself to solving crimes and apprehending suspects. He explained to a young Dick Grayson that "the people we're after have broken the law. It's our job to find them, stop them, and arrest them. Do your job well, and you make that arrest stick. Do your job badly… and you might not get a second chance."[1] Even the classic images of Batman thwarting a mugging or robbery, and then leaving the assailant tied up and hanging from a lamp pole with a note attached to the police with a bat-symbol on it, symbolize this aspect of his behavior—as does his reputation as the World's Greatest Detective, solving crimes already committed and helping the police find the suspect.

Furthermore, Batman acknowledges that no one person can pursue criminal justice alone; when Alfred made a snide comment about the similarities between Batman and the homicidal political activist Anarky, the

M. D. White (✉)
Department of Philosophy, College of Staten Island/CUNY,
New York City, NY, USA

D. K. Picariello (ed.), *Politics in Gotham*,
https://doi.org/10.1007/978-3-030-05776-3_9

Dark Knight told his old friend, "His cause may be just but his methods certainly aren't. … The fact is, no man can be allowed to set himself up as judge, jury, and executioner."[2] Occasionally Alfred must remind his employer of this. After reading a newspaper report of the Joker's latest confinement in Arkham Asylum—from which he will inevitably escape—Batman lamented that "I can catch them, Alfred… but that's it. I can't keep them locked up," to which Alfred added, "Nor can you prosecute them nor defend them nor help them seek out the root of their criminal drives. Yours is a singular task you've set for yourself, Master Bruce. It starts at this [Batcave] tunnel… and it ends at the front of the police station… where you drop off the trash."[3]

Despite noble proclamations, however, in practice Batman does often go too far, taking more liberties with the legal system and criminal justice than he sometimes admits, and more than even his good friend Commissioner James Gordon is comfortable with. In this chapter, I discuss several aspects of this conflict. I start with Batman's lawbreaking in general, exploring his justifications for it and his claims to exclusivity. Next, I turn to Batman's status as a vigilante and how it affects his relationship with the police, including his claim that he can do their job better and their reactions to it (which vary more than you may expect). Finally, I discuss Batman's distinction between justice and the law, and how it leads him to go too far when it comes to dealing with criminal suspects.[4]

Batman's Lawbreaking

Although there is some philosophical debate over the exact reasons, there is a general presumption that citizens have an obligation to obey the law (with the important but rare exceptions of extreme necessity or the injustice of certain laws or their enforcement). Laws help restrain our antisocial impulses and ensure a certain level of stability to everyday interactions, often reinforcing commonsense morality in prohibiting murder, assault, and theft, or regulating routine but potentially dangerous situations such as traffic.[5]

Batman is in a peculiar situation here, in that he claims to enforce the law and help official law enforcement while frequently violating the same laws, especially in the context of extreme violence and trespass. These tools are available to police officers, but only with official permission—

either *ex ante* in the case of trespass, in the form of a warrant, or *ex post* in the case of violence, after review—neither of which applies to Batman.

One of the reasons citizens agree to sacrifice some of their freedom to obey the laws of the state is that everyone agrees to this, which makes those who deviate from the law particularly concerning: not only are they breaking the law, but they may weaken adherence to the social contract by which everyone agrees not to break the law. This can also be stated in ethical terms using Immanuel Kant's categorical imperative, one form of which requires that we "act only according to that maxim whereby you can at the same time will that it should become a universal law."[6] In other words, we should only consider a plan of action (or maxim) as ethically permissible if we can allow everyone to do the same with contradiction. In fact, a federal agent once asked Batman, "We don't approve of your brand of vigilantism, unofficially sanctioned as it is by local law enforcement. Where would we be if every citizen decided to take the law into their own hands and prowl the streets in a cape and cowl?"[7] Batman's choice to break the law fails this test, because if everyone felt free to break the law, the law itself is rendered meaningless, along with Batman's plan to break it. In order for his breaking the law to work, providing him with an advantage over criminals (and the police, as we shall discuss later), Batman needs everyone to obey the law. (Curiously, this logic also applies to criminals, who rely on general levels of trust and lawfulness to enable their activities.)

The ethical implication of this is that when Batman chooses to break the law, he is carving out an exception for himself that he would deny to others, which is immoral per se, at least according to Kantian ethics as well as most social contract accounts. How does Batman justify his violation of the laws he helps to enforce? As many people do, he justifies it with reference to a greater good, which in the terms of moral philosophy is a consequentialist reason for violating a deontological rule, or what amounts to the use of one moral system to compromise another. When Batman enlisted Alfred's help in hacking into a government computer, which prompted Alfred to say, "I'm sure I don't need to tell you this is illegal, sir," Batman answered, "It's in a good cause, Alfred."[8] Even Commissioner Jim Gordon has to concede this point when he confronted Batman, arguing in their early days that "we both want to clean up Gotham—but you're going about it the wrong way." When Batman asked if he really believed that, the young Gordon admitted, "That you're breaking the law? Of course, but… damn it, you work."[9]

Although this moral strategy is noble in that it does actually promote a greater good rather than his own self-interest—as a common thief's use of it would do—it does cause potential problems because this gambit is available to anyone who wanted to break the law, without any type of moral accountability. The legal doctrines of justification and excuse in the criminal law are well established and detailed for precisely this reason, and they can actually be included in the maxims that are evaluated by the categorical imperative. A maxim to steal food when your family is starving, or to break into an abandoned cabin in the woods to avoid freezing, is usually understood to be acceptable because the exception is built into the maxim and therefore unlikely to be abused. Providing an ad hoc justification for lawbreaking "for the greater good" is too convenient, even if sincerely invoked (as Batman presumably does).

This sincerity explains why Batman takes his singular permission to violate the law very seriously. In one tale, a woman named Judy Koslosky trapped a murderer and killed him, telling the police and Batman later that "it might not have been legal… but it was right," serving a higher purpose, namely justice (another basis for Batman's lawbreaking that we will discuss shortly). When Robin said he agreed with her, Batman argued that she was wrong: "People can't set themselves above the law. That way leads to anarchy."[10] Although this seems hypocritical on its face, we can understand it as Batman believing that people can only to be allowed to break the law if they do it the right way and for the right reasons, as he does, using judgment and character to make the decision when promoting the greater good justifies breaking the law. We see this in the care he takes in selecting and training his partners, as well as those he rejects, such as Jean-Paul Valley, his chosen replacement after the villain Bane broke his back. When Valley become reckless and negligent, killing a man and threatening to kill more, Gordon reminded him that "we have a system of law," to which Valley added, "which the Batman has always worked outside of. I still do. Your rules do not apply to me!"[11] Valley believes he is acting as Batman did, but he lacks the judgment to know in what circumstances breaking the law is justified (and under no circumstances would Batman justify killing).

Batman as a Vigilante

Batman's frequent lawbreaking contributes to his reputation as a vigilante in the eyes of many readers in the real world as well as countless people in Gotham, including much of the police force, and one television reporter, Arturo Rodriguez, who went on television to complain about

> Batman and his secret cadre of unelected, unaccountable vigilantes. Answerable to no one, least of all the citizens they claim to protect, many authorities now openly question whether we wouldn't be better off without Batman and his gang. This reporter, for one, now joins that chorus of voices, asking when Batman will submit himself to the lawful oversight of our civil authorities.[12]

In what sense can Batman be called a vigilante, and how does this aspect of what he does affect his relationship with the police force of Gotham City?

In general, vigilantism refers to any activities similar to law enforcement that take place outside the official law enforcement system, taking it upon themselves to act as judge, jury, and executioner—what Batman warned about with Anarky. Not only does this circumvent the system (however imperfect) instituted by society to handle transgressions, but more practically it implies a lack of safeguards or protections such as humane treatment of suspects, a fair trial by dispassionate parties, and proportionate (and again, humane) punishment, all of which the vigilante takes advantage of and often relishes in. In particular (and especially in fictional accounts), the vigilante engages in hyper-violent behavior that police officers are legally prohibited from, as well as breaking the law in various other ways, including trespass and breaking-and-entering. Although vigilantism is often associated with killing, such as with the Punisher, this does not apply to Batman, who famously (and controversially) refuses to kill, but the aspects of lawbreaking and violence in particular certainly do—all things Batman does to pursue his mission, a mission shared by the police who are restricted from the same behaviors.

This circumvention of official restrictions are what people most likely have in mind when they describe Batman as a vigilante—and although he may dispute the terminology, he takes a certain amount of pride in this aspect of what he does. He thinks of himself as helping the police in their shared mission, but using different methods; as he once told Robin,

"Gordon must do what he can. We must do what he cannot."[13] And what Gordon and his people cannot do is practice extreme violence, which Batman takes it upon himself to decide he can. As he repeatedly smashes a thug's hand in the trunk of his car, the thug cried, "You ain't the cops!" to which Batman replied, "That's right, I'm not the cops—that's why I can get away with treating you like the slimy little reptile you are."[14] When drug suppliers repeatedly escaped legal prosecution, Batman asserted, "Maybe the law can't touch them… but the Batman can!"[15] In the same story, he pushed a criminal attorney's face into a bowl of soup while telling the drug dealer, "Maybe the police can't get anything on you—but now you're dealing with the Batman."[16]

The Gotham City Police Department is certainly aware of the ways that Batman gets around the restrictions they must follow. As Lieutenant Sarah Essen—who was later commissioner as well as the wife of Jim Gordon—told him, "You're a vigilante, Batman. By rights you should be locked up! If it wasn't for the way Jim Gordon feels—and the good he swears you've done this city—I'd arrest you myself!"[17] Gordon's relationship with Batman, often endorsing and enabling his vigilantism, is intriguing. Batman is surprisingly honest with Gordon about what he does. When the Joker escaped from Arkham Asylum (again) and Gordon said he was putting his best detectives on the case, Batman told him, "Go ahead, Commissioner—if it'll make you feel better! But I have an idea official methods will be too slow to prevent further killings—so I'll be investigating on my own."[18] The two are even more blunt when Gordon said to Batman, "I'm under orders," and Batman replied, simply, "I'm not."[19]

Even though Gordon thought to himself, upon first becoming aware of Batman's existence, that "he's a criminal. I'm a cop. It's that simple," he came to realize fairly quickly that it is not that simple at all, because many of his fellow police also break the rules (if not engaging in outright corruption), and also that the unique nature of crime in Gotham City sometimes requires extra-legal help.[20] As Gordon once told Batman, "There are factions in the department who've been complaining that I tend to rely on you a little too often—but there are certain cases that seem far more suited to you than to the average cop on the beat!"[21] However, Gordon suffers reputational damage from his embrace of the local vigilante. When he tried to find a job in another city, according to Essen, "they all laughed at him… all because of the 'B.' They told him—we don't want a chief who needs a bogey-man to help fight crime. We want somebody who's good enough to do it himself."[22] As Gordon himself explained to Batman,

> No one would give me work. They didn't want a cop who needed an "urban legend" to do his policing for him. They laughed at me. Some of them behind my back. Some to my face.[23]

Michael Akins, Jim Gordon's successor as police commissioner, had similar concerns about Batman from the beginning. Gordon tried to assure him of the value of the Batman for a police officer in Gotham City:

> Some cops think he's more of a hindrance than a help. Some think he should just mind his own business. They think he's some vigilante in this for kicks. They're wrong. He's the best man I've ever known. I know you're going to make changes, Mike. It's your department now, you'll do things your own way. But trust me on this, there are times when he'll be the only option. You're going to want a friend like him. Let him be your friend… he's the best one I've ever had.[24]

For a while, Akins managed to avoid relying on Batman, but when he did, he told him:

> I should explain why I haven't… called you before now. It's not that I disapprove of you… but I feel that my department has to… we have to be more self-sufficient. We can't rely on you all the time. We have to trust ourselves, you understand? And we have to be worthy of the city's trust. We shouldn't look to you for all the answers…[25]

Akins seems to appreciate what Gordon only learned after years of supervising a police department overly reliant on Batman.

Batman's Relationship with the Police

It is not only top-ranking personnel such as Akins and Essen who have their doubts about Batman; as a beat cop told him, early in his career, "Stay off my beat, Batman! Us professionals keep the peace here!"[26] Some resent Batman's interference in what they do, and find themselves, like Gordon, having to acknowledge the necessity of his presence. When the police failed to bring Mr. Freeze in for questioning on the murder of a police detective, the detective's partner, who was particularly resentful of Batman, acquiesced to calling him in, saying, "I'm a cop in Gotham. I can't afford to live in denial."[27] Gordon feels this way also. When Harvey Bullock—a police detective who once told Batman, "I think you're a freak and a menace. But Gordon thinks you serve a purpose so I go along"[28]—said to Gordon, "I gotta wait to do things by the book, meanwhile the Batman's free to roam the night and do things the way they oughta be done—and he'll prob'ly make my collar. Gettin' so's I hate that costumed gink all over again!" Jim replied, "I felt that way once, Sgt. Bullock… before I realized the Batman has to do what he does." When Harvey asked why, Jim simply answered, "Because he's good at it. The best. And because I'm… only a cop."[29] However, as he told another police officer, Renee Montoya, "being a vigilante was easier than being a cop," presumably because of the restrictions on what the police can "get away with."[30]

One has to appreciate the unique position Jim Gordon is in, being tasked with running a police department with a great deal of corruption (at least when he joined it), fighting costumed criminals (some with superpowers), and operating in a city with little respect for law and order—including his best friend, who exemplifies a lax attitude toward the law. And he does reach his breaking point on occasion. In one such case, Batman broke Two-Face out of jail, expressly without Gordon's permission, to try to clear the name of an innocent man, Freddie Richards. When Two-Face later escaped, Gordon confronted Batman:

> You broke a homicidal maniac out of the nuthouse and then lost him in the Caribbean somewhere. And for what? To save "an innocent man"? What makes you think Freddie didn't kill that John Doe they left in the house? What makes you think the city's any safer with him free? What the blazes makes you so right?!! How many people do you think Two-Face will kill before he gets nabbed again?[31]

Just because Batman thinks he has sufficient judgment to decide when it is justifiable to break the law does not mean he is right, nor that anyone has to agree with him—especially the person who actually has legal authority, Jim Gordon, raising issues about the limits of Batman's own authority to decide when to break the law.

To his credit, Batman understands the way the police feel about him; as he told Alfred:

> Bear in mind that some cops don't really like the Batman. Some cops don't care for the Batman's methods—for the way he cuts through red tape to steal their thunder. I even think it's safe to say… some cops hate the Batman—for being what they can only dream.[32]

He even said the same thing to Gordon once: when the commissioner complained that a criminal's puzzles were "embarrassing" him, Batman told him, "We're the ones who embarrass you, Jim. Cut free from the restraints of bureaucracy, we show the police up with every case we solve. But Robin and I aren't a replacement for the police. We could never be."[33] Unfortunately, this statement is difficult to reconcile with Batman's repeated claims that he can do what the police cannot, leaving us to wonder what function he believes the police serve (other than filing paperwork).

Batman does more than simply embarrass the police—he actively hinders their work by interfering with legal procedure regarding apprehension, interrogation, and trial. He exempts himself from the rules binding the police, and he boasts of the advantages this gives him, but his unlawful actions also compromise police work itself—as he knows, based on what he told Robin about doing their job correctly so they "make the arrest stick." Nonetheless, he regularly absconds with evidence from crime scenes; once, when he returned a bullet he took from a crime scene to Detective Renee Montoya, she told him, "Swell. The coroner said the slug was missing. Convictions are easier when masked vigilantes don't tamper with crime scenes, you know."[34]

Before he became the villainous Two-Face, Harvey Dent was the district attorney of Gotham City, and worked closely with both Batman and Gordon, with a similarly pragmatic view of the law. As he told Batman,

> Our problems are essentially the same. We both want to put Gotham's criminals behind bars. But to do that, I need evidence. I don't want to impede your work—I just want our indictments to stick. I can be at your disposal for consultation. Whenever you get close to a collar, call me and tell me what you've got. If it's enough, you get to do your thing. The police will clean up after you.[35]

This is the ideal, with Batman helping the police investigate and apprehend suspects, while preserving evidence untainted for the prosecutors. But it does not always work this way, as Gordon explained, early in his partnership with Batman:

> Ever wonder what happens to the creeps you bring in? The system has treated them very kindly. At least a dozen felons apprehended by you are back on the streets—and the reason is always the same—insufficient evi-

> dence. It's hard enough explaining to the mayor why we're coddling Gotham's resident vigilante… the fact that your conviction rate isn't any better than ours doesn't help one bit.[36]

Dent's successor as district attorney, Janice Potter, had less affection for Batman; as she told Gordon when she saw the Dark Knight at a crime scene, "This is an ongoing investigation. Just his presence here contaminates the crime scene." When Gordon defended Batman, saying, "His presence here helps solve crimes. Let the man do his job," Porter replies, "Let me do mine! I saw him take evid[ence]—he's gone."[37]

Another area in which Batman potentially compromises investigations is also often at the invitation of the police (however reluctantly): interrogation. Batman famously has his own methods for getting suspects and informants to talk, many of them crossing the line from "mere" violence to torture, methods that are clearly forbidden to the police. Nonetheless, the Gotham City police department often relies on Batman to get information they cannot get themselves. Sometimes, Batman offers his assistance; one time he did this, Gordon hesitated but accepted: "It's against regulations, but… No violence. Remember that." After Batman quickly returned, confirming that "he talked," Gordon asked, "Just like that?" to which Batman answered, "just like that."[38] (Our imaginations can fill in the rest.) Simply the threat of being interrogated by Batman is too much for some police, such as Detective Crispus Allen, to condone. When it is suggested that they call in Batman to question a man suspected of shooting Gordon, Allen shows particularly nuanced concerns:

> It's not that I mind scaring a guy into confessing. That's what the box is for. It's what I do. But we're basically telling this perp he's going to get killed by a vigilante we refuse to stop. That's like putting a gun against his head to extract a confession.[39]

Here, Allen acknowledges that the threat of violence or death, if credible, can be just as torturous as the acts themselves, and represents as such much of a moral (and legal) dilemma for those who choose to work on the right side of the law.

Justice Versus Law

As well as weighing costs and benefits in individual situations, Batman often justifies his lawbreaking more generally by emphasizing the distinction between justice and the law. As commonly understood, justice is the more foundational concept, an ideal of fair and equal treatment, and law is merely its imperfect representation as crafted by legislators and judges over time. According to legal legend, a fellow judge, upon passing Supreme Court Justice and author Oliver Wendell Holmes, Jr., implored him to "do justice!" to which Holmes snapped back, "that's not my job."[40] According to Holmes, his job was to enforce the laws as written by legislators, not abstract ideas about justice as defined by philosophers.

As many vigilantes do, Batman disagrees, proclaiming himself one who sees the justice that underlies the law, and takes it upon himself to disregard the latter in pursuit of the former. As a young man, he said to his parent's graves that he could not become a policeman because "they're too hamstrung by the very laws they're sworn to uphold!"[41] As we have seen, this viewpoint manifests itself often in his discussions with Gordon and others. Early in their relationship, Batman told Gordon that "the only difference between us is that my hands aren't bound by red tape!" Gordon argued that this "red tape" is actually the law, and Batman answered, "I love the law as much as you do… but if I have to bend it to see that justice is done, I won't hesitate!"[42] Much later, after Gordon retired as commissioner, the two were still discussing this topic. When Batman proclaimed that "justice and the law are, sadly, two different things," Gordon remained ambivalent, saying, "I won't tell you you're wrong. But I'm still not convinced you're right, either."[43] The issue here, as with his lawbreaking in general, is that Batman presumes to have sufficient judgment and character to decide under what circumstances the pursuit of justice is sufficient justification for setting aside the law—which, again, is a prerogative he reserves for himself, and maintains regardless of the opinion of Gordon or other officers of the law.

Some of Batman's fellow heroes disagree, not only with his presumed right to break the law when he chooses and judge others when they do the same, but also with his vision of justice. For instance, he criticized Green Arrow, who is normally portrayed as an anti-establishment anarchist, for engaging in an illegal plan with his partner Black Canary to bring down a corrupt company. When Batman questioned his judgment,

Green Arrow fought back, elaborating on their different approaches to justice and "the system":

> Yeah, sure! You can break and enter without a warrant, conduct illegal surveillance, coerce confessions, and violate each and every point of the Miranda rule night in and night out—but it's "different" because you're sustaining the system whose rules you can't abide! … But… I'm wrong because I'm not a hypocrite about it—because I bellow from the rooftops about how warped and corrupt and twisted and sick the system really is—because right along with coming down on the creeps who violate the system's good rules, I come down on the system's bad rules themselves![44]

This passage suggests that although Batman chooses when to break certain laws in pursuit of justice, he believes that the legal system as a whole is just, whereas Green Arrow is skeptical about the entire system and is more proactive about challenging it. Such an interpretation can explain why Batman can cooperate with the police as closely as he does, walking both sides of the fence with impunity while judging others who do the same.

Another critic of Batman's behavior along these lines is Catwoman, who is both an important member of his rogues gallery as well as his frequent love interest (the two having been, very recently, engaged to be married). As such, she often comments on Batman's dual nature as a crimefighter and lawbreaker, and especially where he draws the line between what he will do and what he will not. Once, she suggested that they break into an accountant's office to steal records to protect Batman's identity, but he objected, saying "I have no problem with breaking and entering on a case-by-case basis—but you're talking about larceny… and that means crossing a line." When he reiterated that "I have no innate objection to breaking and entering in the name of justice," she interjected: "There you go again. You call it justice—the system still considers you a criminal, whether you like it or not." When he argued that what she was proposing was wrong, she told him, "everything you do is wrong," emphasizing that even though he may justify his illegal activity on the grounds of justice or the greater good, he is nonetheless breaking the law, which is wrong to anybody that does not share his particular point of view—including the law itself and its official agents, the police and the courts.[45]

Justice as Punishment

For a man so devoted to justice, even at the expense of legal niceties, it is hardly surprising that Batman would not want to stop at merely apprehending criminals and letting the courts handle conviction and punishment. He often speaks passionately of his goal more generally as pursuing justice or vengeance against wrongdoers: "as a youth I swore eternal vengeance of all criminals."[46] Other times he sounds almost biblical, such as when he told Alfred that he hopes to "even the balance between the world's evil and the world's good just a bit."[47] The narration to another tale describes the very meaning of Batman's life as "a never-ending quest for justice. A never-ending war against evil."[48] At one point he even went so far as to quit the Justice League of America because they were insufficiently proactive, telling his fellow Leaguers that

> I've heard the cries of the dying… and the mourning… the victims of crime and injustice… I swore I'd do everything in my power *to avenge those deaths…* to protect innocent lives… and if I fail to keep that promise… my entire life is a lie![49]

All of these quotes point to a hero driven to exact vengeance himself, rather than leaving it for the authorities, which contributes to Batman being characterized as a vigilante (even if he stops short of killing wrongdoers).

Batman's quest for vengeful justice also leads to a focus on punishment rather than mere apprehension. On one occasion, he thought to himself, "with luck, I'll prevent or punish one or two of the night's small crimes."[50] His mission was once described by someone as "trying to shield the innocent" but also "striving to punish the guilty."[51] Although he famously refuses to kill—perhaps the ultimate punishment—and he obviously cannot sentence wrongdoers to prison, his regular use of extreme violence and torture carries significant punitive connotations, made even worse by the fact that not only were none of his subjects convicted in a court of law, but many of them are merely potential informants, not even accused of crimes themselves.[52]

There are significant problems with this from the perspective of the philosophy of punishment, which draws a strong distinction between personal vengeance and retributivist justice. At times, Batman demonstrates an appreciation of the difference between retributivist justice and personal vengeance. As he once told a murderer, "you don't seek justice. You seek vengeance. They're not the same."[53] When the second Robin, Jason Todd, learned that Two-Face may have been responsible for the death of this father, Batman told him that "learning how to temper revenge with justice, well… that's hard even for an adult."[54] While vengeance is seen as a vicious emotion that drives people to engage in illegal and immoral activities, retributivist justice emphasizes the importance of institutions and laws to ensure the dispassionate exercise of deserved punishment within the bounds of human dignity and due process. As opposed to deterrence, which justifies punishment of past crimes based on the prevention or discouragement of future ones, retributivism justifies punishment of past crimes for the sake of right and justice, holding wrongdoers accountable for their actions. Retributivist justice also emphasizes proportionate punishment, based on moral desert, and the determination of guilt before punishment is imposed, both of which require a fair trial conducted by disinterested parties.[55]

Batman's impulse to punish criminals may be motivated by vaguely retributivist principles but has little concern for the guarantees usually associated with it. More obviously, the punishment he metes out is not the result of an investigative and deliberative trial process and was not determined by a judge sworn to follow the law. As said before, even more startling is Batman's willingness to "punish" individuals whom he does not suspect of particular crimes, but are instead likely informants that he beats senseless or dangles off rooftops until they talk. On a more personal level, Batman's mission to fight crime is usually couched in terms of saving the citizens of Gotham City from the suffering he endured as a young boy watching his parents killed in Crime Alley, a motivation in line with the utilitarianism that underlies deterrent approaches to criminal justice. His continued focus on vengeance, however, belies a more retributivist orientation that focuses less on preventing crime and harm and more on punishing wrongdoers himself, which may compromise his broader utilitarian mission to the extent he spends a disproportionate amount of time on cases to which he has a personal connection, rather than focusing his attention on the areas in which his efforts can save the most lives.

Conclusion

Batman walks a fine line with respect to the law, taking it upon himself to decide when illegal activity on his part is justified to fight those who perform illegal activity for their own ends, and to promote the cause of justice as he defines it. Although this is true of most superheroes, few work as closely with law enforcement as Batman does, going so far as to count the police commissioner himself as one of his closest friends and colleagues. This relationship is of tremendous benefit to Batman, granting him access to crime scenes and information he needs in his own personal war against crime. Simply by cooperating with him, though, the police validate his existence and his methods, and in the process they compromise their own legal and moral authority as keepers of the peace and enforcers of the law. Aside from the practical difficulties Batman introduces to the criminal justice process, to the extent the police rely on an illegitimate accomplice, they sacrifice their own legitimacy as the only persons officially sanctioned to use the methods, such as violence and forced entry, that Batman uses with impunity.

Although Commissioner Gordon and other longtime members of the Gotham City Police Department are resigned to Batman's presence in their city, if not enthusiastic about it, their expressed concerns usually focus more on pragmatic issues of conviction rates than more general issues of legitimacy. It is notable that relative newcomers to Gotham, such as Michael Akins, Janice Porter, and Crispus Allen—as well as a young Captain Jim Gordon, years ago—are far more skeptical about interacting with Batman and more cognizant of the deeper problems with this "partnership." These characters provide the reader a valuable perspective from outside the cloistered world of Gotham City law enforcement, refocusing the Batsignal on the implications of cooperating with a known vigilante for police legitimacy and efficacy.

Notes

1. Marv Wolfman and Pat Broderick, *Batman* #438 (September 1989). All comics referenced in this chapter were published by DC Comics, which was located at the time in New York. The listed creators include writers and pencillers only, and story titles are provided only when there are multiple stories in an issue. If no volume number is given, the comic is from the first volume of the title.
2. Alan Grant and Norm Breyfogle, *Detective Comics* #608 (November 1989).
3. Andrew Kreisberg and Scott McDaniel, *Batman Confidential* #25 (March 2009). Although Alfred seems rather harsh in this passage, it can also apply to Batman's desire not only to stop crime but also to reform criminals; as

he wrote in a journal, he wishes he could do more about "the lack of emphasis on reparation or rehabilitation. The revolving doors of the penal system" (Devin Grayson and Paul Ryan, "Locked," in *Batman: Gotham Knights* #5, July 2000).

4. This chapter is based on material I discuss in a different fashion in my book *Batman and Ethics* (Hoboken, NJ: Wiley Blackwell, 2019). Here (as well as in the book), I focus on Batman's portrayal in the mainstream comics from the early 1970s to 2011 (when the entire DC Universe was rebooted during the "New 52" initiative). This is not to discount other versions of Batman, but merely to focus on a lengthy period of fairly consistent and mainstream characterization during which, among other things, his conflicts with the law and the police are well displayed.
5. On this point, see Leslie Green's entry on "Legal Obligation and Authority" at the Stanford Encyclopedia of Philosophy at https://plato.stanford.edu/entries/legal-obligation/, and Christopher Heath Wellman and A. John Simmons, *Is There a Duty to Obey the Law?* (Cambridge: Cambridge University Press, 2005). For a profound argument for civil disobedience in the case of unjust laws, see Dr. Martin Luther King's 1963 "Letter from Birmingham Jail," available at http://www.africa.upenn.edu/Articles_Gen/Letter_Birmingham.html
6. Immanuel Kant, *Grounding for the Metaphysics of Morals*, trans. James W. Ellington (Indianapolis, IN: Hackett Publishing Company, 1785/1993), p. 421.
7. Larry Hama and Scott McDaniel, *Batman* #575 (March 2000). Batman's answer—"if every citizen felt that much responsibility for law and order there wouldn't be any need for either of us"—is well taken but misses the point of the question.
8. Alan Grant, John Wagner, and Norm Breyfogle, *Detective Comics* #594 (December 1988).
9. Doug Moench and Paul Gulacy, *Batman: Legends of the Dark Knight* #12 (November 1990).
10. Jim Starlin and Mark Bright, *Batman* #422 (August 1988).
11. Alan Grant and Bret Blevins, *Batman: Shadow of the Bat* #28 (June 1994).
12. Bill Willingham and Kinsun, *Batman* #632 (November 2004).
13. Chuck Dixon and Tom Lyle, *Batman* #467 (Late August 1991).
14. John Wagner and Chris Brunner, *Batman: Legends of the Dark Knight* #175 (March 2004).
15. John Wagner, Alan Grant, and Norm Breyfogle, *Detective Comics* #583 (February 1988).
16. John Wagner, Alan Grant, and Norm Breyfogle, *Detective Comics* #584 (March 1988).
17. Alan Grant and Norm Breyfogle, *Batman* #460 (March 1991).

18. Denny O'Neil and Neal Adams, *Batman* #251 (September 1973).
19. Andrew Donkin, Graham Brand, and John Higgins, *Batman: Legends of the Dark Knight* #58 (March 1994).
20. Frank Miller and David Mazzucchelli, *Batman* #406 (April 1987).
21. Len Wein and John Calnan, *Batman* #308 (February 1979).
22. Bob Gale and Alex Maleev, *Batman: No Man's Land* #1 (March 1999).
23. Greg Rucka and Rick Burchett, *Batman: Legends of the Dark Knight* #125 (January 2000).
24. Greg Rucka and Rick Burchett, "Officer Down, Part Seven: The End," in *Batman: Gotham Knights* #13 (March 2001).
25. Greg Rucka and Shawn Martinbrough, "Unknowing, Part One," in *Detective Comics* #758 (July 2001).
26. Denny O'Neil and Michael Golden, "I Now Pronounce You Batman and Wife!" in *DC Special Series* #15 (June 1978).
27. Ed Brubaker, Greg Rucka, and Michael Lark, *Gotham Central* #2 (February 2003). After the police manage to capture one of Batman's costumed villains by themselves, Driver gloated to Batman, saying, "we did it alone, without your help." Batman simply responded, "Good. Thank you" (Ed Brubaker and Michael Lark, *Gotham Central* #5, May 2003).
28. Chuck Dixon and Graham Nolan, *Detective Comics* #651 (Early October 1992).
29. Doug Moench and Don Newton, "Boxing," in *Detective Comics* #539 (June 1984).
30. Gale and Maleev, *Batman: No Man's Land* #1.
31. Christopher Priest and Michael Bair, "Faces," in *Batman Annual* #13 (1989).
32. Doug Moench and Gene Colan, "Hill's Descent," in *Detective Comics* #546 (January 1985).
33. Chuck Dixon and Tom Lyle, *Detective Comics* #647 (Early August 1992).
34. Russell Lissau and Brad Walker, "A Friend in Need," in *Batman Allies Secret Files and Origins 2005* (August 2005).
35. Andrew Helfer and Chris Sprouse, *Batman Annual* #14 (March 1990).
36. Ibid.
37. Jeph Loeb and Tim Sale, *Batman: Dark Victory* #8 (July 2000).
38. Marv Wolfman and Jim Aparo, *Detective Comics* #625 (January 1991). Never mind the fact that the suspect invoked his right to a lawyer; I don't have room to go into that!
39. Nunzio DeFilippis and Mike Collins, "Monster in a Box," in *Detective Comics* #754 (March 2001). This sentiment was on display regularly in the series *Gotham Central*, in which resentment of their resident vigilante was a central theme; see, for instance, issue #36 (December 2005), by Ed Brubaker, Greg Rucka, and Kano.

40. For more on this story, see Michael Herz, "'Do Justice!' Variations on a Thrice-Told Tale," *Cardozo Law Review*, 82(1996): 111–161, available at http://www.uniset.ca/terr/art/82VaLRev111.pdf
41. Len Wein and John Byrne, *The Untold Legend of the Batman* #1 (July 1980).
42. Len Wein and Jim Aparo, *The Untold Legend of the Batman* #3 (September 1980).
43. Andersen Gabrych and Pete Woods, "Alone at Night," in *Detective Comics* #800 (January 2005).
44. Doug Moench and Gene Colan, *Detective Comics* #559 (February 1986).
45. Howard Chaykin, *Batman/Catwoman: Follow the Money* #1 (January 2011).
46. James Owsley and Jim Aparo, *Batman* #431 (March 1989).
47. Dennis O'Neil and Sergio Cariello, *Batman: Legends of the Dark Knight* #129 (May 2000).
48. Alan Grant and Eduardo Barreto, *Batman: Shadow of the Bat* #72 (March 1998).
49. Mike W. Barr and Jim Aparo, *Batman and the Outsiders* #1 (August 1983), emphasis added.
50. Doug Moench and Kelley Jones, *Batman* #525 (December 1995).
51. Greg Rucka and Rick Burchett, *Batman: 10-Cent Adventure* (March 2002).
52. For more on Batman's use of extreme violence and torture, see chapter 7 in my *Batman and Ethics.*
53. John Ostrander and Tom Mandrake, *Batman* #659 (January 2007).
54. Max Allan Collins and Dave Cockrum, *Batman* #411 (September 1987).
55. For a survey of philosophies of punishment, see Thom Brooks, *Punishment* (London: Routledge, 2012). On the difference between retributivism and vengeance, see Robert Nozick, *Philosophical Explanations* (Cambridge, MA: Harvard University Press, 1981), pp. 366–68.

CHAPTER 10

The Retributive Knight

Mohamad Al-Hakim

Whatever chance you gave us at fixing our city dies with Harvey's reputation. We bet it all on him. The Joker took the best of us and tore him down. People will lose hope.
James Gordon, *The Dark Knight*

For if justice goes, there is no longer any value in human beings' living on the earth.
Immanuel Kant, *Metaphysics of Morals*

Introduction

Harvey Dent's death in *The Dark Knight* marks the key turning point of Christopher Nolan's popular trilogy. It is a death with substantial consequences for Gotham, as the already fragile relationship between the city and its vigilante further deteriorates when Batman intentionally, but falsely, takes responsibility for Dent's demise. As a result, Batman retires, not to be seen for nearly eight years, and even his resurfacing in *The Dark Knight Rises* is intended to be brief as he battles his inner guilt, fears, and their further exploitation by Bane and the League of Shadows.

M. Al-Hakim (✉)
Florida Gulf Coast University, Fort Myers, FL, USA
e-mail: malhakim@fgcu.edu

D. K. Picariello (ed.), *Politics in Gotham*,
https://doi.org/10.1007/978-3-030-05776-3_10

The death of Harvey Dent is also significant in another way. It symbolically opens up a unique political and legal space that Batman rarely, if ever, operates within. This space concerns the application of punishment. Batman's role, however defined, has mainly been confined in its application. That is, Batman's legal powers are somewhat analogous to that of a police officer; he is traditionally an enforcer of the law but not its legislator or adjudicator. Unlike a police officer, however, he applies non-conventional methods to combat crime and, moreover, does not limit his jurisdiction to Gotham. He is willing to capture criminals even if they are outside the city limits, as he does when he travels to Hong Kong to retrieve the criminal, Lau. He leaves Lau outside Gotham City Police Department (GCPD) with a delivery note for James Gordon. In short, it is left to the law to determine what ought to be done with criminals. The death of Harvey Dent disrupts this traditional role for Batman.

In this chapter, I am interested in exploring this unique space in order to sketch an account of Batman's view of punishment as offered in Nolan's trilogy.[1] My interest is motivated by two main factors. First, in comparison to the ethics, psychology, politics, and sociology of Batman, far less attention has been given to any account of punishment or legal theory more generally.[2] Second, Batman's account of punishment, as I argue later in this chapter, cannot be divorced from a larger politico-legal framework as punishment is properly one of the effects that follow from the very nature of a civil union. Situating punishment requires that we account for the political framework that best fits with Nolan's story. This will help shed light on the sort of political philosophy that informs the politics of Gotham.

In what follows, the section "The Significance of Dent's Death" provides more detail on the significance of Dent's death in Nolan's narrative. I argue that Dent's death generates a unique political and legal space for Batman. Furthermore, I suggest that this space severely undermines the legitimacy of Gotham's legal system after Dent's demise. In section "The Problem of Punishment", I draw on Kant's view of punishment and its underlying political and legal philosophy to further highlight this unique space and the sort of special obligations it places on Batman to re-secure the conditions of freedom. In section "The Retributive Knight Rises", I draw the connection between Kant's system of equal freedom and Batman's approach to punishment. I focus on two important scenes that gesture toward this reading of Nolan's narrative. I suggest that Batman takes on the role of an embattled political authority attempting to secure the rightful omnilateral will of its citizenry. In the absence of Dent, there is still a retributive form of punishment and justice that categorizes Batman's actions as being consistent with a system of equal freedom.

The Significance of Dent's Death

Harvey Dent represents the best of Gotham in Nolan's trilogy and his death is as much symbolic as it is physical. The physical death takes place at the end of *The Dark Knight*, followed by Gordon's pronounced sense of moral defeat, telling Batman that "whatever chance you gave us at fixing our city dies with Harvey's reputation. We bet it all on him. The Joker took the best of us and tore him down. People will lose hope." This physical death also marks a finality of a symbolic death that occurs earlier in the film. For the purposes of this chapter, the symbolic is of greater interest since I argue that it shifts the status of the entire political community and the relationship of its citizenry. However, before I provide a more detailed account of the basis of this relationship, let me first briefly outline what Dent comes to represent in the film and how his death forces Batman to take on a public official role.

It is reasonable to assume that Dent's symbolic death occurs the very moment that the character Two-Face is born. This is captured by Nolan through the tragic explosion orchestrated by the Joker that kills Dent's love interest, Rachel. Prior to this specific moment, Dent was a symbol of hope, justice, and fairness. He is presented as Gotham's "White Knight," who captures a sense of goodness tied to a form of procedural and substantive justice. It is procedural insofar as Dent conducts himself through the proper legal channels to achieve his end. It is substantive insofar as it is a type of justice motivated by some conception of right and fairness rather than mere vengefulness. This all changes with the death of Dent and the birth of Two-Face. Two-Face is the antithesis of Dent. The actions of Two-Face are not lawful; moreover, his decisions are determined through a conception of "luck as justice" (coin toss), and his motives are grounded in personal revenge rather than public interest.

Dent's death is also not singular but takes place through a series of scenes aimed at representing the entire disruption of Gotham's legal framework. This is important because while Dent represents the best of the law (prior to becoming Two-Face), he is not the totality of Gotham's legal system. Dent is still merely a single legal official that represents the interest of the public through his office. Thus, law, which is manifested through a collection of institutions (e.g. judiciary, policing), cannot be totally undermined with the death of Dent. Rather, Nolan represents the collapse of the system in two other scenes. The first involves the initial attempt to kill Dent while he is attending a fundraiser held by Bruce Wayne. This failed attempt is designed by the Joker to take place alongside the killing of Police Commissioner Loeb and District Judge Surillo. Though Batman foils the Joker's initial plan, Nolan returns to this representation in a second scene that features the explosion that changes Dent forever. It is worth noting that the explosion is paired with the bombing of a Gotham police station.

The deaths of Commissioner Loeb, Judge Surillo, and Harvey Dent, and the physical destruction of the police station collectively symbolize the undermining of Gotham's legal system. This generates an interesting void in legality that is normatively problematic even if it is not immediately or practically worrisome. That is to say, as a matter of practicality, the death of Dent, and the symbolic undoing of legality tied to it, does not produce negative outcomes. In fact, near the start of *The Dark Knight Rises*, there is a banquet held in honor, recognition, and celebration of "Harvey Dent Day." In a brief speech, Commissioner Gordon recognizes that over a thousand inmates are currently behind bars and the streets of Gotham are safer because of the impact of the Harvey Dent Act. But Gordon is at conflict with himself, as his mind flashes through the truth about Dent as Two-Face. Normatively, there is something unsettling about the Harvey Dent Act as it is grounded in a figure who (unbeknownst to the citizens of Gotham) no longer represents the public. It appears that punishment is carried out in Gotham in honor of Dent/Two-Face, but the legitimacy of such an Act is normatively problematic.

The Problem of Punishment

This politico-legal disruption generates a unique problem for Batman if we understand punishment as a public right derived through a rational agreement between free and independent moral agents entering into a civil condition. Batman taking on such a public role, however, appears to be inconsistent with such a public right. He is not a legal official, and he does not represent the will of the public in any meaningful sense. In short, Batman simply does not have the authority to punish.

However, the State, that is to say, a political community governed by a set of fundamental principles of justice and responsible for distributing various duties and obligations, is in the business of doing so. Yet, punishment raises a familiar moral problem, namely, on what grounds can the intentional harming of another be justified?[3] This question itself is tied to broader political themes concerned with legitimacy, authority, and the justification they offer for the State's monopoly over the use of coercion. The subject indirectly comes up in *The Dark Knight* when an inspired vigilante wearing a homemade bat suit asks, "What gives you the right? What is the difference between you and me?" to which Batman replies, "I am not wearing hockey pads." Though the response is not a serious one, the question remains important. What differentiates Batman's actions from any other vigilante? Moreover, what differentiates Batman's brand of justice from that of the State (or any public official such as Harvey Dent)? Nolan's Batman struggles often with this question, trying to distinguish his actions from mere vengefulness or, worse, from the very villains he takes on.[4] As I will argue in section "The Retributive Knight Rises", this is what largely attracts Bruce Wayne to Gotham's "White Knight," as Dent represents the legitimacy of the State and the legitimacy of its authorized coercive action toward criminals. Similarly, Kant views the right to punish as a public right that belongs properly to the omnilateral will of the citizens, whereby omnilateral is represented through a civil union. The omnilateral will is a type of normative authorization fulfilled through a rational contract to transfer certain powers over to the State to maintain and secure conditions of individual freedom. The omnilateral will is intended as an extension of individual freedom but one that binds the entire political community and not only those in close or immediate proximity. After Dent's death, and the disruption of law, Batman's approach to criminals (such as Bane) needs to center on securing this rightful condition of freedom if it is to maintain any sort of legitimacy.

The problem of punishment has generated much writing in criminal legal theory. The subject is often taken up alongside broader normative concerns with responsibility, which in turn focus on identifying the conditions of criminality. Leaving aside the importance of identifying the class of persons that may be properly held responsible for purposes of assigning blame (or praise), discussions of punishment focus instead on aim, that is, what is the goal or purpose of punishment? One response is that doing so improves the overall utility of society by deterring harmful criminal behavior. Another response is that punishment is owed to moral agents by virtue of the wrongfulness of the motive itself regardless of utility or expected benefits; or perhaps we ought to strive at restorative goals, aimed at reconciling and healing the relationship between perpetrators and their victims.

Keeping separate questions of responsibility from punishment, my interest is to outline a retributive account of punishment drawn from Kant's political and legal philosophy. This is because Kant's view of retributivism is intimately tied to a broader account of justice concerned with protecting the external (juridical) freedom of individuals. For Kant, punishment is not an externality to law that is consequently added for the purpose of fulfilling some particular function. Rather, as I explain below, Kant's account of coercion and punishment is grounded in a broader theory of individual freedom that justifies the use of force only to secure the equal freedom of others. As Kant put it, "if a certain use of freedom is itself a hindrance to freedom in accordance with universal laws (i.e., wrong), coercion that is opposed to this (as a *hindering of a hindrance to freedom*) is consistent with freedom in accordance with universal laws, that is, it is right."[5]

But what exactly does Kant mean by saying that coercion is right if it is a hindrance to a hindrance to freedom? How is punishment tied to individual freedom?

Kant's view of the right to punish appears in *The Metaphysics of Morals* in a section titled "General Remarks On the Effects with Regard to Rights That Follow from the Nature of the Civil Union."[6] The view is motivated by two core retributive notions, *desert* and *proportionality*. These help differentiate retributive from other normative accounts, such as deterrence theories.[7] First, retributivism is backward-looking, such that "committing an offence in the past is sufficient to justify punishment now," regardless of whether doing so will produce any beneficial outcomes in the future.[8] This is because retributive accounts maintain that punishment is *deserved* (and thus in some sense owed) to a moral agent by virtue of the motive (or intent) of his or her action. Punishment, says Kant "*must always* be inflicted upon him only *because he has committed a crime*…[and] can never be inflicted merely as a means to promote some other good for the criminal himself or for civil society."[9]

In addition to desert, there is also a concern with proportionality. Aside from the question of "what" we are punished for, there is also a question of "how much," generally guided by some principle of fairness or equality. For Kant, this is linked to the *law of retribution* (*ius talionis*), or the creed of "eye-for-an-eye, tooth-for-a-tooth." When one commits a crime, and thus engages in a public wrong, she is also inflicting the wrongfulness on herself. The law of retribution holds that "if you insult him, you insult yourself; if you steal from him, you steal from yourself; if you strike him, you strike yourself; if you kill him, you kill yourself."[10] This does not mean that every crime must be awarded a similar punishment, as it would be problematic if, say, an individual who is rightly found guilty of torture is tortured in return. Working out the contours of proportionality need not occupy us; we merely highlight that retributive theory is concerned with determining the sort of principles that ought to inform the question of "how much" punishment is warranted.

However, it is impossible to discuss Kant's account of punishment (and public right more generally) without discussing the underlying substantial account of moral agency and rational autonomy that informs the justification and the limits of punishment. Setting up Kant's political philosophy will be useful for explaining in the final section how Batman's actions square with a political framework akin to Kant's system.

In the first part of the *Metaphysics of Morals* (*Doctrine of Right*), Kant sets out to work out the requirements of what he calls "a rightful condition." In general, Kant identifies two types of freedom, external and inner. External, or juridical, freedom concerns actions and can be rightfully coerced in accordance with a universal principle of freedom. Inner freedom, on the other hand, concerns the determination of the will in accordance with an ethical maxim and can never be coerced. Inner freedom is taken up in Kant's *Doctrine of Virtue*, which we need not concern ourselves with in this chapter.

The *Doctrine of Right* is concerned with the external (juridical) freedom of individuals and the proper determinative relation between individuals under universal conditions. As Kant states, "the sum of those laws for which an external lawgiver is possible is called the *doctrine of right* (*ius*)."[11] An action is said to be right "if it can coexist with everyone's freedom in accordance with a universal law, or if on its maxim the freedom of choice of each can coexist with everyone's freedom in accordance with a universal law."[12] Thus, individuals' external freedom can be coerced only insofar as use of force does not contradict itself (i.e. violate the universality test). One could not, for example, hold a principle that awarded a greater degree of external freedom for oneself than others. The universalization of such a principle would simply contradict itself as it would be inconsistent with a like freedom for others. Thus, individual freedom to set and pursue ends is restrained only by the reciprocal freedom of others. While it is possible for individuals to unite in their will, the subjection of any individual to the arbitrary preferences of another are never justified. This is because all rational agents have the same postulated inherent innate right said to belong "to everyone by nature, independently of any act that would establish a right," namely the freedom of being one's own master (*sui juris*).[13]

Kant's discussion of right moves from innate to private right and takes up the concern of how individuals can acquire objects external to themselves. There are two ways by which one can come to possess (or acquire) objects. One can do so physically or intelligibly, where the latter entails having a "merely rightful possession" of the same object.[14] One major contrast between physical and intelligible possession is that only the former requires that the object actually be in my immediate possession while the latter, intelligible, is "possession of an object *without holding it*."[15] So, one way to secure property is to have it directly in my possession. However, if left as such, the right to the property would cease upon leaving my possession. Furthermore, the only way another could wrong me in respect to my possession is by trying to physically take the object from my person. So, the alternative way one can lay claim to some property is to do so intelligibly, by way of exercising some choice or power over the object even when such an object is not in one's immediate possession. If, for example, I have an intelligible right to my laptop, then even when it is not in my possession, no other individual has a right to use it or make use of it without my permission or consent. Even if one was to make use of my laptop to further my personal or professional interest—say, someone uses my laptop to complete a paper on Batman and Kant that would be far better than anything I could produce—the action would still be wrongful even if not harmful. This is because the harmfulness of action is not what informs Kant's philosophy. Rather, it is a concern with the *wrongfulness* of an action, understood as a violation of the external freedom of others, that generates a problem. Thus, his view of coercion justifies the use of force only when it is "a *hindering of a hindrance to freedom*."[16] Thus, someone who is coerced through the power of the State to return some private property to its original owner is not wronged. The State, in other words, does not wrong when it uses its power to conclusively secure the property of citizens from those who are wrongfully in possession or use of it.

Kant's account of acquired private rights and possession eventually encounters similar difficulties to those often raised within the social contract tradition, namely in conditions akin to the state of nature, the conclusiveness of property rights and assurance against the encroachment of others remains insecure. Insofar as rational agents remain in such a state, acquired possessions remain provisional and never conclusive. The resolution of the assurance problem (and the securing of rights more generally) requires that agents leave the state of nature and enter into a civil rightful condition (a condition of public right). Kant also postulates this idea of public right, stating that from "private right in the state of nature there proceeds the postulate of public right: when you cannot avoid living side by side with all others, you ought to leave the state of nature and proceed with them into a rightful condition, that is, a condition of distributive justice."[17] Kant holds that individuals do no wrong to one another if they elect to remain in a state akin to the state of nature but that they "in general … do wrong in the highest degree by willing to be and to remain in a condition that is not rightful, that is, in which no one is assured of what is his against violence."[18] Civil society is marked by an omnilateral rational will by all who are part of the contract. For Kant, the social contract is an expression of a rational will and not an empirically grounded claim in some actual agreement. This omnilateral will establishes, in effect, the normative powers of the State to secure and assure the equal conditions of external freedom. This agreement also establishes the normative relation among all citizens with respect to contracts, marriages, and property rights. When the status of one citizen changes in respect to another (e.g. purchasing property), the normative relation of all citizens shifts, as now I have exclusive right to that property to the exclusion of all others. The State secures my property right such that anyone who hinders my freedom in respect to it can be rightfully coerced by the State from doing so as a means of securing my external freedom to exercise my choice (or power) over my property.

All of this squares with Kant's concern to secure the independence of citizens and respect their moral powers to set and pursue their ends without hindrance by others. As Kant recognizes, in a civil condition, *freedom*, *equality*, and *independence* are present. *Freedom* is:

> …the attribute of obeying no other law than that to which he has given himself consent; civil *equality*, that of not recognizing among the *people* any superior with the moral capacity to bind him as a matter of right in a way that he could not in turn bind the other; and third, the attribute of civil *independence*, of owing his existence and preservation to his own rights and powers as a member of the commonwealth, not to the choice of another among the people.[19]

Thus, when citizens unite and normatively alter their condition, they effectively hand over certain powers that authorize the State to act on their behalf to secure the rightful condition of freedom. As Kant scholar, Arthur Ripstein, points out, "any powers a state has must be traced to its claim to speak and act for all…The institutions that give effect to systems of equal freedom must be organized so that they do not systematically create a condition of dependence."[20] For Ripstein, any rationale tied to State action is "immanent in the requirements of a rightful condition," whereby the rightful condition is one that removes the reliance of some citizens on the arbitrary choices of others, that is, secures independence of person.[21] In effect, force and freedom are two sides of the same coin for Kant.[22] When the State applies force (e.g. punishment), it does so in light of hindering a hindrance to freedom. More importantly, it is justified in its action as it acts in accordance with the will of each citizen.

The Retributive Knight Rises

How does Kant's view of punishment and its underlying political philosophy relate to Batman? First, let's take stock of what has been set out so far. I suggested that the death of Dent (and other key legal figures) represents a symbolic undermining of legality in Gotham. This is normatively problematic given the public aspect of punishment and the need to ensure that the State acts in accordance with the will of its citizens. Understanding the public right to punish required taking a detour through Kant's *Doctrine of Right*. Kant's view of the State is premised on the inherent right of individuals to set and pursue their own ends. Protecting the external freedom of persons to exercise their choices generates a right to use coercion only to secure individuals from wrongful hindrances on their freedom. Kant eventually postulates a public right, derived through an omnilateral will among free, independent, rational persons to conclusively secure property and authorize the State to act on their behalf.

In this final section, I bring together the strands of sections "The Significance of Dent's Death" and "The Problem of Punishment" to offer two observations. First, Nolan's Gotham appears to function on a system of universal freedom grounded in a Kantian conception of right. To support this reading of Nolan's film, I will draw on one key scene from *The Dark Knight* to illustrate Batman's acknowledgment of the wrongfulness of violating the external freedom of others, and the serious tone in which this transgression is presented. Second, I will situate Batman's actions in the final film as being consistent with a retributive account of justice that uses coercion to secure public right and not to merely enforce Batman's personal revenge on Bane and the League of Shadows. In short, Batman is able to apply a form of retribution while remaining consistent with justice.

Wrongfulness, as suggested earlier, is not necessarily tied to harmfulness in Kant's framework. As Arthur Ripstein notes in his brief discussion of slavery, our moral outrage against slavery is not restricted (or perhaps even informed) by the treatment of the slave, since, conceptually speaking, one can imagine a benevolent slave owner who cares for the welfare and happiness of his or her slaves and maximizes such happiness at every possible opportunity. Rather:

> [...] the moral outrage of slavery is the way in which one person is subject to the choice of another; not only that what the slave must do, but that what he or she may do, and whether he or she may even continue to exist, is solely at the discretion of the master.[23]

Such dependence reduces the status of a person to that of a *thing*. That is, it reduces our status as persons and the dignity associated with exercising choice by placing an individual at the arbitrary preference of another. This is also why having a system of strict private ownership would lead to no citizen having any freedom beyond their private property. As Ripstein explains, if all land was private then there would be a classic "landlocking" problem generated. This is because any attempt to travel would require that one gain permission from others prior to trespassing on their property. Given that each individual has discretion (power) over the use of his or her property, each individual would be at the arbitrary preferences of others, thereby leading to "landlocking." The solution for this problem is the creation of public roads, the use of which can never be obstructed for private interest. This allows citizens to travel across destinations in pursuit of their ends without needed permission of others. This is because at its core, Kant's political philosophy is concerned with protecting independence, such that the violation of private freedom for the purposes of producing some social utility or preferred set of outcomes (however determined) are never justified under Kant's framework. Undermining the private rights of citizens is simply never permissible regardless of the welfare generated.

This sort of concern is illustrated by Nolan in a brief, but crucial, exchange between Batman and Lucius Fox, who is best known for overseeing Wayne Enterprises's more lucrative projects. In a desperate attempt to locate the Joker, Batman resorts to an action that conflicts with a system of equal freedom, raising serious moral concern for Lucius. Batman modifies Lucius's bat sonar technology to spy on all of Gotham's citizens in an attempt to locate the Joker. The exchange goes as follows.

Batman: Beautiful, isn't it?
Lucius: Beautiful. Unethical. Dangerous. You've turned every cell phone in Gotham into a microphone.
Batman: And the high frequency generator receiver.
Lucius: You took my sonar concept and applied it to every phone in the city. With half the city feeding you sonar, you can image all of Gotham. *This is wrong.*
Batman: I've got to find this man, Lucius.
Lucius: At what cost?
Batman: The database is null-key encrypted. It can only be accessed by one person.
Lucius: This is too much power for one person.
Batman: This is why I gave it to you. Only you can use it.
Lucius: Spying on 30 million people is not part of my job description…I will help you this one time, but consider this my resignation. As long as this machine is at Wayne Enterprises, I won't be.
Batman: When you finish, type in your name.

This exchange reveals much in terms of the recognition of the wrongfulness of violating private rights in the interest of capturing the Joker. More importantly, Batman never challenges Lucius's claim that "this is wrong." The wrongfulness of the act is acknowledged by Batman's premeditated actions, such as limiting access to this database to Lucius and, secondly, not protesting Lucius's resignation on principle due to the wrongfulness of the act. Finally, the inputting of Lucius's name initiates a self-destruct sequence of the entire database, which further suggests that Batman has no intention of violating private rights again. Even if the consequences (i.e. capturing the Joker would spare many lives) are good, the moral wrongfulness of the act remains fully intact. As Kant reminds us, "justice ceases to be justice if it can be bought at any price whatsoever," even through an act that would be beneficial to all of Gotham.[24] It is difficult to deny the deontological constraints, that is, the sort of constraints grounded in duties and obligations, applied in Nolan's narrative. Batman is clearly not motivated by outcomes, and the rare exception he makes should not count against that framework but indeed reinforce it. This was the exception and not the norm. Batman recognizes that Gotham's political framework is grounded in securing the independence of its citizenry.

Batman's wrongful use of the bat sonar technology interestingly enough occurs in the disruptive legal void I suggested exists following the symbolic death of Dent and others. Batman's actions are even more dangerous, as Lucius rightly points out, under this condition. Although law is temporarily disrupted, the permissibility for someone (even Batman) to take on an authority-like role for purposes of protecting Gotham risks undermining the entire system of freedom. It is not far-fetched to worry that Batman will initially fill the void left by Dent but then decide to maintain his newfound authority against the will of the citizenry. The creation of such a powerful authority strikes against the core of Kant's view. This is because the authority of the State is intended as a continuation of the private right of citizens but with an added assurance and security that property rights and external free choice are guarded against encroachment by others or by the State. The legal disruption coupled with the ability to undermine private right through technological means set up a normatively dangerous set of circumstances.

I believe there is a way out of this difficulty for Batman, but it requires that he fulfill two distinct duties. The first is to step in and fill the void left by Dent by ensuring that the omnilateral will of the citizens is re-secured. The second is that Batman must relinquish his temporary authority once the rightful conditions of freedom have been restored. Otherwise, Batman risks the possibility of becoming Caesar-like insofar as being one who is temporarily entrusted with power to protect the political community from external enemies but then elects not to relinquish such power after the threat has been removed. This idea—that it might be permissible to allow someone to operate in a capacity like Caesar—is entertained by Harvey Dent in a valuable discussion he has upon first meeting Bruce Wayne. In the only scene where Wayne and Dent meet, the following exchange occurs over dinner with Rachel and Natasha (Wayne's date):

Natasha: I'm talking about the kind of city that idolizes a masked vigilante.

Dent: Gotham City is proud of an ordinary citizen standing up for what is right.

Natasha: Gotham needs heroes like you, elected officials. Not the man who thinks he's above the law.

Wayne: Exactly, who appointed the Batman?

Dent: We did. All of us who stood by and let scum take control of our city.

Natasha: But this is a democracy, Harvey.

Dent: When their enemies were at the gates, the Romans would suspend democracy and appoint one man to protect the city. It wasn't considered an honor. It was considered a public service.

Rachel: Harvey, the last man that they appointed to protect the Republic was named Caesar and he never gave up his power.

Dent: Okay, fine. You either die a hero or you live long enough to see yourself become the villain. Look, whoever the Batman is, he doesn't want to do this for the rest of his life, how could he? Batman is looking for someone to take up his mantle.

There is valuable insight in this exchange between Dent, Wayne, Natasha, and Rachel. First, Dent defends Batman's actions within certain limits, even claiming them to be "right." There is a sense of approval by Dent of a citizen who functions outside the law for the purpose of securing the conditions of the State. Dent seems to think that such a role, if enacted, ought to be limited and relinquished when the task is complete: "You either die a hero or you live long enough to see yourself become the villain." Caesar, as we know, lived long enough to become the villain, but the suggestion here is that one who temporarily takes on such a public service and relinquishes it appropriately is acting justly by Dent's standards. Dent's view is that Batman was (unofficially) elected when citizens allowed criminals to take over their city. Moreover, he claims that such a role is not an honor but a public service.

I argue that this is precisely what takes place in Batman's approach to Bane in the trilogy's final film, *The Dark Knight Rises*. Bane re-establishes the vulnerable conditions we are left with in *The Dark Knight* by taking the entire city hostage as represented by the shutting down (and blowing up) of the bridges to Gotham and trapping Gotham's police underground.

This is a physical reconstruction of the symbolic disruption we are left with in *The Dark Knight*. But now, Bane creates the condition explicitly, effectively leaving Batman temporarily in a position to administer punishment. It is left to Batman to re-secure the conditions of individual freedom and to administer a form of justice to Bane and the League of Shadows. But the main element of this is that upon doing so and restoring such conditions, the temporary legal powers entrusted to Batman ought to be relinquished. This is why I believe Nolan elects to end his trilogy the way he does: with Batman faking his death and thereby leaving Gotham back in the hands of the proper legal authority.

Conclusion

Batman's personal interests aside, his treatment of crime is not marked by vengefulness but rather by an entrusted temporary legality to act on behalf of Gotham's citizens to remove them from the conditions they were placed under by Bane and the League of Shadows. This situates Batman's approach as being consistent with a retributive form of justice, as one limited to returning Gotham back to a normatively proper condition to which its legal institutions can return to operating properly again. Nolan's Batman can be said to be a retributive knight. Nolan's gesturing toward personal freedom resonates with Kant's philosophy, as evidenced by numerous exchanges and events in the trilogy. Batman's treatment of crime after Dent's death is informed by a public conception of justice that authorizes the State to act only in ways that are consistent with the free will of each citizen. Batman's actions are temporarily authorized within the unique set of conditions in which he finds it necessary to take on the role of the State. However, the upper limits of such a role are reached when the rightful condition of freedom is re-secured. Anything beyond this would place Batman on the wrongful side of justice. His decision to remove himself from Gotham after defeating Bane gestures to his retributive approach. Batman restores public right by securing the conditions of independence, and we are left at the end of the trilogy with the image of a joyous and celebratory Bruce Wayne. Perhaps he has finally restored a sense of justice and dignity to himself and Gotham after years of torment following Dent's death. As Kant aptly reminds us, "For if justice goes, there is no longer any value in human beings' living on the earth"[25] (6:332). Batman's retirement is well deserved.

Notes

1. I limit my focus to Nolan's films. Themes from the film have been explored in numerous comics, some of which clearly inspire iconic images used by Nolan. For example, the rooftop scene featuring Gordon, Dent, and Batman in *The Dark Knight* mimic images from the comic *The Long Halloween.* Also, Bane's isolation of Gotham shares similarity with ideas explored in the comic, *No Man's Land.* The author would like to thank Robin and Kamilia Al-Hakim for their generous support and feedback.
2. Many of these themes are explored in great detail in Mark White and Robert Arp (eds.), *Batman and Philosophy: The Dark Knight of the Soul* (New York; *Blackwell Publishing*, 2008).
3. I use a general definition of punishment as the intentional harming of another, where harm entails a setting back of some interest. I leave aside conceptual issues relating to defining punishment, for more on the definition see David Boonin, *The Problem of Punishment* (Cambridge; Cambridge University Press, 2008); also see Thom Brooks, *Punishment* (UK; Routledge Press, 2012).
4. In the comic book, *Hush*, Batman nearly kills the Joker, on the grounds that he ought to have done so long ago as revenge for the harm the Joker has done to Batman's closest allies (Jason/Robin, Barbara, etc.). Gordon, who stops Batman in time, reminds him that this is the single act that differentiates him from criminals. It worries Gordon as he realizes that Batman had indeed thought this through.
5. Kant, *Metaphysics of Morals*, 6:231.
6. Immanuel Kant, *The Metaphysics of Morals*, (Oxford: Cambridge University Press, 1996).
7. The distinction is conceptual but mixed deterrence-retributive views do exist. Kant is interpreted as offering one such mixed view. For a defense of Kant as a mixed-theorist, whose theory is retributive in principle but deterrent in action, see Sharon Byrd, "Kant's Theory of Punishment: Deterrent in its threat, Retributive in its execution," *Law and Philosophy*, Vol 8, No.2 (Aug 1989), pp. 151–200.
8. Boonin, p. 85.
9. Kant, *Metaphysics of Morals*, 6:331.
10. Kant, *Metaphysics of Morals*, 6:332.
11. Kant, *Metaphysics of Morals*, 6:229. Moreover, Kant's ethical principle is first outlined in the *Groundwork on the Metaphysics of Morals* and then substantially taken up again in his *Critique of Practical Reason.* The universal test of the maxim informs his principle of external freedom as well.
12. Kant, *Metaphysics of Morals*, 6:230.
13. Kant, *Metaphysics of Morals*, 6:237.

14. Kant, *Metaphysics of Morals*, 6:245.
15. Kant, *Metaphysics of Morals*, 6:245.
16. Kant, *Metaphysics of Morals*, 6:231.
17. Kant, *Metaphysics of Morals*, 6:307.
18. Kant, *Metaphysics of Morals*, 6:308. Kant also holds this wrongfulness to possibly be in the formal and not material sense. See footnote in the *Metaphysics of Morals* at 6:308.
19. Kant, *Metaphysics of Morals*, 6:314.
20. Arthur Ripstein, *Force and Freedom: Kant's Legal and Political Philosophy* (Massachusetts; Harvard University Press, 2009), p. 272.
21. Ripstein, *Force and Freedom*, 267.
22. Coincidently enough, prior to becoming Two-Face, Dent would flip a two-headed coin which means that the outcome of the coin would always be the same, such that justice was never left to chance. He only scratches out the one side after becoming Two-Face, thereby creating a condition of chance in the outcome.
23. Ripstein, *Force and Freedom*, 281.
24. Kant, *Metaphysics of Morals*, 6:332.
25. Kant, *Metaphysics of Morals*, 6:332.

CHAPTER 11

Politics as "the Product of Everything You Fear": Scarecrow as Phobia Entrepreneur

Christina M. Knopf

First appearing in *World's Finest Comics* #3 in 1941, "the Scarecrow"—criminal alias for Dr. Jonathan Crane, professor specializing in the psychology of fear—is one of Batman's oldest villains. Though he appeared only five times in his first three decades, his presence grew throughout the 1970s and 1980s. By the 1990s, he was a regularly recurring member of Batman's Rogue Gallery, thanks in part to the animated Batman series. He achieved a kind of stardom in the 2000s and 2010s as the only villain to appear in all three films of the Christopher Nolan *Dark Knight* trilogy, as a central villain in the *Arkham* video game series, as one of the earliest featured villains in the *Gotham* television series, and as a playable character in the *Injustice 2* video game.

Throughout this multi-mediated history, the story and image of the Pharaoh of Phobias, the Duke of Dread, has seen a number of revisions. More than just narrative variations, subtle changes to the Scarecrow's background and appearances are reflective of the socio-political concerns of their era. The differing details of his origins and various vengeances suggest

C. M. Knopf (✉)
SUNY Cortland, Cortland, NY, USA
e-mail: christina.knopf@cortland.edu

D. K. Picariello (ed.), *Politics in Gotham*,
https://doi.org/10.1007/978-3-030-05776-3_11

that the Scarecrow not only preys on the personal fears of his victims, but also plays with the political fears of his audiences.

Superheroes are often perceived as civic models of right feeling and action and embodiments of national identities.[1] Their nemesis, the supervillain, is thought to be a threat to those ideals, a representation of deviance from society or a criticism of its norms.[2] The supervillain is the individual threat to the superhero's collective good. The Scarecrow, whose expertise in psychology represents sociological problems and whose personal vendettas challenge communal welfare, characterizes this relationship—as revealed in narration from *Batman/Daredevil: King of New York*, "While New York's finest are distracted by the trivia of individual deaths, Scarecrow waits for the conditions that will allow him to blanket the whole city with madness."[3] The exploitation of personal phobias is part of the Fear Doctor's *modus operandi*—and a number of stories present narrative glossaries of anxiety disorders from algophobia to taphephobia.[4] The appearances and plots of the Tyrant of Terror also broadly utilize political fears—apprehensions about the collective well-being or uncertainties that arise from conflicts within or between societies.[5]

David Altheide observed that the "pervasive use of fear is part of the social construction of reality in the modern age," what Barry Glassner calls "the culture of fear" and Hisham Ramadan and Jeff Shantz label "social phobias."[6] Social phobias are anxieties regarding others within contemporary society, as related to such issues as terror, cultural decay, invasion, religion, and so on. These contain several recurring themes including fears of poverty, contagion, and violent disorder. Such threats are constructed by social actors—what Shantz and Ramadan term "phobic entrepreneurs"—often decision-makers who use fears to control populations.[7] Politics of fear result from perceived social chaos, though, as Corey Robin notes, fear hinders, rather than helps, democracy.[8]

This chapter argues that Batman's nemesis Dr. Jonathan Crane, aka the Scarecrow, is a phobic entrepreneur who manipulates fear in besieged Gotham City in ways that are historically analogous to the politics of fear in troubled America. If the superhero reflects social ideals, the supervillain reflects social ills, and Scarecrow symbolizes the political production and idea of fear. Echoing the moral panics of the decades, Crane's character matured to represent fears of poverty-caused criminality in the guise of the scarecrow (1940s); drug culture with his use of hallucinogens (1960s–1980s); mass violence linked to domestic abuse, bullying, and post-traumatic stress through his motives (1980s–1990s, 2010s); religious zeal and moral corruption as a cult leader (1990s); higher education as indulgent (1940s–2010s); terror through fear-inducing gases and biological weapons (1960s, 2000s); and social decay as an anarchist (2010s). As the Scarecrow says in *Batman '66* #28, what lies beneath the veneer of civilization "is what drives every choice you make. Your fear."[9]

Fear Itself

Scarecrow first appeared the same year that the Great Depression ended and the United States entered World War II. The preceding decade's unemployment had not only been an economic hardship but also a spiritual one; the jobless prematurely felt, acted, and looked old and impoverished.[10] In March 1933, Franklin Roosevelt assured Americans, "The only thing we have to fear is fear itself—nameless, unreasoning, unjustified terror which paralyzes needed efforts to convert retreat into advance."[11] Exactly ten years later, *Detective Comics* #73 proclaimed, "What do men fear most? Things they do not understand – cunning tricks that seemingly do not 'make sense' and so cannot be warded off by ordinary intelligence! None knows this better than the Scarecrow."[12] Both President Roosevelt and Professor Crane understood the devastating effects of fear on society during the era.

Thus, "a scarecrow [...] a symbol of poverty and fear combined"[13] accurately reflected the mood and trappings of the decade. Similar to those who had been unemployed during the Depression, Crane donned pauper's rags after losing his teaching position at Gotham University. His connection between fright and finance was reaffirmed in 2007, the year the Great Recession began, when "a changed man [...] a new Scarecrow" launched a campaign of horrific homicides and mental mayhem that placed Gotham City on the brink of economic collapse in "Absolute Terror."[14] This symbolism highlights the ways in which Scarecrow's psychology represents sociological concerns, as explicitly expressed in *Batman: Terror* when Bruce Wayne decided to increase funding to the charitable Wayne Foundation "for the victims of crime... and for the victims of poverty which spawns crime," even though he suspected neither charity nor opportunity would have helped Crane.[15]

Demons in Angel Dust

It was not until Scarecrow's next appearance in 1967, that he first used a chemical spray to induce fear—"a special concoction of the tyrant of terror."[16] The compound was sprayed from a small remote-controlled submarine, calling to mind chemical weaponry, which was prominent in the United States' 1961–1971 herbicidal warfare program in South Vietnam.[17] The government was not alone in its political use of chemicals during the era; hallucinogenic compounds, such as LSD in the 1960s and PCP in the 1970s, were part of the counterculture that used drugs to express or establish alienation from society.[18] *Batman* #200 in 1968 introduced drugs to Scarecrow's bag of tricks when he perfected a fear-radiated pill. The use of drugs to instill fear meshed with social taboos surrounding drug use and concerns about drugs triggering a relapse into a primitive state of existence.[19] The concept of drugs as frightening and evil, beyond Scarecrow's diabolical application of them, was reflected in *Detective Comics* #503 through Barbara Gordon's pursuit, both as Batgirl and as a Congressional Representative, of a chemical company she suspected of manufacturing PCP. In the 1969 *Detective Comics* #389, Scarecrow used a percutaneous substance, administered to Batman through a pressurized ring. He again struck his victims through their skin in 1978's "The Sinister Straws of the Scarecrow," with straws treated with a compound that "penetrates the labyrinth of the human brain."[20] Around this same time, rumors circulated about children's transfer-tattoos being laced with LSD that could be absorbed through the skin.[21] By 1981, in *Detective Comics* #503, hallucinogenic drugs were explicitly part of Scarecrow's compound.[22]

While Scarecrow was established as a recurring villain in the 1960s–1970s, anxiety disorders, such as phobias, were a common mental diagnosis and an anti-psychiatry movement was on the rise, challenging the power of psychiatrists to detain and treat individuals, believing that institutions distorted and repressed the human spirit mislabeling difference as deviance.[23] Indeed, the development of the Scarecrow character suggests that it is Dr. Crane who is mad, and that his psychological expertise was selfishly procured and harmfully employed. The idea that someone can affect "certain sensory portions of [the] brain,"[24] or could target the "parasympathetic nervous system… …the part of the human body that controls involuntary emotions"[25] is disturbing.

The twenty-first-century Scarecrow, as depicted in the *Arkham* video game franchise, depended on the use of syringes, attached to a macabre glove, to administer his toxins through an injection. Read one way, Scarecrow's syringes could simply reflect the needle phobia (also called Trypanophobia) that afflicts about 20 percent of adults in a merger of the drug and phobia themes of the earlier decades.[26] It is, however, notable that his hypodermic glove debuted amid the rise in prominence of the anti-vaccine movement during the 2010s. As Ramadan and Shantz observe, social phobias about invasion extend not only to fears of contagion but also to "anxieties over *proper* inoculation" [emphasis added].[27] Scarecrow's injections are, therefore, symbolic of the debate around risks and hidden dangers in vaccines—anxieties that the cure could be worse than the disease, or may even become the disease itself.[28]

Vengeance Is Mine

During the 1990s, much attention was given to the roots of the sinister Scarecrow's supervillainy, specifically the snubbing he suffered in society. In a 1992 episode of *Batman: The Animated Series*, Scarecrow sent Gotham University into a panic as revenge for being fired from his position as professor of subliminal psychology[29]; harassment by his colleagues for his appearance and dismissal for his unorthodox teaching strategies was likewise an element of the original Scarecrow origin story. A renewed origin story in 1995 fully explored the taunting he received as a child for being awkward and studious. He learned about fear in order to conquer it, and used his knowledge to scare two of his main tormenters, resulting in the death of one and the crippling of another.[30]

From this point on, bullying by school classmates and workplace colleagues played a larger role in Scarecrow's criminal activity. The same scenes were playing out in schoolyards and workplaces across the country. More than 20 incidents of deadly workplace rage occurred across the United States between 1983 and 1997.[31] School violence also became a prominent socio-political concern of the decade. Between 1993 and 2001, America witnessed 15 deadly school shootings perpetrated by students. In 13 of the incidents, the shooters were socially excluded through ostracism, bullying, or romantic rejection.[32] Scarecrow's own twisted brand of justice for bullying was reinforced with a character redesign in the animated *New Batman Adventures* in 1997. With a black duster coat, flat-top cowboy hat, and broken noose around his neck, the new Scarecrow embodied violent, Old West, vigilante justice.[33]

The bullied Crane was a more sympathetic villain, as Jason Todd (Robin) observed of Scarecrow, "nobody likes to be laughed at."[34] Rescuing one of Scarecrow's victims who had been one of Crane's high school bullies, Batman scolded, "You tormented and shunned someone who was already different – until he became almost alien. You taunted Jonathan Crane's strangeness. Now you've been haunted by it."[35] And again, while rescuing two more of Crane's former classmates from Scarecrow's vengeance, Batman reprimanded them, "Remember that all the f-fear… you felt in this h-house… is the s-same fear… …you gave to J-Jonathan Crane… in high school."[36] Nonetheless, a better means of handling bullies was presented by Becky Albright, a Gotham University student victimized by both the Scarecrow and by bullies, when she refused to get even with her tormentors by becoming the Mistress of Fear in *Scarecrow (Villains)* #1.[37]

As violence seemed to be on the rise, America's confidence in organized religion began to decline in the 1980s and beyond.[38] Fear of religion correspondingly appeared in several prominent Scarecrow storylines. In 1993, *Shadow of the Bat* #16–18 ran "The God of Fear" story arc in which Scarecrow attempted to create a cult of personality with himself as the god of fear. He explained:

> I've read that the present parlous state of world affairs may be a direct result of mankind's long slow drift away from religion. I intend to rectify that sorry fact. Before the night is over, a million voices will sing my praise – a million knees bend in homage – a million screams beg me to release them from my awful reign of terror. Beware… for tonight the god of fear stalks Gotham City![39]

During the same year, religious cults came under scrutiny with a siege at the Branch Davidian compound in Texas that left 80 people dead, prompting comparisons to the 1978 massacre at the "Jonestown" Peoples Temple community in Guyana.[40] The 1998 *Batman/Scarecrow 3-D* again raised the specter of the dangerous cult through a character using hallucinogenic drugs to overcome the trauma of his parents' death by fire in a religious cult's mass suicide.[41] The theme of "Fear of Faith"[42] was introduced in the 1999 No Man's Land crossover event, just a couple short years before the Roman Catholic Church began publicly investigating thousands of child abuse allegations against its clergy.[43] The 2005 reboot of Scarecrow's origins used religious abuse to further explore connections between faith and fear. Crane's abusive great-grandmother believed "T'was God's will [...] to face our childhood fears" and terrorized Crane for his supposed sins.[44]

Psychoses 101

In addition to illustrating declining belief in organized religion, the Scarecrow—described as a "renegade college professor and authority on the psychology of terror"[45]—has long represented ongoing tensions between society and the institution of higher education. The character of Jonathan Crane is based on Washington Irving's Ichabod Crane in "The Legend of Sleepy Hollow"—a gangly, bookish teacher. Martin Staples Shockley argued that Irving's story helped to establish a standard teacher stereotype: a "wholly unfavorable characterization," reflecting common social attitudes, of arrogance, greed, cruelty, and weakness.[46]

Over the years, the allusion to Irving's tale was emphasized in the Scarecrow stories, including the Crane name, the gawky appearance, and the implicit negative characterizations of the pedagogue. In "Year One: Scarecrow Masters of Fear" flashback sequences reveal that the villain was a lanky and awkward youth, bullied by his peers. A loner, he found solitude in books. Inspired by the dancing agility of Ichabod Crane, he learned the Crane Style of Kung Fu, but was ultimately dismayed at the cowardice exhibited by Ichabod. In college and graduate school, he studied psychology and chemistry and soon became covetous of the life of a professor—"a life of study and books."[47] Impatient for a job opening, he murdered his mentor to take his position, but was soon dismissed from the university for firing a gun in class as part of a lecture about fear. In the "God of Fear" story arc, Scarecrow masquerades as a visiting university researcher, Professor Rance (an anagram of Crane), in order to brainwash followers under the guise of his experiments. *Batman: The Animated Series* introduced the Scarecrow as "a professor of psychology, specializing in phobias" who "became [a] leading professor of subliminal psychology" at Gotham University until his extreme "experiments on fear and its subsequent effects" resulted in his dismissal.[48]

Time and again these stories represent college professors as callously competitive, personally petty, and morally missing. Research is presented as wasteful or useless, serving personal agendas rather than intellectual or public goals. And teaching strategies are called into question through Crane's psychological manipulation of his students. Just as Irving's Crane reflected unfavorable attitudes toward teachers in his society, DC Comics'

Crane highlights unfavorable attitudes toward higher education in this society—or at least the political criticisms raised in the so-called "War on College." These criticisms, or fears, include arguments that the professoriate is populated by ideologues "trying to brainwash everyone" into their worldview while not adequately teaching useful skills to students.[49] Such worries have become increasingly pronounced in the political climate of the 2010s which has been marked by the politics of fear, as evidenced by such headlines as "How Trump Can End Brainwashing on College Campuses" and "Donald Trump and the Politics of Fear."[50] Robin sums up the issue in *Batman/Scarecrow 3-D* when he declares, "People my age are already bombarded with teachers and parents and politicians trying to tell us how to act and what to think – We really don't need maniacs like Crane [...] adding to the chaos and trying to tell us what to feel."[51]

Real Terror

The 2013 documentary *Necessary Evil: Super-Villains of DC Comics* asked, what is villainy to us in the present? Comics professionals argued that real evil has become darker and scarier.[52] The terrorist attacks in the United States on September 11, 2001, with their subsequent anthrax scares and wars, shaped American society, politically, psychologically, and culturally.[53] In the comics, supervillains became metaphors for the real evil of the new age and the uncertainty of fearful times. Order and chaos replaced dichotomies of good and evil.[54] Scarecrow's sinister scenarios similarly swayed from little larcenies and lively larks to comprehensive confusion and killing in the community.

The critically acclaimed film *Batman Begins* explored post-9/11 fears of chemical terrorism when Scarecrow was part of a plot to contaminate Gotham City's water supply with his fear toxin.[55] While other Scarecrow stories in the new century used terrorist-related themes of mob violence, mass hysteria, and massacres—such as the 2007 novel *Fear Itself* and the 2013 youth novella *Scarecrow, Doctor of Fear*[56]—the film reinforced the reality of terrorism through Scarecrow's realistic appearance; as a psychiatrist, Jonathan Crane dressed like a professional with a suit and tie. He used only a simple burlap mask to torment those he poisoned with his toxin. The look of a terrorist was blended with Scarecrow's more classic burlap-and-straw costuming in the Arkham video game series—particularly *Arkham Knight* in which he appeared with a gas mask and suicide-bomber-style vest of toxin canisters.[57] By the time of the 2017 release of the *Injustice 2* fighting/role-playing video game from NetherRealm Studios and Warner Brothers Entertainment, public trust in the government was at historical lows.[58] This is reflected in the description of the game's version of Scarecrow. No mere terrorist now, he is specifically an *anarchist* attempting to use the chemistry and psychology of fear "to sow panic on a global scale."[59] No longer sporting a gas mask or suicide-bomber vest, he now wears a burlap mask with a jack-o-lantern grin and rags covered in crow feathers, often considered a sign of furtiveness, misfortune, or death. The anarchist characterization amid historically low confidence in the government is made more significant by the fact that the Scarecrow in *Injustice 2* is not merely a character in the game's story, as he had been in earlier video games but is actually a playable character that gamers can choose to "be" or control, allowing the audience to take on the guise and goals of an anarchist (Figs. 11.1 and 11.2).

In the aftermath of terrorism and war, America became more attuned to post-traumatic stress disorder. Correspondingly, childhood trauma began to take on a more prominent place in the characterization of the Scarecrow. In the 2005 "Year One" story, Crane was abandoned by his father, rejected by his grandmother, and abused by his great-grandmother.[60] In the 2013 *Detective Comics* #23.3 issue, it is revealed that he was abused by his father.[61] In two episodes during the 2015 season of the television

Fig. 11.1 Scarecrow in the *Arkham Knight* videogame wears a gas mask and suicide-bomber vest reminiscent of terrorist imagery. (Screen shot from video game trailer)

Fig. 11.2 Scarecrow is an anarchist in the *Injustice 2* videogame; his crow-feathered costume suggests misfortune and death. (Screen shot from video game trailer)

drama *Gotham*, Crane endured the death of his mother to a house fire and the subsequent madness of his father.[62] Emphasizing the role of the super-villain as the antithesis to the superhero, comparisons were made between Batman who, because of childhood trauma, used fear to fight crime, and Scarecrow who, because of childhood trauma, used fear to commit crime. Even Batman noted, "The irony is not lost on me."[63]

In the midst of all this horror, Scarecrow became immune to fear. Overexposed to his fear toxins, nothing frightened him anymore. Desensitization to violence was, similarly, a real fear surrounding the fictional and nonfictional narratives of espionage, mass destruction, and tortured bodies in post-9/11 media.[64] Scarecrow's inability to feel fear is a key part of his characterization in the 2008–2009 *Blackest Night* event, in which the dead rise and are challenged by the Green Lantern Corps in cooperation with the other Lantern Corps. When Scarecrow was deputized by the Sinestro Corps, the Yellow Lanterns who wield fear as their power, he again felt afraid. It was this fear which he noted in earlier stories is what "reminds us we're alive" and "provides our every motive and governs our every response"—that prompted him to fight with the others to save Earth.[65] It was fear that motivated his civic response.

The Product of Our Fears

Politics of fear, or phobic discourses, often seek to identify and demonize an "other" to advance a political goal or achieve economic or social gain. The 1941 debut of the Scarecrow illuminates this process, and its consequences. Jonathan Crane is stigmatized by his peers because of his impoverished appearance. Shantz and Ramadan write, "phobic discourses portray the poor as a social contagion, an infection of the social body, with *visible poverty* being infectious" [emphasis added].[66] Crane is, therefore, cast out from the social body of the university. His response is to retaliate. In so doing, he embodies the very social phobia to which he fell victim—anxieties of the poor as a scourge on society. He sees no choice but to turn to a life of crime. This is the first instance in Scarecrow's multi-mediated history which demonstrates that fear is antithetical to democracy. As Robin writes, "Philosophers and politicians, scholars and pundits [deem] fear the great evil of civilization, the most lethal impediment to freedom, to be fought at all costs."[67] For Crane, the phobic discourses of poverty restricted his access to, and possibilities in, the socio-economic system.

When he stops living within the confines of law and, significantly, ethics—when he becomes the Scarecrow—Crane positions himself to *direct* Gotham's phobic discourses. A caricature of the phobic entrepreneur, Scarecrow exposes the corruption and deception inherent in the politics of fear. His motives of revenge, his purpose of creating chaos, and his results in instigating violence hint at the tandem persuasive forces of fear and anger made apparent in post-2016 political discourse.[68] In "The 6 Days of Scarecrow," Crane uses a "fear-pheromone" to make Gotham afraid of Batman, turning even his closest allies against him.[69] In "Fear for Sale," Scarecrow plays on Batman and Robin's deepest anxieties, making them hostile toward one another.[70] Likewise, Corey Robin observes that the Trump regime's "resurrection" of political fear has resulted in Americans turning against one another. "Vulnerable populations, from the undocumented to the LGBT community, from Muslims to Mexicans, are facing intensified harassment on the street, and surveillance, scrutiny and worse from the state."[71] In such a climate, it is important to remember Batman's advice that, "*Knowledge* is [a] thing that helps us fight fear" [emphasis added].[72]

In the *Arkham Knight* video game, Scarecrow tells Batman and, by extension, the player controlling Batman, "You are the product of everything you fear. Violence. Darkness. Helplessness."[73] This was a recurring theme of Scarecrow's monologues. As he argues in *Batman Annual* #19, "The very act of living is nothing but a conditioned response to the fear of death!"[74] Scarecrow, in turn, is the embodied manifestation of our political fears. He represents our unresolved sociological problems, including, but likely not limited to, poverty, mental health, addiction, medical care, child abuse, bullying, religious intolerance, mass violence, and unequal opportunity. He also represents elite exploitation of those problems for economic and political gain. Just as his character highlights the darker aspects of Batman, fear and trauma, it also highlights the darker aspects of society, terror and rage. Batman is community-minded; he is the city. Scarecrow is selfish; he is the individual. Batman is hope and authority. The Scarecrow is horror and anarchy. More than this, though, Gotham City is the United States and Scarecrow is a phobia entrepreneur "who work[s] to fix meanings in ways that resonate economically or politically with [his] own concerns."[75] Through his machinations to achieve financial gain, personal satisfaction, social standing, or political ends, he identifies and amplifies people's fears in order to master them; a frightened citizen is one who will more easily submit to authority. When the Scarecrow asks, "What has my delicious fear gas shown you?"[76] we might answer, "ourselves."

Notes

1. For example: Jason Dittmer, *Captain America and the Nationalist Superhero* (Philadelphia: Temple University Press, 2013).
2. Chris Deis, "The Subjective Politics of the Supervillain," in *What is a Superhero?*, ed. Robin S. Rosenberg and Peter Coogan (New York, NY: Oxford University Press, 2013), Kindle edition, loc. 1934–2034; Stanford W. Carpenter, "Superheroes Need Superior Villains," in *What is a Superhero?*, ed. Robin S. Rosenberg and Peter Coogan (New York, NY: Oxford University Press, 2013), Kindle edition, loc. 1812–1933.
3. Alan Grant, Eduardo Barreto, and Matt Hollingsworth, *Batman/ Daredevil: King of New York* (New York, NY: DC Comics, 2000), 37.
4. David V. Reed and Sal Amendola, "The Sinister Straws of the Scarecrow," *Batman Arkham Scarecrow* (Burbank, CA: DC Comics, 2016), 89, 76, 79. (Originally published in *Batman* #296 1978).
5. Corey Robin, *Fear: The History of a Political Idea* (New York, NY: Oxford University Press, 2004).
6. David L. Altheide, *Terrorism and the Politics of Fear*, 2nd edition (Lanham, MD: Rowman & Littlefield, 2017), Kindle edition, loc. 43; Barry Glassner,

The Culture of Fear: Why Americans are Afraid of the Wrong Things, Tenth Anniversary Edition (New York: Basic Books, 2009); Hisham Ramadan and Jeff Shantz, "Phobic Constructions: An Introduction," in *Manufacturing Phobias: The Political Production of Fear in Theory and Practice*, ed. Hisham Ramadan and Jeff Shantz (Toronto: University of Toronto Press, 2016), 3–14.

7. Jeff Shantz and Hisham Ramadan, "Phobic Constructions: Psychological, Sociological, Criminological Articulations," In *Manufacturing Phobias: The Political Production of Fear in Theory and Practice*, ed. Hisham Ramadan and Jeff Shantz (Toronto: University of Toronto Press, 2016), 51–68.
8. Robin, *Fear*.
9. Jeff Parker and Lukas Ketner, *Batman '66* #28 (Burbank, CA: DC Comics, December 2015).
10. Robert S. McElvaine, *The Great Depression: America, 1929–1941* (New York, NY: Three Rivers Press, 2009), Kindle edition.
11. Franklin D. Roosevelt, "Inaugural Address," March 4, 1933, in *The American Presidency Project*, edited by Gerhard Peters and John T. Woolley, accessed January 6, 2017, http://www.presidency.ucsb.edu/ws/?pid=14473
12. Don Cameron, Bob Kane, and Jerry Robinson, "The Return of the Scarecrow," *Batman Arkham Scarecrow* (Burbank, CA: DC Comics, 2016), 24. (Originally published in *Detective Comics* #73 1943).
13. Bill Finger, Bob Kane, Jerry Robinson, and Roussos, "Riddle of the Human Scarecrow," in *Batman Scarecrow Tales* (New York, NY: DC Comics, 2005), 7. (Originally published in *World's Finest Comics* #3 Fall 1941).
14. John Rozum and Tom Mandrake, *Detective Comics* #835 (New York: DC Comics, October 2007), np.
15. Doug Moench, Paul Gulacy, and Jimmy Palmiotti, *Batman: Terror* (New York, NY: DC Comics, 2003), 85. (Originally published in *Batman: Legends of the Dark Knight* #137–141 2001).
16. Gardner Fox, Bob Kane, and Joe Giella, "Fright of the Scarecrow," *Batman Scarecrow Tales* (New York, NY: DC Comics, 2005), 27. (Originally published in *Batman* #189 February 1967).
17. Arthur H. Westing, "Herbicides in War: Current Status and Future Doubt," *Biological Conservation* 4, no. 5 (1972): 322–327.
18. J.A. Inciardi and J.L. Goode, "Oxycontin and Prescription Drug Use," *Consumers Research* 86, no. 7 (2003): 17–21; J. Jonnes, *Hep-Cats, Narcs, and Pipe Dreams* (New York, NY: Simon and Schuster, 1996).
19. Erik van Ree, "Fear of Drugs," *International Journal of Drug Policy* 8 (1997): 93–100.
20. Reed and Amendola, "The Sinister Straws of the Scarecrow," 75.

21. Jean-Bruno Renard, "LSD Tattoo Transfers: Rumor from North America to France," *Folklore Forum* 24, no. 2 (1991): 3–26.
22. Gerry Conway, Don Newton, Dan Adkins, and Ben Oda, "The 6 Days of Scarecrow," *Batman Scarecrow Tales* (New York, NY: DC Comics, 2005), 78–102. (Originally published in *Detective Comics* #503 June 1981).
23. Rick Nauert, "Diagnostic Trends in Mental Health," *Psych Central*, March 29, 2010, accessed January 1, 2017, http://psychcentral.com/news/2010/03/29/diagnostic-trends-in-mental-health/12411.html; Adrian Furnham, "The Anti-Psychiatry Movement," *Psychology Today*, May 7, 2015, accessed January 10, 2017, https://www.psychologytoday.com/blog/sideways-view/201505/the-anti-psychiatry-movement
24. Fox, Kane, and Giella, "Fright of the Scarecrow," 31.
25. Denny O'Neil, Ernia Chua, and Dick Giordno, "The Scarecrow's Trail of Fear," *Batman Scarecrow Tales* (New York, NY: DC Comics, 2005), 48. (Originally published in *The Joker* #8 July–August 1976).
26. Jerry Emanuelson, *The Needle Phobia Page*, 1997–2016, accessed April 21, 2018, http://www.needlephobia.com/
27. Ramadan and Shantz, "Phobic Constructions," 11.
28. The College of Physicians of Philadelphia, "History of Anti-vaccination Movements," *The History of Vaccines*, January 10, 2018, accessed April 21, 2018, https://www.historyofvaccines.org/content/articles/history-anti-vaccination-movements
29. "Nothing to Fear," directed by Boyd Kirkland, *Batman: The Animated Series* (September 15, 1992; Burbank, CA: Warner Home Video, 2008), Kindle Fire.
30. Doug Moench, Bret Blevins, and Mike Manley, "Year One: Scarecrow Masters of Fear," *Batman Arkham Scarecrow* (Burbank, CA: DC Comics, 2016), 141–186. (Originally published in *Batman Annual* #19 1995).
31. Mark Ames, *Going Postal: Rage, Murder and Rebellion from Reagan's Workplace to Clinton's Columbine and Beyond* (Brooklyn, NY: Soft Skull Press, 2005).
32. Mark R. Leary, Robin M. Kowalski, Laura Smith, and Stephen Phillips, "Teasing, Rejection, and Violence: Case Studies of the School Shootings," *Aggressive Behavior* 29 (2003): 202–214.
33. Introduced in "Never Fear," directed by Kenji Hachizaki, *The New Batman Adventures* (November 1, 1997; Warner Home Video, 2008), Kindle Fire.
34. Mike W. Barr, Alan Davis, and Paul Neary, "Fear for Sale," *Batman Scarecrow Tales* (New York, NY: DC Comics, 2005), 111. (Originally published in *Detective Comics* #571 February 1987).
35. Doug Moench, Kelley Jones, and John Beatty, "Scarecrow Part Two: Haunted House of the Head," *Batman Arkham Scarecrow* (Burbank, CA: DC Comics, 2016), 226. (Originally published in *Batman* #524 1995).

36. Moench, Gulacy, and Palmiotti, *Terror*, 106.
37. Peter Milligan, Duncan Fegredo, and Bjarne Hansen, "Mistress of Fear," *Batman Scarecrow Tales* (New York, NY: DC Comics, 2005), 127–148. (Originally published in *Scarecrow (Villains)* #1 February 1998).
38. Lydia Saad, "Confidence in Religion at New Low, but Not Among Catholics," *Gallup*, June 17, 2015, accessed January 9, 2017, http://www.gallup.com/poll/183674/confidence-religion-new-low-not-among-catholics.aspx
39. Alan Grant, Bret Blevins, and Adrienne Roy, *Shadow of the Bat* #17 (New York: DC Comics, late September 1993), 6.
40. Darcey Steinke, "God Rocks: SPIN's 1993 Feature on the Siege in Waco, Texas," *SPIN*, November 6, 2015, accessed January 9, 2017, http://www.spin.com/featured/david-koresh-waco-texas-1993-siege-feature/
41. J.F. Moore, C. Critchlow, and S. Buscema, *Batman/Scarecrow 3-D* #1 (New York: DC Comics, December 1998).
42. Devin Grayson, Dale Eaglesham, Aaron Sowd, and Matt Banning, *Legends of the Dark Knight* #116 (New York: DC Comics, April 1999).
43. Saad, "Confidence in Religion."
44. Bruce Jones, Sean Murphy, and Lee Loughridge, "Year One: Batman Scarecrow" *Batman: Two-Face and Scarecrow Year One* (New York: DC Comics, 2009), 19. (Originally published in *Year One: Batman Scarecrow* #1–2 2005).
45. BAS 20.
46. Martin Staples Shockley, "The Teacher in American Literature," *The South Central Bulletin* 31, no. 4 (1971): 218.
47. Moench, Blevins, and Manley, "Year One," 167.
48. "Nothing to Fear."
49. Daniel W. Drezner, "Everyone Thinks the Current State of Higher Education is Awful. Who is to Blame?" *Washington Post*, August 14, 2015, accessed April 21, 2018, https://www.washingtonpost.com/posteverything/wp/2015/08/14/everyone-thinks-the-current-state-of-higher-education-is-awful-who-is-to-blame/?noredirect=on&utm_term=.45601756c96c
50. F.H. Buckley, "How Trump Can End Brainwashing on College Campuses," *New York Post*, January 9, 2017, accessed April 21, 2018, https://nypost.com/2017/01/09/how-trump-can-end-brainwashing-on-us-campuses/; Molly Ball, "Donald Trump and the Politics of Fear," *The Atlantic*, September 2, 2016, accessed January 20, 2018, https://www.theatlantic.com/politics/archive/2016/09/donald-trump-and-the-politics-of-fear/498116/. Also: Corey Robin, "How Political Fear Works," *The New Republic*, February 6, 2017, accessed April 21, 2018, https://newrepublic.com/article/140431/political-fear-works

51. Moore, Critchlow, and Buscema, *Batman/Scarecrow 3-D*, 33.
52. *Necessary Evil: Super-Villains of DC Comics*, directed by JM Kenny and Scott Devine (Burbank, CA: DC Comics, 2013), DVD.
53. Tom Pollard, *Hollywood 9/11: Superheroes, Supervillains, and Super Disasters* (New York, NY: Routledge, 2016), Kindle edition.
54. *Necessary Evil.*
55. *Batman Begins*, directed by Christopher Nolan (2005; Burbank, CA: Warner Home Video, 2005), DVD.
56. Michael Reaves and Steven-Elliot Altman, *Batman: Fear Itself* (New York, NY: Ballantine Books, 2007); Matthew K. Manning, Erik Doescher, Mike DeCarlo, and Lee Loughridge, *Batman: Scarecrow, Doctor of Fear* (North Mankato, MN: Stone Arch Books, 2013).
57. Rocksteady Studios, *Batman: Arkham Knight* (London: Eidos Interactive, 2015), Microsoft Windows.
58. Pew Research Center, "Public Trust in Government: 1958–2017," *Pew Research Center: U.S. Politics & Policy*, May 3, 2017, accessed April 21, 2018, http://www.people-press.org/2017/05/03/public-trust-in-government-1958-2017/
59. "Scarecrow," *Injustice 2*, 2017, accessed February 14, 2018, https://www.injustice.com/characters/scarecrow
60. Jones, Murphy, and Loughridge, "Year One: Batman Scarecrow."
61. Peter J. Tomasi and Szymon Kudranski, "Double Jeopardy," *Batman Arkham Scarecrow* (Burbank, CA: DC Comics, 2016), 257–276. (Originally published in *Detective Comics* #23.3 2013).
62. "The Fearsome Dr. Crane," directed by John Behring, *Gotham* (February 2, 2015; Warner Home Entertainment, 2015), Blu-ray; "The Scarecrow," directed by Nick Copus, *Gotham* (February 9, 2015; Warner Home Entertainment, 2015), Blu-ray.
63. Jeph Loeb and Tim Sale, *Batman: Haunted Knight* (New York, NY: DC Comics, 1996), 11.
64. Juliette H. Walma van der Molen, "Violence and Suffering in Television News: Toward a Broader Conception of Harmful Content for Children," *Pediatrics* 113, no. 6 (2004): 1774–1775.
65. Moore, Critchlow, and Buscema, *Batman/Scarecrow 3-D*, 17; Moench, Blevins, and Manley, "Year One," 170.
66. Shantz and Ramadan, "Phobic Constructions," 51.
67. Robin, *Fear*, 3.
68. Ball, "Donald Trump."
69. Conway, Newton, Adkins, and Oda, "The 6 Days of Scarecrow."
70. Barr, Davis, and Neary, "Fear for Sale."

71. Robin, "How Political Fear Works," para. 2.
72. Fox, Kane, and Giella, "Fright of the Scarecrow," 35.
73. Rocksteady Studios, *Batman: Arkham Knight.*
74. Moench, Blevins, and Manley, "Year One," 170.
75. Ramadan and Shantz, "Phobic Constructions," 3.
76. Johns, Reis, Albert, and Prado, *Blackest Night* #6, n.p.

CHAPTER 12

#FAKENEWS in Gotham City

Salvatore James Russo

"This house," a stoned Mad Hatter leers at Batman in the graphic novel *Arkham Asylum: A Serious House on Serious Earth*, "It…does things to the mind."[1] While there is little doubt that the cursed walls of Arkham must wreck havoc on the minds of the poor souls confined therein, what about those residents of Gotham City who are not so confined? How do Gotham's citizens form opinions about their city—and Batman's place therein—and what forces work to shape and refine these opinions? This chapter explores these questions, and then asks why it is that Gotham City's citizens continue to place so much trust in the news media, while, in reality, Americans' trust in the media only decreases.

Looking at the cinematic Batman universe, as well as the Batman universe as represented in comic books and graphic novels, it seems as though traditional mass media has a great deal of influence in shaping the beliefs and behavior of Gotham's citizens. Crucially, not only does the mass media have the ability to shape Gothamites' views on their world, generally, it also has the ability to influence their views on Batman. Other forces that social scientists have traditionally recognized as having influence over mass publics, such as "political parties, churches, unions, and service organizations," have comparatively little sway over Gotham's citizens.[2]

S. J. Russo (✉)
California State University-Dominguez Hills, Carson, CA, USA
e-mail: srusso@csudh.edu

D. K. Picariello (ed.), *Politics in Gotham*,
https://doi.org/10.1007/978-3-030-05776-3_12

This relationship is most striking today, as Americans' trust in news media has been plummeting for decades, with little sign of abatement. Is the trust that people in Gotham have in the media simply a convenient plot device? Or, does it speak to something integral to the Batman mythos?

This chapter explores these questions in three parts. Part one looks at the media as Batman and his friends and foes use it to communicate with each other, and with the citizens of Gotham City. In other words, in part one, we look at the media as being a passive receptacle, where messages are dropped off by one party, and then are picked up by others. Part two addresses how the mass media in Gotham City can shape the citizenry's views specifically on Batman, for good or for ill. Thus, in part two, the media is seen as an active player, showing agency and assigning benevolent or malevolent motives to Batman. In part three, the final part, the question is "why?" Why does mass media play such an outsized role in the lives of Gothamites?

Media as Megaphone: How Heroes and Villains Use Mass Media to Communicate with One Another—And the Masses—In Gotham City

In Tim Burton's film, *Batman* (1989), we see the mass media being the primary means of communication between relevant actors—meaning Batman and the Joker—both in terms of their communicating with each other and in terms of their communicating with the masses.[3] The Joker is shown to be an avid consumer of mass media messages about Batman. Early in the film, the Joker wipes the blood of a fresh victim off a copy of *The Gotham Globe* to reveal the headline, "WINGED FREAK TERRORIZES GOTHAM'S GANGLAND." The Joker reads the headline and murmurs, "Winged freak…terrorizes…?" before delivering the memorable line, "Wait 'til they get a load of me." In the context of the scene, it seems as though the "they" to which the Joker is referring is not to "Gotham's Gangland" but rather the Gotham City mass media. Further demonstrating the Joker's desire for media coverage, later in the film, the Joker destroys a television set after watching a news report about Batman, angry that Batman is "getting all of (his) press!" The viewer is left wondering if the Joker engages in some of his malevolent activities just so he can revel in the attention the media pays him. When considering the Joker's relationship with the mass media, it is hard not to recall real world debates over whether the names and manifestos of serial killers and school shooters should not be given media coverage, a topic inelegantly detailed in Oliver Stone's *Natural Born Killers* (1994). Finally, the viewer is also presented with the battle between Batman and the Joker for Vicki Vale, a reporter for whom both men have fallen. This battle is highly symbolic of the struggle between Batman and the Joker over the attention—and affection—of the mass media. Rather than just idly flirting, or being captivated with Miss Vale's appearance, both Bruce Wayne and the Joker demonstrate themselves to be sophisticated consumers of media messages, and express to Miss Vale a knowledge of, and appreciation for, her work as an investigative journalist.

While the above examples demonstrate the Joker as a more reactive consumer of mass media, almost incidentally communicating with Batman through his exploits as covered by the local media, at other times, Batman and the Joker actively manipulate the media. At one point in the film, in a sequence that recalls Mario Bava's *Danger: Diabolik!* (1968), the Joker uses his knowledge of chemistry to create a deadly compound called "Smylex." The Joker then laces batches of toiletry and cosmetic products with elements of Smylex. When an unknowing victim then wears a combination of cosmetic products that have been tainted with Smylex agents, a lethal chemical reaction occurs—the victims laugh hysterically before quickly dying, their faces frozen in a hideous grin. A true sadist, the Joker wants to spread fear, as well as inflict mass casualties, so he informs the people of Gotham of his actions. How? By waiting for a news anchor to succumb to Smylex on live television, and then interrupting the broadcast with a faux-advertisement for "Smylex." The Joker's commercial is complete with spokes-corpses, and concludes with a macabre warning to Gotham City, "I know what you're saying! 'Where can I get these fine new items?' Well, that's the gag: chances are, you bought them already!"

It stands to reason that the Joker had to engage in this transmission jamming and fear-mongering during a live broadcast; for maximum terroristic impact, he needed the first Smylex victim to die live and on-air before pirating the television signal. It is noteworthy, however, that the Joker did not interrupt a sporting event, or a live comedy program, or any other form of live television. In the Batman universe, Gotham citizens are gathered around their television sets for nightly news, not live professional wrestling, a concert, or college basketball. This stands in contrast to present-day America, where the most popular network nightly news broadcasts, which are generally watched by about seven million Americans each night, draw far fewer viewers than scripted sitcoms or live sporting events.[4] Cable news shows, as much as scholars and media critics, seem to pay attention to them and discuss them, are less watched than network news programs. Fox News, currently the most watched cable news channel, averages about 2.4 million viewers during prime time, and, as with CNN and MSNBC, these viewers are overwhelmingly over 50 years old.[5] Thus, Burton's *Batman* recalls an era where citizens had a common communications culture, one where watching a nightly news broadcast was a ritual shared by neighbors and fellow Americans throughout the nation alike rather than the fractious media landscape we now inhabit.

Batman and his foes' interest in news media is not restricted to their adventures on the silver screen. A notable example of the degree to which Batman and his rivals are fixated on the news is in *Batman* #66's "The Joker's Comedy of Errors" (1951).[6] In this story, the Joker's robbery of the Gotham Electric Company is foiled when, as when he cut all the power in the building in order to affect the robbery, he forgot that this would also lead to the elevators in the building not functioning. Though he is able to get away from Batman and Robin, the Joker is taunted in the *Gotham Bulletin* and *Gotham Gazette* for his mistake, or "boner," that cost him "the perfect crime."

The Joker's response to this public mocking is to make Gotham's law enforcement officials—and Batman and Robin—look bad by engaging in a series of "boner"-themed crimes, played out in the newspapers and over the radio airwaves. This culminates in Batman seemingly committing a major, boneheaded error of his own—and thus being taunted in *The Daily Blade*, *Gotham Gazette*, and the curiously named *News Globe*—much to the Joker's delight. However, Batman is able to use the Joker's own fixation on embarrassing him and Robin in the press to eventually find the Joker's hideout and bring him to justice. The Joker was so disturbed by his being mocked in mass media, that he was willing to risk capture in order to make sure that the mass media also had a go at Batman. Batman knew that the Joker would be so obsessed with how the media portrayed Batman's actions that he could use this to eventually capture the Joker.

The mass media also plays a central role in Frank Miller's sprawling, multipart series *The Dark Knight Returns*. Miller uses television news broadcasts in the series for purposes of exposition and advancing the story line, as well as to provide a satirical, running commentary on the political landscape and urban life in the late twentieth century. We also see the characters themselves using mass media to reach out to one another, and to the general public. In the first book of the series, Harvey Dent—better known as Two-Face—jams a television transmission to announce that he will blow up "Gotham's beautiful twin towers" if he is not paid USD five million.[7] Like the Joker's terroristic threats in Tim Burton's film, Two-Face is not necessarily intending to communicate with Batman, but he does know that jamming a live television broadcast will guarantee maximum effect. Like the Joker in Burton's film, too, Two-Face jams a news broadcast, in this case, one ironically discussing Batman, "Crusader or Menace?" This further demonstrates the importance of mass media to the people of Gotham City. Once again, Two-Face's choice of television program to jam is telling. Two-Face knows that to spread the most fear, he should jam the most widely watched live broadcast, and in Gotham City, that is a live news broadcast.

In book two of the series, the threat facing Gotham is The Mutant Gang, an anarchistic street gang led by a psychotic mutant with superhuman strength.[8] The gang members, and their leader, are frequently given airtime on the news. They use this time to call out Commissioner Gordon,[9] and Batman himself.[10] After Batman cripples the Mutant Leader in their second battle, the former members of the Mutant Gang now pledge themselves as devotees of Batman and use the airwaves to threaten criminals. Sometimes, Batman's foes do not need to hijack the airwaves to get the attention of the mass media. The limited series *Batman: White Knight* features the Joker playing the role of a politician, running a sophisticated media campaign to turn the citizens of Gotham City against Batman.[11]

Neither Batman nor Gotham's Rogues' Gallery needs to be so overt in using the media to communicate to an intended target. Sometimes, simply by behaving in a certain manner, it can be assured that the media will report on their behavior, and, in a kind of implied bargaining, they can be confident that their action will produce a certain reaction.

Media as Manipulator: How Mass Media in Gotham Influences Citizen Perceptions of Batman

In addition to serving as both a tool and a means of communication for Gotham's heroes and villains, mass media in Gotham also shapes the opinions of Gothamites about the Caped Crusader. Social science research on the media as a factor in shaping opinions has reached mixed conclusions. Philip Converse, in a highly influential article from over 50 years ago, stated that Americans have "belief systems," or configurations of ideas and attitudes that are somehow linked together, in varying degrees of coherence.[12] Converse asserted that the more informed Americans do *not* then provide cues or knowledge to their less informed fellow citizens. While Converse's work remains highly influential, his conclusion as to the irrelevance of elites has been challenged, often convincingly. A large body of literature suggests that elite discourse within and outside of mass media *can* and *does* influence the behavior of mass publics. Robert Huckfeldt found that citizens are capable of recognizing expertise—in his article, knowledge about politics—in other citizens, and will seek those people out in order to learn more about politics from those experts.[13] Empirical works in the social sciences have also suggested a "filter hypothesis," or the idea that the influence of mass media messages can be highlighted, mitigated, or obviated depending on the discussant network of the media consumer.[14] John Zaller has also argued that media effects on a viewer will be mitigated depending on, among other factors, viewers' preexisting beliefs and the interpersonal networks to which that viewer belongs.[15] In short, empirical work in the social sciences suggests that media effects can be mitigated or filtered, and that the media is but one of many other sources of potential influence upon an actor's behavior.

This elite-driven influence seems lacking in Gotham. Gotham citizens seem to rarely ask witnesses to Batman's exploits whether Batman was behaving heroically or malevolently in a given situation. Instead, they trust the mass media to tell them how to react. Those in more official elite roles in society play little role in the lives of Gothamites, either. For example, we rarely see local elected leaders able to influence the decision-making processes of the citizens of Gotham in any meaningful way. If anything, elected officials matter little to the story arcs in the Batman universe, and figure even less into the lives of the average Gotham City resident. While Commissioner James Gordon has remained a consistent—and heroic—figure in the Batman universe, the Mayor of Gotham City tends to be an afterthought. On the 1960s television series *Batman*, 11 out of 120 episodes featured the mayor, once simply as "The Mayor," played by Al McGranary, and then 10 episodes featured "Mayor Linseed," played by Byron Keith.[16] In the initial revival, pre-Christopher Nolan Batman films (from 1989 to 2008), each film introduced a new Mayor of Gotham City. Only starting with Mayor Anthony Garcia, who survived Nolan's *The Dark Knight* (2008), but was killed in *The Dark Knight Rises* (2012), has a Mayor of Gotham City been brought back for an encore performance.

Most of Gotham's cinematic executive officers are not even afforded the honor of a dramatic death; some are unnamed—as in Joel Schumacher's *Batman Forever* (1995)—and even Mayor William Borg from Tim Burton's film that brought Batman back to the silver screen in 1989 was ignominiously replaced by an unnamed successor for 1992's *Batman Returns*. Neither in 1997's *Batman & Robin* nor in 2005's *Batman Begins* do we see the Mayor of Gotham City at all.

The Mayor of Gotham City is afforded little more respect in print than he does on the silver screen. In the Batman comic books,[17] Gotham has seen a rotating cast of mayors, from corrupt pawns of mob bosses,[18] to plot devices existing only to be assassinated or otherwise meet gruesome ends,[19] to vaguely anonymous figures behind desks who might have a line of dialogue, and, if they're lucky, a last name assigned to them for an issue or two.[20] In Frank Miller's *The Dark Knight Returns*, there are two, seemingly interchangeable, incompetent mayors. The first unnamed mayor's most defining characteristic is his refusal to make a decision.[21] Deputy Mayor Stevenson succeeds the first unnamed mayor after the first mayor has his throat ripped out by the leader of the Mutant Gang during a negotiation session, and promptly announces that the city is still open to negotiating with The Mutants.

The Mayor of Gotham City is not the only executive official finding himself all but forgotten by the citizens of Gotham City and the writers of Batman adventures alike. Gotham City's religious leaders, too, seem to lack any influence over the citizenry. Gotham Cathedral has been an imposing backdrop for many a Batman film or comic book. Even with this massive edifice serving as a constant reminder of the faith in Gotham City, church attendance seems an afterthought for the average Gothamite; the cathedral is most famously portrayed as deserted and abandoned, and despite the stress and terror that seem to come with living in Gotham City, we rarely see Gothamites—including heroes like Batman or Commissioner Gordon—turn to religion for solace. As Gotham City hosts a cathedral—and as there have been, as we're about to see, a handful of Cardinals and one Archbishop of Gotham City seen in Batman comics and television programs—it can be concluded that Gotham City is an Archdiocese of the Catholic Church, and the center of an Ecclesiastical Province in the United States. Despite the prominent role Gotham City would thus play in the Catholic Church, organized religion does not seem to play a strong role in the lives of Gotham's citizens. In Tim Burton's *Batman*, the cathedral is abandoned, and left to serve as atmospheric ruin porn. Filled with cobwebs and crumbling statues, the deserted church serves as the location for the Joker and Batman's final (for the time!) battle. More recent incarnations of Gotham Cathedral have seen it in no better condition. In fact, in the video game versions of the Batman universe, Gotham Cathedral is not only abandoned but is used by villains for creating and storing weapons.

Quantitative research in the social sciences has demonstrated that religious elite cues can shape adherent beliefs. Paul Djupe and Brian Calfano demonstrate in their book *God Talk: Experimenting with the Religious Causes of Public Opinion* that exposure to the decision-making process from religious elites impacts public opinion on political issues.[22] However, religious leaders in Gotham City seem to hold little sway over the public.[23] Despite the parallels often made between the fictitious Gotham City and the real world New York City, Gotham City never has politically powerful clergymen in the mold of New York Cardinals Hayes, Spellman, O'Connor, or Dolan.[24] Much like Gotham's mayors, the very few times Gotham City's religious leaders appear, they tend to only be in the background, and are usually killed off as quickly as they appear. The television series *Gotham* briefly introduced an Archbishop of Gotham City, only to have him killed off shortly thereafter. The same series also featured a news report that introduced Cardinal Quinn, a priest facing charges of child molestation, who was in the process of being killed by the vigilante Balloonman. The animated anthology film *Batman: Gotham Knight* introduced the heroic Cardinal O'Fallon in a vignette, and while he proved more durable than his brothers in the cloth from the live action television series *Gotham*, he has not been seen again.

Members of the academy, too, wield little influence over the citizenry.[25] Gotham University[26] first appeared in print in 1941, and while it has produced the delightfully deranged Harley Quinn, and the less-delightful Scarecrow, it seemingly otherwise has done little in terms of producing elite cues for citizens to follow.[27] We rarely see academics performing cue-giving functions in Gotham City. Even fraternal and sport clubs, perhaps paralleling Robert Putnam's findings in *Bowling Alone*, seem to lack membership and do little to build social capital or aid in citizen decision-making in Gotham. One can assume that Gothamites join labor unions, the Freemasons, or rugby teams, but there is little to suggest that these labor unions, Fraternal orders, or amateur sport clubs are building social cohesion or aiding Gothamites in making decisions. When the mass media tells the people of Gotham City to turn against Batman in Christopher Nolan's *The Dark Knight* (2008), the citizenry essentially just turns against

Batman. We do not see citizens asking their confessors, professors, lodge Masters, team captains, or shop stewards about what to do. They've received information from their information source, and they are going to use solely that source, the mass media, to make a decision.

Being that the institutions we might expect to shape the views of Gothamites (political leaders, religious institutions, higher education) seem ineffectual, how do Gotham's citizens form opinions about their city and the Batman's place therein, and what forces work to shape and refine these opinions? The one institution that is able, repeatedly, across time and space, to influence Gothamites is that of mass media. While media effects scholars have convincingly argued that print and television media has a significant impact on those receiving mass messages, none have argued that print and television media has a monopoly on opinion-shaping and shaping social discourse.[28] However, this seems to be exactly the case in Gotham City.

Batman is not unique in the comic book landscape in assigning to mass media great power to influence the populace. Nor is Gotham the only city where the media can be fickle—if not hostile—toward costumed superheroes. Superman, in his alter ego as Clark Kent, a mild-mannered reporter for a major metropolitan newspaper, can control his own press at Metropolis' *Daily Planet*. Spider-Man, on the other hand, even as photographer Peter Parker, is unable to stop publisher J. Jonah Jameson from maligning Spider-Man at every opportunity, seemingly for no real reason other than out of sheer perverse pleasure.[29] Batman, however, has no "pull" with the mass media in the role of a sympathetic friend working for the press, much less full-time employment at a media outlet. Instead, when Batman wishes to get better coverage, he generally must get a little more hands on.

This chapter would be incomplete if it did not describe the entry into the Batman universe wherein the mass media's ability to manipulate Gothamites is embodied in one, villainous form. Pepe Moreno's *Batman: Digital Justice* (1990) is an entirely digitally rendered graphic novel that takes place in "Gotham Megatropolis. Sometime into the next century." The dystopian future is one wherein Gotham, while nominally led by a mayor called Madam X, is actually ruled by a secret cabal called The Interfaces "who supply the drugs, entertainment, muscle—and information—that keep the megatropolis as it is."[30] While two of the Interfaces ("MobLord" and "LawMan") show the traditional balance of "crooked cops" and "ascendant thugs" that are often running Gotham, it is the third Interface that draws our attention in this chapter. The third Interface is named "MediaMan," and he controls the news media in Gotham Megatropolis. MediaMan is able to digitally alter news reports in order to keep the population of Gotham docile and trusting in the technology that runs their lives.[31] We can view Gotham Megatropolis, at least, in terms of what factors influence its citizens, as not being very different from contemporary Gotham City. What matters to the lives of Gotham's citizens? As always, what matters are the criminals, those who fight the criminals (or, are at least supposed to fight them), and the mass media. There is no Interface in charge of overseeing schools, no Interface given jurisdiction over organized religion. The mass media is again seen as having no competition in its influence over Gotham's citizens.

When Sergeant James Gordon—grandson of Commissioner Gordon—assumes the Batman identity in order to solve a string of murders, Madam X and the Interfaces grow fearful that the resurrection of the Batman mythos may inspire Gotham's citizens, and consequently loosen their own grip on the city. MediaMan begins to digitally alter footage to make it appear as though Batman's "vigilante activities" resulted in the death of two senior citizens. MediaMan's actions—coupled with a Madonna/Lady Gaga-like entertainer, "Gata," taking on the role of Cat Woman—cause the citizens of Gotham to turn against Batman as quickly as they championed him and anointed him a hero earlier in the graphic novel.[32] This is not the only time in the Batman universe that we see Gotham City's citizens turning on Batman because media messages tell them to do so. In Nolan's *The Dark Knight*, for example, the media turns against Batman after the Joker threatens to continue his killing spree unless Batman reveals his identity. In Miller's *The Dark Knight Returns*, shortly after Batman's final struggle with the Joker, the media labels Batman a "murderer" for the death of the Joker, and blames him for the police who were killed in the melee.

The outsized role that the news media plays in the lives of Gotham citizens—from the average denizen to the costumed heroes and villains who do battle in the streets—stands in marked contrast to how present-day Americans view the news media. Starting in 1972, Gallup has asked a random sample of Americans the following question:

> In general, how much trust and confidence do you have in the mass media—such as newspapers, T.V., and radio—when it comes to reporting the news fully, accurately, and fairly—a great deal, a fair amount, not very much, or none at all?[33]

This question was asked in 1972, 1974, and 1976, and then yearly starting in 1997. We see a decline in respondents saying they trust media "A great deal" or "A fair amount" decline from 72% in 1976 to 53% in 1997, a *nineteen-point drop.*

During the 1980s and early 1990s, while Gallup eschewed asking the above question, they did ask another series of questions that are still illustrative. In 1981, and nearly yearly since,[34] Gallup asked respondents:

> Now I am going to read you list of institutions in American society. Please tell me how much confidence you, yourself, have in each one—a great deal, quite a lot, some, or a little?[35]

"Newspapers" were one of those institutions in the abovementioned years, and starting in 1993, "Television news" was also asked about on a yearly basis. From just 1979 to 1981, we see respondents going from trusting newspapers either "A great deal" or "quite a lot" from 51% to 35%, and never again getting above 40%. Television news' highest watermark was 1993's 43%, as it then tumbled to 35% by 1994, and has never gotten above 36% in the ensuing decades. Gothamites, on the other hand, remain as susceptible to media messages as they ever have. Nobody in futuristic Gotham Megatropolis thinks it's odd that Batman has gone from saving the city to causing the death of senior citizens; the television said it's true, so it must be true. We do not see Gothamites in *The Dark Knight* stopping to wonder if Batman, who risks life and limb to fight organized crime kingpins and The League of Shadows for no pay, might have reasons for not revealing his identity. The media has turned against The Caped Crusader, so they must turn, too.

Media as Motor or Media as Mirror? Is the Mass Media in Gotham Simply a Useful Plot Device, or Does It Reflect the Values of the Batman Universe?

The earlier sections looking at how the mass media is portrayed in Gotham City bring up a valid question: why? Why does Gotham City continue to be portrayed in a universe where the news media has such a monopoly on the public's attention, even as here in reality, public trust in the media continues to plummet? There are two plausible explanations. One explanation is more practical, the other a bit more abstract. Let's begin with the practical explanation. News media remains a convenient means of exposition, or vehicle for moving the story forward, in dramatic writing. How did Batman find out about The Mad Hatter's latest act of villainy? He read it in the newspaper or saw it on television. How did The Penguin convey his demands to Gotham City? He had them announced over a news broadcast on the radio, conveniently overheard by Bruce Wayne. It is then easy to start moving the story along. Even in *Digital Justice*, Jim Gordon learns about the original Batman's actions by reading old copies of *The Gotham Times* that were packed with some of his grandfather's old belongings. Later, Jim Gordon is rescued by The Batcode, a computer code version of Batman, created by Bruce Wayne in the distant past. The Batcode then brings Jim Gordon to speed as to the threat that the Joker Virus poses. How does The Batcode do this? By showing Jim Gordon old news clips.[36] Of course, the writers of Batman are far from alone in using conveniently overheard news bulletins to move a story from Point A to Point B. Even the writers of *South Park* have used the trope of a news report as exposition, to the point where they have satirized their own usage.[37]

But, there is also a less cynical explanation for Gotham City's continued fixation on the news media. Even as the world of Batman has moved from Detective Comics to Alan Moore and Frank Miller's often-brutal graphic novels, to Tim Burton's gothic vision on the big screen to Christopher Nolan's unflinching films dealing with Gotham as a target of terrorism, there remains a fixed, almost old-fashioned, morality. Americans are losing their faith in the media, but the people of Gotham still gather around their television sets and daily newspapers to learn the latest; even the Joker starts his mornings off by reading the headlines. We, the consumers of Batman media, can trust that Batman will never decide to just hang up his cape and cowl and enjoy the idle pleasures of being Bruce Wayne, (at least, not without designating a successor, as seen in *The Dark Knight Rises*), that the stress of being Batman will never overcome Batman to the point where he intentionally kills a helpless Riddler. In fact, a crucial part of the morality of the Batman universe is the morality of Batman himself.

In *The Dark Knight Returns*, Batman has numerous chances to kill dangerous and deadly villains such as the head of The Mutant Gang, Two-Face, and the Joker. Each time Batman has one of these evil men at his mercy, Batman makes a point of not crossing that self-imposed line. The Joker revels in the knowledge that Batman blames himself for each one of the Joker's new victims, Batman knowing that each innocent victim would still be alive if only he had finally killed the Joker.[38] During their climactic showdown, Batman decides that the only way he can stay true to his code, but also ensure that Gotham City will really be safe from the Joker, is to paralyze the Joker. Batman breaks the Joker's neck, and the Joker taunts Batman for being unable to bring himself to killing. In a final "joke," the Joker twists his own neck and kills himself, making it appear as though Batman killed the Joker.

The highlighting of the internal conflict Batman feels about potentially having to take a life sharply contrasts with Miller's *Holy Terror*, a graphic novel about a vigilant superhero combating Al Qaeda, written in the aftermath of 9/11. Miller began *Holy Terror* as a Batman comic but decided to make it instead about a new masked superhero, "The Fixer," one that Miller said is "…much more well adjusted in committing terrible acts of violence on very evil people." The fact that *Holy Terror* began life as a Batman comic is evident from not just the title—a play on Robin's catchphrase on the 1960's *Batman* TV series: "Holy [pun], Batman!"[39] —but also from the characters themselves, including a Selena Kyle-like cat burglar love interest for The Fixer, Natalie Stack. Miller was not comfortable with either the idea of Batman fighting a real world threat (like Al Qaeda) or committing "terrible acts of violence"[40] upon them.

As realistic as newer, "darker" visions of Gotham City come into being, they can still only push the envelope so far. The world of Batman is, ultimately, not a transgressive world, but one of good and evil, of "white hats" and "black hats." Gothamites' trust in news media reflect this familiar, early twentieth century, "square" world; people in Gotham trust their news media because that's the way things are *supposed* to function. Even when the news being provided is "fake news," such as that dished out by MediaMan, Gothamites still go to MediaMan for their information, because you're supposed to be able to go to your media to get the news, rather than go to other, competing sources of information. Taking this a step further, there are not even competing *media* sources of information in Gotham City. In reality, we have numerous sources of mass media messages. We can even tailor our media consumption habits in accordance with which ideological filter we want used to spin the day's events, or which version of reality we want presented to us. In Gotham City, we do not see competing media messages; there is no underground newspaper in Gotham Megatropolis reporting the facts that MediaMan will not, or non-exploitative television news channel in *The Dark Knight Returns*, allowing for an intelligent presentation of information. Again, seemingly reflecting a mythologized postwar America, there is simply "the news" in Gotham City, and "the news" is sometimes fake news being used to manipulate the citizenry. Fortunately for the somewhat gormless Gothamites, they have Batman to (correctly!) decide for them what is and is not fake news, and then to stop the flow of fake news. In today's climate of mistrust of the mass media, perhaps it is this function of Batman we most desire in the real world?

Notes

1. Grant Morrison, *Arkham Asylum: A Serious House on Serious Earth*, (United States: DC Comics, 1989).
2. L.W. Bennett and Shanto Iyengar, "A New Era of Minimal Effects? The Changing Foundations of Political Communication," *Journal of Communication* 58, (2008).
3. *Batman*, directed by Tim Burton (1989; Westwood, CA: Warner Bros. Company), Film.
4. Lynette Rice, "The Top 50 Most-Watched Shows of the 2017–2018 Season," Entertainment Weekly, May 31, 2018, https://ew.com/tv/2018/05/31/top-50-most-watched-shows-2017-18-season/
5. A representative weekly example can be seen at: Mitch Metcalf, "Showbuzzdaily's Top 150 Tuesday Cable Originals & Network Finals: 8.7.2018," Showbuzzdaily, August 8, 2018, http://www.showbuzzdaily.com/articles/showbuzzdailys-top-150-tuesday-cable-originals-network-finals-8-7-2018.html
6. Bill Finger, "The Joker's Comedy of Errors!" *Batman #66*, (United States: DC Comics, 1951) *Dial B For Blog*, http://www.dialbforblog.com/archives/136/; *Blah Blah Blah* (Blog), February 14, 2009, https://cacb.wordpress.com/2009/02/14/the-jokers-comedy-of-errors/

   Very special thanks to the websites, "Dial B for Blog," and "Blah Blah Blah," for hosting images for this Golden Age comic book online.
7. Frank Miller, *Batman: The Dark Knight Returns*, (United States: DC Comics, 1986).
8. Frank Miller, *Batman: The Dark Knight Strikes Again*, (United States: DC Comics, 2001–2002).
9. Ibid. Page 44.

   "We will kill the old man Gordon. His women will weep for him. We will chop him. We will grind him. We will bathe in his blood."
10. Ibid. Page 85.

    "Batman is a coward. I broke his bones. I conquered the fool. I made him beg for mercy. Only by cheating did he escape alive."

11. Sean Murphy, *Batman: White Knight*, (United States: DC Comics, 2017).
12. Philip E. Converse, "The Nature of Belief Systems in Mass Publics," *Ideology and Its Discontents*, (1964).
13. Robert Huckfeldt, "The Social Communication of Political Expertise," *American Journal of Political Science* 45, no. 2 (2001).
14. Elihu Katz and Paul F. Lazarsfeld, *Personal Influence: The Part Played by People in the Flow of Mass Communication* (Glencoe, Illinois: The Free Press, 1955), Rudiger Schmitt-Beck, "Mass Communication, Personal Communication, and Vote Choice: The Filter Hypothesis of Media Influence in Comparative Perspective," *British Journal of Political Science* 33, no. 2 (2003).
15. John Zaller, *The Nature and Origins of Mass Opinion* (New York: Cambridge University Press, 1992); "The Myth of Massive Media Impact Revisited: New Support for a Discredited Idea," in *Political Persuasion and Attitude Change*, ed. D. G. Mutz, P.M. Sniderman, and R.A. Brody (Ann Arbor, MI: University of Michigan Press, 1996).
16. *Batman*, 23, "The Ring of Wax," directed by James B. Clark, aired March 30, 1966.
17. When referring to the Batman comics, this chapter will include both the series' named after Batman and devoted to the Caped Crusader solely, as well as anthology-type titles such as "Detective Comics." For the sake of brevity, both will be referred to as "Batman comic books."
18. Gerry Conway, "The 'I' Of the Beholder," *Detective Comics #511*, (United States: DC Comics, 1982).
19. Chuck Dixon, "The Factor of Fear," *Batman: Gotham Knights #1*, (United States: DC Comics, 2001).
20. Don Cameron, "Brothers in Crime," *Batman #12*, (United States: DC Comics, 1942); Bill Finger, "The Man Who Led a Double Life," *Detective Comics #68*, (United States: DC Comics, 1942); David Vern Reed, "The Menace of the Fiery Heads!," *Batman #270*, (United States: DC Comics, 1975).
21. "...You'd think all there is to running a city is **making decisions...!**"
22. Paul A. Djupe and Brian R. Calfano, *God Talk: Experimenting with the Religious Causes of Public Opinion* (Philadelphia, PA: Temple University Press, 2013).
23. The one-shot Elseworlds title "Batman: Holy Terror" that features an alternate universe inspired by an ascendant Oliver Cromwell is noted but also takes place outside of any "canon" Batman universe.
24. Batman writers have stated that, spiritually or emotionally, Gotham City is "...Manhattan below 14th Street at eleven past midnight on the coldest night in November" (Dennis O'Neil, afterword to *Batman: Knightfall, A Novel* (New York: Bantam Books, 1994), 344) and "...New York at night"

(Barry Popik, "Metropolis is New York by day; Gotham City is New York by night," *The Big Apple* (blog), March 29, 2008). Geographically, however, DC Comics have traditionally placed Gotham City in New Jersey ("All About the Justice League of America," *Amazing World of DC Comics #14*, ed. Paul Levitz (United States: DC Comics, 1977)). The Archdiocese of Gotham City could thus parallel either the Archdiocese of New York, or the Archdiocese of Newark, New Jersey.

25. One can argue, of course, that Dr. Jonathan Crane, Professor of Psychology at Gotham University, is able to exert a great deal of influence over the citizens of Gotham when he terrorizes them in the guise of Scarecrow. This point is conceded. Considering that the academy has little influence over Gothamites when its members are not donning fanciful costumes and unleashing "fear gas," I think it is safe to make the assertion that the institution of higher education, nonetheless, has little sway in the day-to-day lives of the citizens of Gotham City.
26. It is not clear if it was rechristened Gotham City University (GCU; as seen in 2016's *Batman v. Superman: Dawn of Justice*), or if GCU is a cross-town rival for Gotham U.
27. Jerry Siegel, "Superman: The Case of the Death Express." *World's Finest Comics #3*, (United States: DC Comics, 1941).
28. Larry M. Bartels, "Messages Received: The Political Impact of Media Exposure," *The American Political Science Review* 87, no. 2 (1993); Walter Lippman, *Public Opinion* (United States: Harcourt, Brace and Co., 1922); Maxwell E. McCombs and Donald L. Shaw, "The Agenda-Setting Function of Mass Media," *The Public Opinion Quarterly* 36, no. 2 (1972); Diana C. Mutz, *Impersonal Influence: How Perceptions of Mass Collectives Affect Political Attitudes* (Cambridge, UK: Cambridge University Press, 1998); Elisabeth Noelle-Neumann, "The Spiral of Silence: A Theory of Public Opinion," *Journal of Communication* 24, no. 2 (1974); John R. Zaller, *The Nature and Origins of Mass Opinion* (Cambridge, UK: Cambridge University Press, 1992); "The Myth of Massive Media Impact Revived: New Support For a Discredited Idea," in *Political Persuasion and Attitude Change*, ed. Diana C. Mutz, Paul M. Sniderman, and Richard A. Brody (Ann Arbor, MI: University of Michigan Press, 1996).
29. Various motivations for Jameson's hostility toward Spider-Man have been retconned into different Spider-Man story lines, ranging from Jameson's inability to trust "heroes" due to the abuse he suffered from his war-hero father, to a simple jealousy of Spider-Man. Whatever underlying motive an individual story arc or motive has been ascribed to Jameson, however, no reader of the Spider-Man series, or fan of J.K. Simmons' portrayals of Jameson throughout media, can deny the malevolent glee J. Jonah Jameson takes in turning New York City against the web slinger.

30. Readers eventually discover that even the powerful Interfaces bend to the will of a mysterious entity called the Joker Virus.
31. MediaMan's role here is not dissimilar from the villainous mass media monopoly in the 1987 action/adventure film *The Running Man*.
32. Even Gata's motivations seem more driven by a need for positive media coverage than anything else. Toward the climax of the novel, she snarls, "Of course there are no cameras! You've stolen all the cameras! But I'm going to get them back! Even if I have to kill you to do it!" before attacking Batman with a deadly electronic whip.
33. Art Swift, "Americans' Trust in Mass Media Sinks to New Low," Gallup, September 14, 2016, http://news.gallup.com/poll/195542/americans-trust-mass-media-sinks-new-low.aspx
34. Gallup did not ask this question in 1982, 1987, or 1992 but did ask it twice in 1991, in a poll taken from February 28 to March 3, and then again from October 10–13.
35. "Media Use and Evaluation," Gallup, http://news.gallup.com/poll/1663/media-use-evaluation.aspx
36. "I'll explain all of it in a moment. First, let me play some old news clips for you. They'll help clarify things, help prepare you for what is yet to come…."
37. "Here, with our latest report, is a midget wearing a bikini." "Thanks, Tom!…."
38. "…It would never be enough. No, I don't keep count. But you do. And I love you for it."
39. Miller stated, facetiously or not, that the book began life titled, "Holy Terror, Batman!"
40. Hunter Daniels (July 23, 2011). "Comic-Con 2011: Frank Miller on HOLY TERROR: "I Hope This Book Really Pisses People Off"". *Collider.com*. Complex Media.

CHAPTER 13

Batgirls and the Politics of Feminism in Gotham

Carolyn Cocca

Introduction

There have been several Batgirls in Gotham City since 1961. Betty, Barbara, Cassandra, Stephanie, and Nissa have roughly tracked the external concerns, the successes and failures, and the internal tensions of the US feminist movement—the push for equal opportunities for males and females in all areas of life, the difficulties of stereotypes of gender pervasive in American culture and institutions, and the diversity of people who identify as women. This movement has often been labeled as having "waves": the First Wave, from 1848 to 1920; the Second Wave from the mid-1960s to mid-1980s, and the Third Wave from that time to the present. While the wave metaphor does not capture the underlying continuities of the feminist movement and uses dates more closely tied to white women's activism than to women's activism in general, it does capture ways in which the movement's emphases have changed over time.

The first Batgirl, Betty, is more representative of First Wave feminism, the notion that women can contribute when given opportunities. Barbara's

C. Cocca (✉)
State University of New York, College at Old Westbury, Old Westbury, NY, USA
e-mail: coccac@oldwestbury.edu

D. K. Picariello (ed.), *Politics in Gotham*,
https://doi.org/10.1007/978-3-030-05776-3_13

initial characterization embodies the Second Wave of feminism, with her self-sufficiency, strength, and professional careers. Both Betty and Barbara also embody white, middle-class, heterosexual concerns as well as their creators' unease with the idea of females subverting cultural expectations of gender. Barbara's later portrayals as the wheelchair-using Oracle, along with those of the new Batgirls (disabled Eurasian-American Cass, working-class Stephanie, and impoverished woman of color Nissa), illustrate Third Wave feminism's emphases on recognizing diversity and celebrating girlhood. However, these characters' youth can also be read as representing cultural discomfort with the idea of equality for women, such that constructing them as "just girls" reduces their impact.

This chapter employs these feminist theories to analyze the Batgirls—their abilities and skills, their physical appearances, their personalities, their challenges, and their relationships to the male characters—and how the politics of gender and power in Gotham have changed over time.

The First Wave: Equality, Difference, and Betty the Bat-Girl, 1961–1963

The long First Wave of Feminism is usually dated from 1848 and the convention in Seneca Falls, NY, which produced the "Declaration of Sentiments and Resolutions." Signed by the women and men in attendance, many, if not most of, were abolitionists as well, the document was modeled on the Declaration of Independence. It declared that "all men and women are created equal" and listed grievances against men who had banned women's right to vote, to own property, to have the same jobs as men, to receive equal pay, to sue for divorce or protest domestic violence, and to obtain an education. It called for an end to moral double standards and to teaching women that they were inferior.[1]

While feminists may have been united in these goals, they had different emphases and approaches. For instance, along with these calls for equality, some feminists acknowledged the idea that women were different from men, that women and men complemented one another by bringing their unique perspectives together. Some cast women—particularly, white, middle-class, American-born women—as morally superior to men. Some noted that the above list of grievances was really more about these already-privileged women, and did not speak about working-class, or impoverished, or enslaved, or immigrant women.[2]

A nod toward equality for women, along with acceptance of the idea that women and men were different and that white, middle-class heterosexual womanhood was both the norm and the goal, is readily seen in the first Bat-Girl, Betty Kane, as well as the first Batwoman, Betty's aunt Kathy. In the wake of psychiatrist Frederic Wertham's 1954 book *Seduction of the Innocent* and his testimony before Congress about the harms of comic books, alleging homoerotic undertones between Batman and Robin, comics industry professionals crafted the content-regulating Comics Code. Among its multiple guidelines were these: "Respect for parents, the moral code, and for honorable behavior shall be fostered... The treatment of live-romance stories shall emphasize the value of the home and the sanctity of marriage...Sex perversion or any inference to same is strictly forbidden." Kathy the Batwoman was created in 1956 and her niece Betty in 1961, by Bill Finger and Sheldon Moldoff. Each of Betty's appearances featured Batman, Batwoman, Robin, and Bat-Girl as a kind of family unit, with the younger white, opposite-sex couple respecting and obeying the older white opposite-sex couple, and Batman acting as the clear decision-maker for all four of them.

Betty swings into action on the cover of *Batman* #139 [4/61] in a short, red, green-belted dress with short-sleeved green cuffs and a cape; red peter pan boots; and an eye mask that frames her pale skin and bobbed blond hair. The costume's colors and design position her as a female version of Robin; her name positions her as a young female version of Batman. She does not have a utility belt, but rather, a stereotypically feminine "crime compact" with a lipstick that contains wires to capture criminals, hair spray that produces a smoke screen, and perfume that she uses as a distraction. Her age and gender are foregrounded in her introductory narration as well: "Criminals Beware! A new crime fighter is coming your way! ...Wait till you come up against a pretty teen-ager!...Here she comes: BAT-GIRL!" But Batman is opposed to her joining the team. He tells Kathy to pretend to train her but never complete her training, and Kathy complies.

Like the introduction that described her as both crime-fighter and pretty teenager, Betty is shown throughout the story as capable, but limited by her girlhood. She analyzes evidence that leads her to the villains, but then she is captured. When rescued by Batman, Batwoman, and Robin, she joins in the fight and asks, "How'm I doing, Robin?" He answers, "Not bad—for a girl." And having her apologize for being captured, the last two panels of the story ignore the fact that it was she who found the criminals. Kathy is pleased that Betty has learned not to act alone, and tells her maybe she'll be on the team someday. Instead of being pleased by the idea of future crime-fighting in and of itself, Betty is more excited to date Robin, saying, "Oh I can hardly wait! Perhaps Robin and I can work on a case together, too! Well, Robin is that a date?" "ULP," replies Robin.

Betty's subsequent appearances follow a similar pattern, embodying the First Wave ideas that women are capable if given opportunity, but have different and stereotypically feminine perspectives and skills. She also embodies resistance to this idea, through the writer and artist underscoring the ways in which she overestimates her abilities and is more interested in romance with a boy than anything else. In terms of the former weakness, Batman not only tries to prevent her from becoming Bat-Girl in the first place, but in a later issue, he tells Batwoman and Robin to tell Betty to stop being Bat-Girl. They do. Batman later explains to her they worried that "too much publicity [about her successes as Bat-Girl] might make you over-confident instead of careful." Instead of being annoyed by this patriarchal underestimation, she sees them as just trying to protect her, so she throws her arms around Robin and kisses him. In terms of the second weakness, both she and Batwoman are the clear pursuers of romance, while the males mostly demure to focus on crime-fighting. Betty allows herself to be trapped with a ravenous tiger (which she distracts with her perfume before throwing a net over it) to impress Robin, and also allows herself to be captured so that Robin can rescue her. When Robin says he is devoted to another woman, causing Betty to feel "heartbroken" and "lovesick," he later reveals he means Lady Justice. A sympathetic Batman gives his permission for the teens to date. Relieved, Betty throws her arms around Robin and kisses him. Another kiss occurs when Bat-Girl and Robin are beamed away to another planet, and she then saves the day as only she could. She asks the green-skinned, bald aliens if they'd mind her putting lipstick on, and one replies, "Ha Ha! A female is the same in any world! When facing a problem, she always resorts to powdering her nose or putting on fresh lipstick!" Then she opens the lipstick, and its trick wires encircle and capture them.

Bat-Girl and Batwoman disappeared when a new editor, Julius Schwartz, found them and other characters like the little imp Bat-Mite to be silly. The next Batgirl would share some similarities to Betty and her First Wave roots, but a cautious embrace of the nascent Second Wave of feminism would influence Barbara Gordon's portrayal as well.

The Second Wave: Equality and Exceptionality for Barbara the Batgirl, 1967–1988

Second Wave feminism dates from around the 1963–1964 publication of Betty Friedan's *The Feminine Mystique*, the release of the report on the Presidential Commission on the Status of Women, the passage of the Equal Pay Act and the Civil Rights Act of 1964, the founding of the National Organization for Women, and the introduction into Congress of the Equal Rights Amendment.[3] This movement was united in its insistence on equal opportunities for women and men and in its deconstruction of the "feminine mystique" that glorified different and unequal roles for women and men, but somewhat divided within due to its focus on white, middle-class, non-queer concerns.[4] Through lobbying, court cases, rallies, publications, alternative institutions and safe spaces, and consciousness-raising, Second Wave feminists did make headway, particularly in changing laws that overtly discriminated against women in terms of work and family planning. Second Wave feminism's achievements were circumscribed, as in the First Wave but to a lesser extent, by cultural expectations and norms of gender and femininity.

Barbara Gordon's earliest portrayals personify both the promises of the Second Wave of feminism as well as its limits at the time. Created as part of a strategy to bring young female and older male viewers to the TV show *Batman*, Barbara's first comic appearance was in January 1967 in *Detective Comics* #359 by Gardner Fox and Carmine Infantino. She is in her early 20s, light-skinned and red-haired, tall, fit, strong, pretty, funny, and bright, and puts her PhD to use as a librarian. In other words, she is a face of Second Wave feminism for young women to look up to (white, professional, middle-class, capable), and for older men to look at (attractive by traditional Euro-American standards, non-queer).

The daughter of the Gotham City Police Commissioner Jim Gordon, she makes her Batgirl costume to annoy and surprise her father at a policeman's masquerade ball. It is black with a yellow bat, has yellow gloves and skinny-heeled boots, and a little red purse hooked to her yellow utility belt. She admires herself in her outfit, and says that despite her "PhD and brown belt in judo," the masquerade ball "will be the highlight of my life!" But along the way, she sees Bruce Wayne being kidnapped. Calling herself Batgirl despite her age, she fights Killer Moth and loses, but she "is having the time of her life—fully alive to this new excitement and danger—and loving it!" Batman and Robin discourage her, saying, "No,

Batgirl! … you must understand that we can't worry ourselves about a girl." She ignores their rebukes and rescues them. Batman protests they could have rescued themselves, but tells Commissioner Gordon that he'll "welcome her aid…she doesn't have to take a back seat to anybody." She decides to continue on as Batgirl because she likes the excitement, has the skills, and wants to do good.

Her independence, her capability, and her drive are established immediately, as are her contrasts to Betty the Bat-Girl—Barbara is older, has a high-level degree and a job, has no romantic interest in Batman or Robin, does not automatically defer to their opinions, and does not require rescue. Later, she will run for Congress and win, serving from 1972 to 1980 in that capacity while still fighting crime as Batgirl. This, along with her PhD, both of which reflected a tiny percentage of white, middle-, and upper-class women at the time, show us that Barbara is quite exceptional, benefiting from the push for equal opportunities by feminism's Second Wave.

There are similarities between Barbara and Betty, reflecting dominant cultural norms of gender and pushback to the calls for equality. First, while Barbara is shown to be quite bright and even have a photographic memory, her resourcefulness is consistently grounded in her skills related to being a librarian, a feminized profession. Second, her heterosexuality is a given. Third, a number of plots in the comics had to do with fashion, even into the 1970s. One from January 1968 (#371) by Gardner Fox has Batgirl stop in the middle of a fight to straighten her headpiece, lamenting that she will have to work to "overcome my feminine instincts by sheer concentration! It wasn't my personal vanity that made me adjust my headgear—it was an instinctive feminine reaction!" Later, when she stops fighting criminals due to a run in her tights, they also stop in order to look at her legs, and thereby get themselves caught. Apparently, as it is women's instinct to care about their appearance, it is men's to look at female legs even if it results in going to jail. Batman praises her, "You see, Batgirl? That was one time where you turned a feminine trait to your advantage—and the disadvantage of the criminals!" Barbara thinks, "I just didn't have the heart to tell Batman and Robin that I tore my tights deliberately—to give me an excuse for showing off my legs and distracting those crooks! The fact that my feminine weakness betrayed me so often in the past—I just had to prove it has its strong points too!" Fox's story, its language, and its assumptions are indicative of a traditional view of womanhood and femininity, and manhood and masculinity, that many still took for granted in the 1960s. One might even assume that the story was meant to be complimentary to Barbara at the time.

Barbara's subsequent adventures in the 1970s usually merged her being a smart career woman and a capable crime-fighter with her being particularly concerned with fashion and dating, showing the promise and the limits of how male writers and artists felt about the feminist movement at the time. Different authorship shifted Barbara's portrayal in the comics in the early 1980s. She continued fighting crime but also was written by Cary Burkett as fighting her insecurities as well. Barbara's appearances begin to dwindle, the most high-profile being that in Marv Wolfman and George Perez's 1985 *Crisis on Infinite Earths*, a mini-series that merged numerous continuities from comics and thereby rebooted the DC superhero universe. A still insecure Barbara tells Supergirl that she feels "useless, so helpless, so worthless" and afraid. She says, "Look at your powers. I-I'm nothing…I-I don't think I was ever cut out for playing hero." While not unheard of with male characters, this trope of female insecurity has been repeated across decades with fictional female characters, undercutting their power.

But before her retirement, Barbara would have two last adventures by Barbara Randall Kesel, the first woman to write the character in 21 years. Kesel was hired after sending DC Comics a long letter about how their female characters could be written better. She was directed to write a sympathetic story for Barbara's last outing as Batgirl because, she was told, Barbara's next appearance in *The Killing Joke* would be tragic. *The Killing Joke,* written by Alan Moore and drawn by Dave Gibbons, was emblematic of the new "grim and gritty" tone of the 1980s–1990s comics. In this story, the Joker shoots Barbara, paralyzing her from the waist down, and then takes pictures of her in various states of undress while she is writhing in pain. It was this story that prompted future *Birds of Prey* and *Batgirl* writer Gail Simone to create the "Women in Refrigerators" website, a list of incidents in comics when female characters were made victims of violence—particularly, sexualized violence—solely to show the violence's effect on male characters. The violence done to Barbara was a classic "fridging," in that no one in the story ever asks her how she's feeling after it happens, nor does the story follow her and her recovery. Rather, the story explores how her father and Batman react to it and feel about it. Fridging is a plot device that treats women as objects rather than as people; it pushes against feminist ideas of equal opportunity and equal treatment. *The Killing Joke* was a huge success for its backstory of the Joker, and the parallels it draws between the Joker and Batman. For Barbara, the story was a low point, but it would also provide the springboard for her new identity and for the creation of new Batgirls.

The Third Wave: Diversity and Girliness for Barbara, Cassandra, Stephanie, and Nissa, 1990s–2010s

Comic writers John Ostrander and Kim Yale forged a new identity for Barbara Gordon, "Oracle." Beginning in 1989, Oracle would use her exceptional intelligence, photographic memory, and facility with information sciences to be a team leader, information broker, computer hacker, master tactician, and wheelchair user—a new kind of superhero. And she would also act as a mentor to the new Batgirls, the disabled Eurasian-American Cassandra Cain; the working-class villain's daughter, Stephanie Brown; and the impoverished teen of color from the future, Nissa.

Barbara as Oracle, and these three Batgirls, engage with Third Wave feminism and its continuities with and critiques of Second and First Wave feminism. Grounded in protest of the 1980s and 1990s conservative backlash to various civil rights movements, the Third Wave of feminism builds on previous feminist activism with its central tenets of liberation and equality, but it also builds on internal critiques of the First and Second Waves as having predominantly white, heterosexual, middle-class, non-disabled standpoints. The Third Wave strives to be more intersectional, to be sensitive to the ways in which different vectors of discrimination combine and overlap in ways that disempower some people more than others. It is more open to continuums of race, gender, and sexuality while also embracing a reclamation of signs of femininity or girliness as empowering, often conveying these values through irony and humor.[5] Barbara and Cass as living with disabilities, Cass and Nissa as young women of color, and Stephanie and Nissa's non-middle-class backgrounds all allow for explorations of Third Wave feminist values as well as the limits of celebrating youth and girliness in a culture that still tends to devalue females.

From Batgirl to Oracle: Barbara Gordon, 1989–2011

Barbara was Oracle for over 20 years, starring in the *Birds of Prey* title with Black Canary for most of that time period. The two main characters complemented one another, with Oracle as the cool methodical planner and

Canary as the warmer, more impulsive, and fishnet-clad "boots on the ground." About half of the issues were written by Chuck Dixon and about half by Gail Simone; there were various artists. Barbara as Oracle is portrayed as young, attractive, intelligent, healthy, white, cisgender, heterosexual, wealthy, independent, and disabled. She stood out from the 1990s' "Bad Girl" art that was enmeshed in a backlash to Second and Third Wave feminism, showcasing hyperviolent and hypersexual female characters to appeal to older, white, heterosexual males who bought comics in local comic shops. Defying conventional wisdom that only those kinds of books would sell, *Birds of Prey* sold quite well, comparable to *Batman* and *Detective Comics* at the time. Dixon would fight against turning out a "cheesecake book," and Simone would fight editorial pressure to have romantic subplots for Barbara, both writers building on the successes of the First, Second, and Third Wave feminist activism that pushed against stereotypical portrayals of women.

Barbara is neither dependent nor isolated, nor self-pitying as stereotypes of people with disabilities would have us expect. Rather, Gail Simone in particular has her surrounded by a rotating roster of superhero women in ways that Barbara-as-Batgirl and Betty-as-Bat-Girl were not. While those Batgirls were made to seem exceptional and unusual and had to carry great representational weight for all women, in *Birds of Prey*, the sheer number of female characters guarantees that neither she nor any of the others has to represent all women; rather, each can be different from one another and represent more of a spectrum of gender.

While centering a female hero with disabilities who successfully leads other heroes is emblematic of Third Wave feminism, it is also the case that Barbara is something of a "supercrip": a fictional disabled hero who accomplishes unbelievable feats and thereby gives the impression that it is easy to "overcome" a disability. Some of this is enabled by her various privileges. She begins with a PhD and obtains a law degree. She hacks villains' bank accounts and gets grants from the Bruce Wayne Foundation (i.e., from Batman); a kind of economic independence which is not a reality for most people. She is unusually strong from the waist up due to her previous training in martial arts, such that almost every time we see her face a foe with her escrima sticks, she wins. And she is privileged via her sexuality, in that we see her have a "normal" heterosexual romantic life with a few men, most notably with the Robin to her Batgirl, Dick Grayson. And because so much of her work is online, Barbara is unseen by villains, which means her gender and her disability are not visible. Across the *Birds of Prey* run, characters who know of her only online or by reputation assume that someone with such intelligence and resources must be male and able-bodied, and afford her respect accordingly. Repeating this misconception as a plot point several times in the 1990s and 2000s, her writers are commenting on intersectional discrimination against women and against people with disabilities in ways that the 1960s–1970s writers of Betty and Barbara were unwilling or unable to do.

But while Barbara is invisible to foes, she is visible to readers, and as noted, her first writer pushed (not always successfully) against her being overly sexualized, a rarity at a time of the 1990s–2000s hypersexualization of female characters in comics. Later, though, during Gail Simone's run as writer, artist Ed Benes would draw Barbara and the female characters in a more sexualized manner, while not doing so with the male characters. This is symptomatic of the overwhelmingly male-dominated production of superhero comics: a male artist drawing a female character more as an object to be looked at than a subject of her own story, undermining her agency and undermining gender equality. But such a portrayal also subverts a stereotype of people with disabilities as being asexual or undesirable because Barbara is treated the same as the other female characters. In the late 2000s, this complication was rendered moot when the first woman to draw Barbara Gordon in an ongoing title, Nicola Scott, would draw her as sexy but not sexualized; her second longer-term female artist, Babs Tarr, would do the same in the mid-2010s. This clearly illustrates the importance of equal opportunity in comics creatorship for the production of more diverse and more nuanced female characters.

Similarly, Gail Simone's writing of Barbara does not portray her femaleness as a weakness, or as central to a desire for romance with men, but just as one part of her complex, multifaceted character. She has Barbara choose to act a maternal figure with the new Batgirls, Cassandra Cain (1999–2008), Stephanie Brown (2009–2011), and Nissa (2013–2017). In this way, Barbara subverts a stereotype of women with disabilities as unable to care for young people, and puts forth the idea that women can be mentors as well as men although they have been rarely portrayed as such in fiction. The way in which Barbara deals with these young women, in that she both embraces her role but also finds it burdensome, is nuanced and compelling, furthering the stories of all of the characters.

The New Batgirls: Cassandra and Stephanie

Cassandra Cain's representation during the Third Wave of feminism, as a young and extremely capable woman of color with disabilities and without constant romantic attachment to a male character, was probably unthinkable to comics creators of the 1960s and 1970s, when female characters such as Betty and Barbara were written as white and middle-class and bounded by their concerns about makeup, fashion, and romance. Introduced in 1999 in *Batman* #567 by Kelley Puckett, Damion Scott, and Jordan Gorfinkel, and the first to headline the *Batgirl* comic title, Cassandra Cain was brought up to be an assassin, like her parents, David Cain and Lady Shiva (Sandra Wu-San). Cain raised Cassandra alone, and had trained her not to read, write, or talk, but rather, to use those parts of her brain to "read" people's body language so that she could defeat them physically. At a young age, he orders Cassandra to assassinate someone, and due to her "reading" skills, she is horrified when she realizes how painful the death is, and she runs away. In Gotham City, she does errands for Barbara Gordon/Oracle, and in a dramatic moment stands in between Commissioner Gordon and her father's gun and speaks her first word: "stop." She becomes Oracle's ward while training to be the new Batgirl.

Her costume has a much different silhouette from the previous two Batgirls, Betty and Barbara; there is no attempt to feminize the outfit with delicate boots or flowing hair or painted lips. Trusting her due to her saving Commissioner Gordon and her incredible martial arts skills, Batman gives her a completely black Batgirl costume, and she sews the mouth shut with wide and visible stitches. Her eyes appear blacked out as well, and she wears black boots and tucks her hair into the cowl. The full outfit conveys her intimidating stealth, and the sewn mouth conveys part of her disability, her difficulty in using speech.

Cassandra's disability is a core part not only of her costume but also of her character. She signs to Batman that she only knows how to speak through violence: she raises her hand, makes a fist, and puts it in front of her mouth. In the *Batgirl* title that she headlined, writer Kelley Puckett had her brain "rewired" by a telepathic character, such that she could speak and understand words better, but even after this she still speaks minimally, often one or two words at a time, and has great difficulty reading due to what is described as a form of dyslexia. Barbara helps her learn to communicate and later, she takes classes to learn to read, write, and speak English as a new language.

As much as the Third Wave of feminism was oriented toward intersectionality, there were some limits to the progressiveness of the Cassandra character in terms of the intersections of her race and gender. As arguably the world's greatest fighter, one whom Batman admits could defeat him, Cassandra falls into a stereotype of Asian female characters as being expert martial artists. Her silence can be construed as alluding to a stereotype of Asian women as quiet and submissive as well. And later, in an editorially mandated plot line, she was written as a villain, falling into a stereotype of Asian female characters as untrustworthy "dragon ladies." At the same time, most artists (but not all) subverted gender and racial stereotypes as well, by not overly sexualizing her depiction.

She considers Barbara to be like a mother to her, and she is legally adopted by Bruce Wayne. But then he dies. So after ten years of being Batgirl, Cassandra gives the mantle to her friend Stephanie Brown, and goes to Hong Kong and continues to work as the vigilante Black Bat. She ostensibly does this because she is disillusioned and grieving, but it would be explained later that she did so on Batman's orders—to boost Stephanie's confidence. Cassandra helps train Stephanie, and in turn, Stephanie helps Cassandra with her reading. Their friendship speaks to Third Wave strategies of inclusion and acceptance, as while their struggles might be different, they have many commonalities as well.

Stephanie's background is quite different from the previous Batgirls, and it engages with Third Wave feminists' concern that the movement must reach beyond middle-class professional concerns and must make public stories of domestic abuse so as to empower survivors and help with their healing. Stephanie's father, Cluemaster, is in jail when she's young. He is abusive to her mother, who struggles with depression and an addiction to painkillers. A friend of her father, babysitting Stephanie when she was young, attempted to rape her. She and her mother do not live with the middle- or upper-class comforts of Betty or Barbara. All of this has an effect on Stephanie: she has some anger and aggression, but she pushes through with an optimistic attitude and a resolve to do good. She does so through her identity of "Spoiler," introduced in 1992 as a young woman clad in purple and seeking to spoil her villain father's schemes. Her creator, Chuck Dixon (along with Tom Lyle), who would write Barbara in *Birds of Prey*, kept her character on as Robin/Tim Drake's love interest. So unlike Betty, Barbara, and Cassandra, not only was Stephanie not created to be Batgirl, but rather, she was created as a villain's daughter and a hero's love interest, an adjunct to male characters.

She dates Robin on-and-off, and when she discovers she is pregnant from a former boyfriend, Robin supports her in her decision to give the baby up for adoption to protect it from Gotham's villains. This may have represented discomfort with the idea of a teen having an abortion, but it also allowed for an exploration of teen pregnancy and the opportunity for a future writer to bring the child back into the story at some point. Even though Stephanie and Robin are clearly close, she still doesn't know his real identity until Batman tells her. More than once, she thinks Robin's cheating on her, and is often positioned as "the girlfriend" not unlike Betty as Bat-Girl. She is not the perfect fighter, the perfect girlfriend, or the perfect daughter; she is not written as a model "strong female protagonist," but as more grounded in real-world concerns.

Stephanie becomes Robin herself, briefly in 2004, and suffers a graphic death, in an editorially mandated story line that was protested by the writers of *Batgirl* and *Nightwing*, Dylan Horrocks and Devin Grayson, and was unpopular with many fans as well. Tim is forced by his father to quit being Robin, and Stephanie demands to take his place. Batman does train her, reluctantly, but in short, she overestimates her abilities, is fired when she makes mistakes, and then while trying to help the situation without full information on what Batman is doing, causes a gang war in Gotham. This is not terribly different from Betty the Bat-Girl's first outings, but the outcome here would be much different from the pat on the head from Batman and the kiss on the cheek from Robin that Betty received. Stephanie, rather, undergoes a violent and sexualized torture and death, a type of "fridging" not unusual for female characters in the 1990s–2000s when male artists and writers tended to feature hyper-muscular and violent male characters and hyper-objectified female characters in their comics, a type of backlash to feminism's push for equality for women and men.

Due to fan outrage and the continuing marketability of the character, Stephanie was brought back to be Spoiler again in 2007, with Batman and Robin still feeling unable to trust her. But it was not long after, following the death of Batman, that Stephanie would be given the title of Batgirl by Cassandra.

Stephanie as Batgirl, as written by Bryan Q. Miller from 2009–2011 and drawn initially by Lee Garbett and Trevor Scott, conforms to Third Wave feminism's celebration of girlhood alongside its push toward ending the devaluation and recognizing the strength of girls—in other words, "girl power," as the phrase was initially used by Third Wave feminists and before it was commercially co-opted to sell merchandise. She is similar in demeanor and appearance to Buffy the Vampire Slayer, whose eponymous TV show had capitalized on the idea of "girl power," aired to critical acclaim from 1997–2003, and had continued on in comic form. Both were slight, perky, quippy teens with blonde hair, initially underestimated by both their allies and opponents.

Like Cassandra, Stephanie's relationship with Barbara Gordon is an integral part of her stories. Stephanie trains hard, works to prove herself, and often accedes to Barbara's guidance, earning the latter's trust. So Barbara designs and gives Stephanie a new purple-and-black costume, reflecting her history as Spoiler and her future as Batgirl. The costume has a yellow thigh pouch and its cowl is shaped like Barbara's rather than Cassandra's, such that Stephanie's long blonde hair streams out from behind it and the lower half of her face is visible. Like Cassandra, Stephanie has flat-heeled, practical, rugged black boots, quite unlike Barbara's 1967 dainty yellow heels. Barbara also installed some tech in the suit, so she can communicate information to Stephanie from behind her computer as Oracle. These two form a trio when Wendy, the tech-savvy wheelchair-using daughter of Barbara's nemesis, the Calculator, joins the team. Here, Barbara is essentially mentoring two younger versions of herself, a new Batgirl and a new Oracle, such that Barbara does not have to represent "all" women as she did in the 1960s, or even all women with disabilities. However, most of the stories with Stephanie as Batgirl feature almost entirely white and heterosexual casts, such that they do not engage with Third Wave feminism's emphasis on intersectionality in terms of gender, race, ethnicity, and sexuality.

Stephanie is shown enmeshed in a variety of relationships other than the ones with Barbara and Wendy. She has friends at college and sometimes hangs out with Supergirl, and is living with her mother who is no longer addicted to drugs and is working as a nurse. Stephanie acts in a sisterly role to the new Robin, Damian Wayne, and works with him and the new Batman (Dick Grayson, the first Robin). Like Barbara, these two are at first wary and skeptical of Stephanie, but come to value her determination and her improved skills. Stephanie's on-and-off boyfriend, Tim Drake (also formerly Robin) tries to win her back, but she rebuffs him; rather, she is interested in a cop named Nick who works with Barbara's father, Commissioner Jim Gordon. But this Stephanie is not a mere girlfriend to a male character, nor an object to be "fridged" to further a male character's story. This story is hers, and her portrayal here showcases the feminist notions that young women from difficult backgrounds are not to be underestimated, and older women with disabilities can serve valuable roles as mentors.

The Future Batgirl: Nissa

Still in a mentoring role in the *Batman Beyond* comic (similar to the 1999–2001 animated series), set about 40 years in the future, Barbara is a much older, white-haired, non-disabled Commissioner Gordon, like her father before her. She works with the new Batman, Terry McGinnis, and in a 2013 story by Scott Peterson and Annie Wu encounters a young woman of color dressing as Batgirl and fighting crime in an impoverished area of Gotham called Crown Point. This Batgirl's homemade costume is gray, with her hair tucked into the cowl like Cassandra but the lower half of her face visible like Barbara and Stephanie, and a large black bat that stretches to her shoulders to become a cape. She criticizes Barbara and the police for ignoring her community, and together they confront and take down a businessman whose company is poisoning the food in Crown Point. Barbara shows up at her high school the next day, having figured out her identity: she is a 15-year-old named Nissa, with brown skin and long dark hair. Her name together with her appearance contribute to the impression that she has family roots in the Middle East or perhaps South Asia.

Nissa reappears in 2017, fighting against drug dealers in her neighborhood who are targeting middle schoolers, and still feels that Barbara has not done enough for Gotham's poor and against indifferent politicians and corrupt cops. She is not silent like Cassandra nor bubbly like Stephanie, and she has no desire to be a detective like Barbara. She has fewer resources than her predecessors and therefore no tech or gadgetry. Her weapon is herself. While this characterization makes her different from the previous Batgirls, and opens up new possibilities for exploring Third Wave feminist concerns about diversity of race, ethnicity, class, and sexuality, her small number of appearances can only tease at the potential of a young, brown, and impoverished Batgirl working with an older Barbara Gordon in a dystopic future Gotham.

Conclusion: Gender and Power in Gotham and Beyond

In 2012, DC Comics rebooted its superhero universe, wiping out the earlier continuities. A younger Barbara Gordon was editorially mandated to be "cured" of her paralysis, and to act as Batgirl. This engendered emotional protests by readers who held dear the character of Oracle and valued her importance to people with disabilities and to women more broadly, two groups radically underrepresented in mainstream superhero comics. The post-2012 Barbara is not a former Congresswoman, JD/PhD, team leader, mentor, and master tactician. Rather, she is a physically slighter, less-experienced college student, like her TV portrayals in the Batman animated series of the 1990s and 2000s, and the print mini-series *Batgirl: Year One* by Chuck Dixon, Scott Beatty, and Marcos Martin. She is more an amalgam of Barbara and Stephanie, younger and wearing a purple-inflected costume, trying to find herself, and often romantically entangled with men. Stephanie was brought back as Spoiler, again underestimated and mistrusted by the Bat-Family and in love with Robin/Tim Drake; Cassandra is called Orphan, again deadly and mostly silent. Neither works with Barbara's Batgirl. None of their previous character development, nor the bonds of family and mentorship between these three are evident in the new books. All of these moves, while still portraying forward female heroes, undercut the greater feminist potential of these diverse female heroes working together toward common goals.

The superhero comics industry of the 2010s, almost entirely male and white, both behind the scenes and on the page, is attempting to respond to broad-based calls for diversifying its creative teams and its characters while also trying to placate a vocal segment of fans who prefer the demographically disproportionate status quo; as such, it is just one of the many arenas in which struggles between dominant and marginalized groups in the United States are taking place today. De-aging female characters may make them appear as less challenging to cultural norms of gender, but it can also subvert the status quo by demonstrating strength and leadership through young female bodies. These new versions of the characters, just like all of the Batgirls since 1961, are doing both simultaneously as feminist ideas about equality and equity are embraced by some and fought by others.

Each Batgirl has been a product of the successes and limits of the feminist movements at the time of her creation, the intent of writers and artists and editors at a profit-oriented company mindful of both feminist ideas and backlash to them, and varying receptions and sometimes pushback by readers. As these variables change and morph over time, so too do the portrayals of Batgirls and the politics of gender and power in Gotham. They may be produced and received as conforming to stereotypes of females as lesser than males, or as embodying feminism's challenges to inequalities of gender, race, class, sexuality, and disability. These powerful females, still as numerically rare in fiction as in company boardrooms and in the halls of Congress, have been and will remain enmeshed in debates over the importance of more equitable and authentic representation in fiction as well as in real-life economic, political, social, and cultural institutions.

Acknowledgements The author would like to thank Stella Bowman and Steven Goodman for their insightful comments on this chapter.

Notes

1. Elizabeth Cady Stanton, "Declaration of Sentiments and Resolutions." 1848. http://ecssba.rutgers.edu/docs/seneca.html
2. See, for instance, "Debates at Equal Rights Association meetings." 1867–69. http://www.womeninworldhistory.com/TWR-16.html
3. NOW [National Organization for Women], "Statement of Purpose," 1966. https://now.org/about/history/statement-of-purpose/
4. See, for instance, Cherríe Moraga and Gloria Anzaldúa, eds., *This Bridge Called My Back: Writings by Radical Women of Color* (Watertown, MA: Persephone Press, 1981); Audre Lorde, *Sister Outsider* (Freedom, CA: Crossing, 1984); Carole Vance, ed., *Pleasure and Danger: Exploring Female Sexuality* (Routledge and Kegan Paul, 1984).
5. See, for instance, Rebecca Walker, ed., *To Be Real: Telling the Truth and Changing the Face of Feminism* (New York: Random House, 1995); Jennifer Baumgardner, and Amy Richards, *Manifesta: Young Women, Feminism, and the Future* (New York: Farrar, Straus, and Giroux, 2000); Daisy Hernandez and Bushra Rehman, *Colonize This! Young Women of Color on Today's Feminism* (Berkeley, CA: Seal Press, 2010); Julia Serano, *Excluded: Making Feminist and Queer Movements More Inclusive* (Berkeley, CA: Seal Press, 2013).

CHAPTER 14

Dawn of Justice: Revisioning, Accountability, and Batman in the Twenty-first Century

Aidan Diamond

Do you know the oldest lie in America, Senator?
It's that power can be innocent.
—Lex Luthor (Zack Snyder, dir., *Batman v. Superman: Dawn of Justice, Ultimate Edition* (Warner Bros., 2016). Subsequent references to and quotations from *BvS* refer to this source.)

The scene plays out like this: A black-gauntleted fist is aimed with unerring accuracy until the recipient submits and tells the assailant what he wants to know. Or, it goes like this: Something gleaming and sharp flies through the air, knocking down the first line of defense, or *thwack*ing just a hair away from skin, or landing mercilessly and excruciatingly in some vulnerable flesh that incapacitates, but certainly doesn't kill. Or: A man is snatched from the street by a bat-masked specter and suspended in terror from the edge of a very tall building, a fall from which will almost certainly prove to be lethal. He is interrogated, threatened, and terrified because the Bat believes his victim knows something that might prove useful to his crime-fighting mission.

A. Diamond (✉)
University of Southern California, Los Angeles, CA, USA

D. K. Picariello (ed.), *Politics in Gotham*,
https://doi.org/10.1007/978-3-030-05776-3_14

Narratively speaking, Batman's vigilante violence is practically always justified. The henchman betrays his boss and reveals the details of a shipment (of drugs, of weapons, of humans), or a plot to poison the water supply (or evaporate the water supply, or fill it with smiling fish), or a scheme to kidnap or murder someone or steal something. The message is that Batman is infallible, and that torture works.

Its representation in popular media aside, torture does not work. American intelligence agencies have known for decades that torture produces neither reliable or actionable information, but rather whatever the tortured thinks will stop the pain.[1] All too frequently, torture results not in an arrested terrorist plot but in more innocent people being tortured.[2] Despite the facts, positive representations of torture pervade American media, often suggesting that even if torture doesn't yield desired information, then the catharsis of hurting a "bad guy" is justification enough.[3] The politics of violence are particularly fraught in superhero narratives, which rely on an easily identifiable hero dispensing justified violence against an easily identifiable villain—the genre's foundational vigilantism. Good guys win by beating up bad guys. Might is Right, at least until one begins to think critically.

Zack Snyder's *Batman v. Superman: Dawn of Justice* (2016; abbreviated hereafter as *BvS*) is the rare exception to this rule. At its heart, the film attempts—much like its source material, Frank Miller's lauded *The Dark Knight Returns* (1986)—a synthesis of and commentary on the politics of the superhero narrative, specifically the violence in those politics.[4] As such, *BvS*'s treatment of violence and its refusal to gloss over or mitigate representations of brutality and torture deserve careful consideration. This is the goal of this chapter.

This chapter is organized into four parts. The first reviews the long tradition of revision and "retconning" in superhero narratives, using Geoff Klock's analysis of *The Dark Knight Returns.* The second illustrates how *BvS* borrows from Miller's comic in order to argue, in the third part, that *BvS* asks no less of its viewers than to consider all past iterations of Batman, and Superman, and every other superhero and infer the same degrees of violence demonstrated in *BvS* as having *always already* been present in each. The final part forms the bulk of the chapter, and closely reads *BvS* via the question of sovereignty and contemporary criticism of Guantánamo and the "War on Terror."

New York Times film critic A.O. Scott memorably described *BvS* as "as diverting as having a porcelain sink broken over your head," alluding to

Batman's doing precisely that to Superman in the film's eponymous conflict.[5] However, to dismiss the film's undeniable violence as merely unentertaining, unwatchable, or unpleasant is to misread *BvS* and its thesis: that violence, particularly in superhero narratives, should be the subject of rigorous interrogation; that it should never simply be a tool to entertain; and that it can, and should, be held accountable for its representation.

Retconning the Bat

Narratives conventionally demand that the exposition's status quo be upset and resettled into something new by the denouement. Superhero narratives stress this essential premise. To fulfill narrative demands, everything must change; to fulfill marketplace demands, everything must remain the same. The mechanism through which this is achieved is a "retcon," a portmanteau derived from "retroactive continuity." Essentially, a new writer retroactively revises a previous narrative by demonstrating that it was incorrectly represented. The updated continuity is then accepted as having always already been true by the readers and the publishers, which, argues Orion Ussner Kidder, is essential to a functional retcon. One must notice what has been changed in order to apply the change.[6] Retcons may be both minute (Grant Morrison's changing Jason Todd's hair to red, for instance)[7] or game-changing, as in the case of Ed Brubaker's declaring that Bucky Barnes had never died; he had been captured by the Soviets and cryogenically frozen.[8] Most rarely, they can revise an entire history. This is the case of *The Dark Knight Returns*.

Comics scholar Geoff Klock declares that Frank Miller's *The Dark Knight Returns* is "one of the most important works in the tradition of superhero narratives" precisely because the scope of its revision "attempts a synthesis of forty-five years of preceding Batman history in one place."[9] Its uncompromising method of doing so has been adopted by nearly every Batman story to succeed it. Accordingly, unprecedented degrees of realism are introduced. Batman has aged the 45 years of his character (since his creation in 1939)[10]; Gotham has mixed feelings about its fascist vigilante; his weaponry and costume are rationalized: "When Batman takes a rifle shot to the chest, which any reader assumes would kill him instantly, it reveals metal shielding. Batman says[,] 'Why do you think I wear a target on my chest—can't armor my head,' and with that one line a thirty-year mystery dissolves as every reader runs mentally through previous stories, understanding that plate as having always been there."[11]

This is the key to Miller's accomplishment: the retroactive decree that something he introduces to the canon for the first time was *always already* there. Similarly, the other elements Miller introduces to Gotham should be understood as having always existed. The violence Batman sustains, as evidenced by his extensive scarring and history of injury, is nothing new, just more explicit; similarly, the violence Batman enacts against others should be understood as having always been crucial to his crime-fighting strategies. "Every convention," Klock writes, "that allows superhero narratives to function, and every intertext, is exposed [by Miller] to the reader with a clarity that at once cleans up comic [...] history and also complicates it."[12] Elided elements elucidated, the history of Batman's vigilante exploits suddenly makes much more sense—and simultaneously demands that the reader ask of previous narratives the questions *Dark Knight* prompts: what is the purpose of a superhero in "the real world"? And can that purpose be achieved without violence?

Dark Knight to *Dawn of Justice*

BvS draws on *The Dark Knight Returns* through verbal, visual, and thematic parallels. Lines and images are quoted directly from Miller's comic to Snyder's film: in both, Alfred wryly remarks that the Wayne wine cellar might not last to the next generation, "not that there's likely to *be* a next generation." Both comic and film note the death of "the American conscience," though only *BvS* includes Martin Luther King, Jr., with the Kennedys. At key moments, Batman states his belief in an opponent's vow to kill someone, before killing the opponent; Batman admits his own criminality; and snarls the lesson his parents taught him—"That the world only makes sense if you force it to"—at Superman.[13] Like *Dark Knight*, *BvS* armors its older, more grizzled and cynical Batman in a mechanical suit, and the Batcave is haunted by an empty Robin costume. Compare Miller's rendering of the Wayne murders to Snyder's and one finds a faithful adaptation of the former, from the fall of shell casings to the rain of pearls. Superman lifts a tank over his head in *Dark Knight* and a rocket in *BvS*; in both, he is decimated in a blazing nuclear explosion that turns the sky yellow, and must wait for the sun to restore him.[14]

Beyond the direct quotations from *Dark Knight*, plot elements and themes are borrowed heavily. A battle between Batman and Superman is staged with Superman attempting to reason with Batman and Batman immediately triggering sonic weapons. An unnamed president orders the release of nuclear missiles, and implicitly expects Superman to save the United States from the fallout. Both comic and film close with a funeral, resurrection, and Batman leading a new movement toward justice. Thematically, both argue the ethics of vigilantism through the media—though unlike *Dark Knight*, *BvS* does not dismiss these ethical concerns out of hand, and is acutely invested in the responsibility of discussion.[15] Senator June Finch, the character who directly interrogates the moral consequences of "unilateral" action—a kind euphemism for vigilantism—says as much to Superman when he appears before her committee: "This is how a democracy works. We talk to each other." Attempts to uphold democracy, the unspoken keystone of "truth, justice, and the American way," must be made, at least in part, through conversation.

A conversation is precisely what *BvS* endeavors to have. It is fundamentally interested in not just quoting *Dark Knight*, verbally or visually (though it does both sufficiently frequently to underscore its lineage) but in adapting Miller's revisionary intervention to the genre of superhero films.

Always Already

BvS, at its most basic level, is the story of Lex Luthor successfully manipulating both Batman and the American government into, respectively, believing Superman to be an agent of unchecked destruction, and doubting Superman's moral authority. Luthor's machinations are instigated following the destruction of Metropolis first depicted in *Man of Steel*,[16] which is re-filmed from Bruce Wayne's perspective in *BvS*. Over the course of the film, Wayne/Batman grows increasingly convinced, in part due to Luthor's manipulations, that Superman represents an apocalyptic threat to humanity; Superman, by doing his job as a reporter, concludes that Batman is a threat to civil rights. After the two trade (verbal) blows, Luthor intervenes and coerces Superman into fighting Batman by holding Superman's mother, Martha, as hostage. When neither hero dies, Luthor unleashes a Kryptonian Frankenstein, the murderous Doomsday, who succeeds in both uniting the DC Trinity (Batman, Superman, and Wonder Woman) and killing Superman.

As we have discussed, *Dark Knight*'s revisionary intervention has two parts: "Miller forces the world of Batman to make sense" by (1) suspending camp and fantastic elements (beyond a dystopic imagining not entirely alien to urban life in the 1980s), thus (2) retroactively forcing this realism into the entirety of the Bat-canon.[17] The armored chest plate is revealed to have always already been a part of Batman's suit. Violent vigilantism has always already taken a physical toll on Batman's body. Most crucially, "even in regard to 'do-gooders,' the threat of paternalism cum fascism is always present."[18] Klock notes that:

> First, superheroes, and Batman especially, always rely on physical violence and intimidation to fight crime. Batman himself is not unwilling to be physically brutal to acquire information, for example, and often relies on the threat or implied threat of violence to keep criminals in line. Second, it is often the case that the superhero is a kind of criminal—a vigilante. [...] Third, superheroes most often occupy a reactionary role, traditionally emerging only to meet a threat to the status quo.[19]

Violence, criminality, and reactionary politics: all ingredients necessary to the propagation of fascism. That Klock identifies each as intrinsic to superhero narratives, and particularly to Batman, is no surprise; the charge of fascism has been leveled against superheroes[20] since Superman was first connected to the Nazis' appropriation of Nietzsche's Übermensch.[21] Violence as governance is the hallmark of a fascist regime—in stark contrast to Senator Finch's insistence that democracy functions as a conversation. Miller, in *Dark Knight*, gestures to the whole of Batman's (extra-) diegetic history when he portrays him as "the worst sort of reactionary fascist terrorizing people into his control with cheap theatrics," and worst of all, Miller and his narrative justify and even glorify Batman's fascistic tactics and worldview.[22] In doing so, he further entrenches fascist acts and philosophy into a genre that should repudiate fascism,[23] but without engaging in Finch's political dialogue; he unveils the "fascistic impulses" that have always already undergirded superheroics, and drops the mic, as it were.[24]

However, mutual recognition is essential to a successful retcon. The reader must recognize the revision in order to apply it, and Klock argues that they do: "both the reader and Batman come to a realization of the role [these fascistic impulses] play in the superhero narrative."[25] Whether or not Batman recognizes the untenability of his politics is a question anyone studying Batman must consider, but critical readers astutely recognize the dilemma of an agent of justice relying on fascistic terror. Cheap theatrics, torture, and murder are the tools Batman uses, and has always used, in his war on crime, and in depicting them so baldly, Miller suggests that like the armor and the scars, Batman has always been a criminal; he has always used a torturer's tools to achieve his ends.[26]

BvS proposes exactly the same intervention: that the film's depictions of violence, torture, and the troubled nature of superheroes are nothing new; that the only changes are the blatancy of representation and the critical dialogue about the role of and right to violence that the film engenders. Crucially, however, *BvS* recognizes the catastrophic nature of the degree of violence Batman enacts against those he finds criminal in three ways: the commentary provided by Gotham's citizens and press; the questioning of Batman's mental health; and the revelation of Batman's fallibility.

From the outset, the commentary surrounding Batman's extraordinary use of violence is couched in the recognition that this use is exceptional, atypical. It is a new development. The Poet, a Gothamite briefly interviewed by Clark Kent, insists that "There's a new kind of mean in him. He is angry. And he is hunting." The implication, of course, is that the degree of anger and the hunting itself is new; that Batman's methods have changed, even if (at least to some spectators) his victim pool hasn't. "Only people scared of him, people got reason to be," retorts the Poet's neighbor, suggesting that the degree of violence and the use of fear is justified because it is only imposed upon the "deserving." Critically, the understanding of Batman's particular violence—revealed in his first scene to include torture and branding—as new is reflected in media coverage in both Gotham and outside of it. The *Gotham Free Press* notes that "Within the past month there have been 18 reports of violent criminals unwillingly being marked with 'bat-brands'—a large bat symbol burned directly into their flesh seemingly for the purpose of attracting violence from other prisoners." The *Daily Planet* and the *Gotham Free Press* coverage also treats the branding as a new phenomenon. In other words, it is not normal; it represents an aberration in Batman's tactics and philosophy, and it attracts (to some small degree) the critical attention such violence should. *BvS* thus argues that the extremes of Batman's violence, which have always already existed in canon, should *never* have been normalized or justified; they should have always been critically interrogated.

The second way through which *BvS* marks the abnormality of Batman's violence is through its subtle questioning of Batman's mental health. Treatment of mental illness in Batman media has never been done well,[27] in large part thanks to editor Denny O'Neil's declaration that "Wayne/Batman is not insane."[28] Many critics have noted that Batman "comes to experience, to varying degrees, bouts of schizophrenia, neurosis, paranoia and psychosis resulting in an inability to balance reason and passion" throughout his history, despite the finality of O'Neil's edict.[29] *BvS* engages in this uncomfortable dichotomy by linking Batman's paranoid dreams and imaginings to the abuse of prescription medication: waking up from a vision of a demon bursting from his mother's tomb, Bruce reaches unerringly for an orange bottle recognizable to anyone who has ever visited an American pharmacy. He shakes out some pills, and washes them down with wine. What exactly the medication is for remains unclear, but it is not difficult to guess that they are at least antidepressants and at most antipsychotics, meant, judging by the timing of the dose, to ward off fear, paranoia, or a sense of unreality. The timing of the dose, not to mention its consumption with alcohol, betrays as well the instability of the treatment. My own prescription for antidepressants directs me to take my dose at the same time each day to accustom my brain to a regular release of chemicals, and to avoid mixing the dose with alcohol. Whether or not Batman takes antidepressants or antipsychotics, the principle is the same: establish a regular dose, and do not mix with other potentially mind-altering substances. This is advice Batman clearly ignores, and, as such, his regimen cannot be effective, nor can it have much of a positive effect. If anything, his medication will further destabilize his sense of security, self-worth, and reality—thus explaining many of Batman's more extreme perceptions and actions throughout *BvS*. As such, *BvS* posits that Batman, a figure whose narratives rely on the confinement and punishment of the mentally ill by a figure of supposedly absolute rationality, is mentally ill himself—*and has always been so*.

The third (and arguably most important) way *BvS* emphasizes the catastrophic nature of Batman's violence is by revealing Batman's fallibility. A sense of unreality, a resurgence of trauma, and a supremely clever manipulator would throw even the World's greatest detective off his game, and this is exactly what happens. Batman is haunted throughout *BvS* by the attack on Metropolis, perhaps especially by the destruction of the Wayne Enterprises tower there (which, as is discussed in the next section, may be read as an assault on Batman's sovereignty), but he is, tellingly, cast back during the attack to a child whose parents have died. Sweeping a girl from the path of collapsing stone, Batman-as-Bruce Wayne promises her that everything will be alright, and that they'll find her mother. But the girl, when asked where her mother might be, points to the razed ground of Wayne Financial, and Batman immediately comes to the most logical conclusion: the mother is dead, much like his own mother was murdered in front of him, but with one crucial visual difference. While *BvS*'s adaptation of the Wayne murders obscures the face of their killer by blurring his face or focusing instead on the gun, Batman has an unimpeded view of Superman and General Zod crashing through the Metropolis skies; the camera even zooms in to focus his gaze. After that, it would have been simplicity itself for Lex Luthor to sow Superman's path with death in order to exacerbate Batman's rage and direct it at Superman. "Ripe fruit, his hate," Luthor says manically, unveiling his machinations to Superman: "Two years in the growing. But it did not take much to push him over, actually. Little red notes, big bang. *You let your family die!*" In the context of Batman's mental health and the horrifying recreation of his foundational trauma, the success of Luthor's manipulations is unsurprising. What *is* noteworthy is the fact that in revealing Batman's fallibility, *BvS* calls into question Batman's other decisions. If he could be so wrong about Superman, what's to say he wasn't wrong about anyone else he targeted? As the *Gotham Free Press* points out, many of those branded had not even faced trial when Batman marked them. Further, *BvS* suggests that this fallibility, like Batman's mental health and the necessity of critically examining Batman's violence, is nothing new: it has always already been a part of the Bat-canon.

The Sovereign

To examine Batman's use of violence, we must first situate him as sovereign within his sphere and define what it means to be sovereign. Of the theorists (Carl Schmitt, Giorgio Agamben, Jacques Derrida, and Michel Foucault)[30] central to modern definitions of sovereignty, we refer primarily to Schmitt and Agamben.[31] Schmitt famously declared, "Sovereign is he who decides the exception," meaning that the sovereign determines a state of normality and a state of emergency, the latter of which is the state under which exceptional power is justifiably exercised.[32] For Schmitt, notes Tracy B. Strong, "the sovereign authority not only was bound to the normally valid legal order but also transcended it," and this is precisely how: the sovereign transcends the state of normality because he is the one who defines it; every state of being in his domain is predicated upon his recognition of that state, and his authority to recognize it.[33] The fascism underlying Schmitt's argument is no accident, given his participation in the Nazi Party, and usefully offers a point of connection to criticism of Batman's own actions in his 20-year state of exception in Gotham.[34]

Agamben's take on sovereignty reverses Schmitt's perspective. Instead of focusing on the power of the sovereign, Agamben analyzes how absolute power affects those bound to the sovereign's will through the figure of *homo sacer*, a Roman term he uses to indicate those subject to the violence of the sovereign's actions and simultaneously unprotected by the sovereign's authority: "*The sovereign sphere is the sphere in which it is permitted to kill without committing homicide and without celebrating a sacrifice, and sacred life—that is, life that may be killed but not sacrificed—is the life that has been captured in its sphere.*"[35] Derek Gregory usefully glosses *homo sacer* as "those who could not be sacrificed according to ritual (because they were outside divine law: their deaths were of no value to the gods) but who could be killed with impunity (because they were outside juridical law: their lives were of no value to their contemporaries)."[36] Essentially, the sovereign has the power to determine "which lives count [and] which ones do not"; "who matters [and] who's worth it."[37] Those "who matter" are protected from violence that either externally threatens or is authorized by the sovereign against those not "worth it"—those subject to the sovereign ban. Crucially, the "banned" are vulnerable to violence not just at the sovereign's hands, but at anyone's. The sovereign ban signals absolute apathy toward those subjected to it; they are worth nothing.[38]

One of sovereignty's most crucial elements is territory. Sovereignty is bound to spatiality, thus proving sovereign instability in international relations. America's "War on Terror" and torture at Guantánamo as opposed to in America, where prisoners would be entitled to legal protections, exemplify this instability very well, especially considering international criticism. Claudia Aradau, situating Guantánamo as the exception, argues:

> Without the concreteness of space, order cannot achieve its validity. One can reverse the statement and say that any constitution of a particular order depends on the imaginary redistribution of spaces, on enclosures and limits. A new order is constituted by the spatialisation of practices that govern disorder and order; law needs the concrete embodiment of space to sustain its ordering function.[39]

Sovereignty does not exist if it cannot be applied to space—sovereignty presupposes territory. A sovereign without territory is inherently oxymoronic.

Based on Schmitt, Agamben, and Aradau's respective readings of the sovereign—that the sovereign defines his own power and the circumstances under which it may be used; that the sovereign determines who is protected by/from the sovereign's power and who is not—we may condense the concept of sovereignty thus: violence is inextricable from sovereignty because the sovereign decides when, how, where, and *against whom* violence is acceptable.[40] Sovereignty is simply another name for the authority to commit violence without consequence.

Given the degree to which superhero narratives rely on violence, the genre and its protagonists are especially suited to sovereign critique, as exemplified by Will Brooker and Neal Curtis. Though Brooker's approach is useful in cohering Batman's cultural history, we follow Curtis's application of political conceptualizations of sovereignty to superheroes in arguing that Batman's actions within *BvS*, especially his eponymous conflict with Superman, are clarified through a sovereign lens, particularly as relates to territory, violence, and risk.

Because "Gotham is his jurisdiction and within that city he is the *de facto* sovereign," Batman is the "character most suited" to the question of sovereignty, especially regarding territory.[41] More than other superheroes, Batman has been inseparable from and territorial regarding Gotham; his "Dark Knight" epithet, along with Miller's chivalric imagery[42] and royal references,[43] emphasize the often-feudalistic nature of Batman's relationship to Gotham.[44] *BvS* does not borrow the feudalistic tradition from *Dark Knight* or its successors per se, but it invokes Batman-as-sovereign both in and out of costume. In the lull of the Battle of Metropolis between Superman and General Zod, Batman-as-Bruce is hailed by one of his company's employees, Wallace Keefe, whose cry for help suggests that such help can only arrive if Bruce permits it: "You're the boss, boss," Wallace says shakily, and with that recognition of Bruce's authority, the fallen beam is lifted from Wallace's damaged legs. Furthermore, the Battle's infamous damage, though not reaching Gotham, does infringe upon and compromise Batman's sovereign territory. One of the building's most violently damaged houses is Wayne Financial, Batman's own company. The camera concludes the Metropolis sequence by reversing slowly from Bruce Wayne, arms protectively wrapped around the newly orphaned girl, with the Wayne Financial sign shattered on the rubble behind him. To couch the Metropolis branch in imperialist terms,[45] this colony lends a perverse truth to Batman's later claim that Superman "brought the war *to us*." Superman's battle literally leveled a territory under Batman's sovereign protection, effectively diminishing Batman's sovereign authority.

Superman's second affront to Batman's sovereignty is twofold. He enters Gotham, infringing on Batman's territory, and he impedes Batman's acquisition of kryptonite. Most importantly, his motive in entering Gotham is to decree that "The Bat is dead." Batman, seething with paranoid rage, is left dethroned in his own kingdom, the Batmobile ripped apart while he was still inside. Perhaps the most galling moment occurs when Batman attempts to speak to Superman—the infamous "Do you bleed?" line—and Superman leaves without answering or acknowledgment, denying Batman's authority, and denying to Batman the same subjectivity that Batman denies others.

Batman denies subjectivity—which we may understand as subjecthood, in opposition to objectness—to others. This is a fact which has always been part of Batman's character, since his original declaration that "criminals are a superstitious and cowardly lot."[46] *BvS* insists upon it from Batman's first costumed appearance, when he flees after torturing César Santos, a human trafficker. The scene is gruesome: two police officers enter an abandoned building, where they find an unlocked dungeon full of women too terrified of their ostensible rescuer (Batman) to escape. Upstairs, a man screams, proclaiming his ignorance. When the officers find Santos, he is stretched across a radiator, bleeding profusely, a bat branded onto his shoulder. He has been tortured, and, found ignorant, reduced to a body unworthy of compassion. This degradation is epitomized in an interaction between Metropolis prison guards and Santos, who has been transferred there to avoid the Bat-brand's death sentence in Gotham prisons. Santos pleads with his captors: "It don't come off! You can't put me in general, man, they're gonna kill me." The guard dismisses Santos apathetically: "*He's only a criminal.*"[47] Santos's life is worth nothing either to the sovereign (Batman) or Santos's contemporaries. By branding him, Batman marks Santos as subject to all the violence Batman represents and none of the protection. The Bat-brand declares Santos unprotected, that violence may be committed against him without consequence, which is exactly what happens, as the prison guards dehumanize him and Luthor orchestrates his murder.

The question Santos's presence in *BvS* raises is: where is the end of sovereign authority? Yes, Santos was a criminal, as his partner acknowledges, but she insists upon his subjectivity as well: "He was a father. He was that, too." Gregory argues, "our horror ought not to be measured by the innocence or guilt of the prisoners—which in any case is subject to the judicial process denied to them—but by the calculated withdrawal of subjecthood from all of them."[48] Santos haunts the film because *BvS* insists upon his subjectivity, even as Batman denies it, demanding recognition of Santos's nuance—someone who perpetuated gendered and racialized violence against women of color, but who was loved and mourned by a partner and son, and who was denied justice in the courts by the same sovereign ban that denied his subjectivity.

As Luthor and Santos's partner point out, Batman acts as judge, jury, and executioner, none of which amounts to the idea of justice embodied in Senator Finch's Superman inquiry. This, too—the "unilateral action" of which Finch is rightfully wary—is part of sovereignty. Aradau, on sovereign spatiality, argues, "What matters in the governing of space is not the distinction between exception and law, but what practices are deployed and how. Law is not suspended in Guantánamo, but its function is changed,"[49] and Curtis agrees: "...the sovereign's use of law is not simply violent with regard to those it treats as criminals, it is violent in relation to the creation of alternative laws."[50] The sovereign's reformation of law within his territory, his authorization of its changing function, is itself an act of violence, because it permits violence at lower levels. *BvS* emphasizes this: inquiring into Santos's death, Clark Kent is arrested at the sight of a political cartoon taped to the reception desk, in which a criminal cowers from a police officer swinging the Bat-signal as a club, and captioned "BAT'er up!" Clark's horror when he insists to Perry White that "the cops are actually *helping*" Batman in his war on crime underscores this point.[51] The violence Batman commits becomes violence committed by others in his name. This same principle saw the "War on Terror" engender Islamophobic crime in the West, and Donald Trump's own racism beget blatant white supremacism in America. Violence by the sovereign signals the circumstances in which violence may be enacted by the less powerful.

Leigh Johnson and Tina Managhan, writing independently on the psychology of risk after 9/11, note that the apparent permission for violence against the Middle East as an undifferentiated bloc was—and, at time of writing, remains—possible due to the sense of risk the West, and particularly America, experienced after the attacks: "post-9/11, the seemingly most powerful and secure [people] on the planet came to be identified as subjects of terror/trauma within the context of a global war..."[52] The same observation translates discomfitingly to Batman, and explains his actions throughout the film—though, refreshingly, this explanation does not function as an excuse. Batman's entire worldview, within *BvS* and beyond, is irrevocably shaped by the death of his parents, thus the film's opening with the Wayne murders; Batman's character arc is unintelligible without explicit recognition of his trauma. The purpose of his vigilantism is to prevent such a trauma from befalling anyone else, a goal which is narrowed after the Battle of Metropolis, during which Batman's sovereignty is threatened, and he is faced with a mirror of his own trauma: the young orphaned girl, looking for her mother, and knowing she won't be found. The entirety of Batman's paranoid rage, which finds convenient target in Superman (thanks, in part, to Luthor's machinations), originates in this moment, as Batman explains to Alfred: "Count the dead," Batman insists. "*Thousands* of people. What's next? Millions? He has the power to wipe out the entire human race, and if we believe there's even a 1% chance that he is our enemy, we have to take it as an *absolute* certainty." To Alfred's protestation that Superman "is *not* our enemy," Batman retorts that it's only a matter of time until he is: "Twenty years in Gotham…We've seen what promises are worth. How many good guys are left. How many stayed that way." Here, Batman masks his risk perception and fear of another catastrophe with a seemingly justifiable cause, a preemptive strike to defend himself against future attacks—the same reasoning that motivated the Bush administration's invasion of Iraq and Afghanistan.[53] But, unlike the "War on Terror," this plan is thwarted because Batman recognizes his failure, where America maintains its righteousness.

BvS's eponymous battle concretizes the always-already retcons pioneered in *Dark Knight* and pursued throughout *BvS*: Batman's authority is tied to his territory, so he summons Superman to Gotham; Batman's violence has always approached torture, so the viewer is forced to confront that reality being enacted upon Superman, the character trying hardest to do good. With kryptonite, Batman eliminates Superman's greatest advantage—his physical invulnerability—and reduces him to a mere body, which "is always already caught in a deployment of power."[54] Superman, thus embodied, is trapped in Batman's sovereign right to violence and his denial of Superman's subjectivity. Batman cements this power in a telling declaration: "You were never even a man," refuting Superman's humanity and reinforcing Batman's righteousness in applying to Superman the sovereign ban.

The execution of the ban is painful to watch, but it is *meant to be so*. The camera focuses on Superman's unmasked, all-too-human and all-too-emotive face; he wears the agony of each blow (expertly dealt, inexpertly deflected) as plainly as a child because this experience is unprecedented to him. Superman has no context for this degree of pain, no way to guard against fearing the next hurt. In giving Superman this primal fear, Batman strips him of all defenses, and the viewer must recognize this cruelty. Each of Superman's cries is involuntary; the sounds are literally punched out of him. Batman's own groans only highlight Superman's agony: Batman growls his pain; the sound is all but indistinguishable from the grunts he makes when he attacks. But Superman's cries evoke Santos's tortured screams because Superman is being tortured: "The aim of torture is to reduce human beings to the point where they [can] no longer participate as the rational [...] agents [upon which] democracies depend..."[55] Batman has reduced Superman to the object of Batman's hate: inhuman, undeserving of compassion. However, the viewer is unable to dismiss or excuse Batman's violence here: unlike Santos, Superman has committed no crimes; Batman seeks no information from him; and Superman is white, which elicits the empathy of the (white) viewer the way Santos may not. But, like Santos, Superman is threatening enough to merit the sovereign ban until the moment that Batman must confront Superman's subjectivity, when Lois Lane throws herself before Superman the way Martha Wayne had cast herself before Bruce, revealing that Superman, too, has a mother; her name is Martha; and she is about to die. The invocation of "Martha" *demands* that Batman see Superman as a subject, a person, not a mere objectified body. "Martha" humanizes Superman by situating him as victim in Batman's formative trauma, and forces Batman to realize that he has become analogous to the same murderous figure who took away his own parents—that he is in the wrong, and that his tactics are, too, and that he must change in order to redeem himself.

Conclusion

BvS proposes key interventions to the Bat-mythos, the foremost being that these interventions are better understood as revealing what already existed. Batman's reliance on torture, his uncertain mental health, and his recognition of his own fallibility have all been denied, obscured, or uncritically celebrated throughout his history until *BvS*, when the three are tied irrefutably together in his conflict with Superman. In grounding these interventions in *The Dark Knight Returns*, *BvS* insists upon the legitimacy of its revisionary interrogation of Bat-canon and the superhero genre.

BvS contributes a critical examination of the politics of violence in popular media and superhero narratives that is worth the attention and analysis of any media scholar, especially considering the dominance of the superhero movie. It suggests that "the righteous are not always innocent of the deeds of the wicked," but more importantly, that this need not be the case.[56] Despite its bleak tone, *BvS* is a profoundly hopeful movie. The Batman who decried men as inexorably corruptible concludes the film by affirming that "Men are still good," and this affirmation is founded upon responsibility, accountability, and reparation. Men are still good, not because they don't fight, kill, or betray one another, but because that vision of humanity is cripplingly blinkered to their kindness, compassion, and faith. In this way, *BvS* signals a new "dawn of justice," but it recognizes that justice is only possible when heroes admit their mistakes, repair their harm, and change for the better.

Notes

1. Mohamedou Ould Slahi, *Guantánamo Diary* (New York, Back Bay Books, 2015); Darcia Narvaez, "Torture, evil and moral development," *Journal of Moral Education* 44 no. 1 (2015), 1–16.
2. Narvaez notes that "Naming people under torture leads to more torture of more innocent people. It is a spreading toxic spill of misinformation and harm" (2).
3. Narvaez, 3.
4. Frank Miller, et al., *Batman: The Dark Knight Returns* (New York, DC Comics, 1986).
5. A.O. Scott "Review: 'Batman v Superman'…v fun?" *The New York Times*, 23 Mar. 2016, https://nyti.ms/2ozvFJv. Accessed 1 Mar. 2018.
6. Orion Ussner Kidder, "Historicizing the Superhero: Alan Moore's *Supreme* and Warren Ellis/John Cassaday's *Planetary*," *Journal of the Fantastic in the Arts* 21 no. 1 (2010), 77–96. Kidder argues that "Superhero comics have, almost since their beginning, gone out of their way to erase their own narrative history," and identifies two types of retcon: the first "alters previous, published comics by disingenuously 'revealing' that the events [depicted within] were depicted incorrectly or incompletely"; the second is the "incremental…update on the settings, characters, and politics…to create the impression of a perpetually contemporary setting" (78–9).
7. Grant Morrison, et al., *Batman & Robin* #4 (New York, DC Comics, 20).
8. Ed Brubaker, et al., *Captain America Omnibus, Vol. 1* (New York, Marvel Entertainment, 2007).

9. Geoff Klock, "The Revisionary Superhero Narrative," *The Superhero Reader*, edited by Charles Hatfield, et al. (Jackson, University Press of Mississippi, 2013), 117, 116.
10. Bill Finger, et al., *Detective Comics* #27 (New York, DC Comics, 1939).
11. Klock, 119, quoting Miller (1986), 51.
12. Klock, 133.
13. Miller (1986), 22, 45, 64–5, 135, 192; Snyder.
14. Miller (1986), 191, 19–20, 22–25, 130, 166–7; Snyder.
15. Soledad O'Brien, Jon Stewart, Carrie Birmingham, Vikram Gandhi, Neil deGrasse Tyson, Anderson Cooper, Dana Bash, Nancy Grace, Erika Erickson, and Andrew Sullivan appear in *BvS*.
16. Zack Snyder, dir., *Man of Steel* (Warner Bros., 2013).
17. Klock, 118. Notably, Miller's means of making Gotham sensible are replete with misogyny, racism, and homophobia.
18. Klock, 127.
19. Klock, 125.
20. See: Chris Gavaler, "The rise and fall of fascist superpowers," *Journal of Graphic Novels and Comics* 7 no. 1 (2015), 70–87; Gavaler, *On the Origin of Superheroes* (Iowa City, University of Iowa Press, 2015); and Bill Peterson and Emily Gerstein, "Fighting and Flying: Archival Analysis of Threat, Authoritarianism, and the North American Comic Book," *Political Psychology* 26 no. 6 (2005), 887–904.
21. Neal Curtis, *Sovereignty and Superheroes* (Manchester, Manchester University Press, 2016), 16.
22. Klock, 130.
23. Superman (1938) and Captain America (1941) responded to Nazism.
24. Klock, 129.
25. Klock, 129.
26. Finger, et al., *Detective Comics* #27, #33.
27. See: Aidan Diamond, "'Stronger than their madhouse walls': Disrupting Gotham's Freak Discourse in 'Mad Love' and 'Harley Quinn,'" *The Ascendance of Harley Quinn: Essays on DC's Enigmatic Villain*, edited by Shelley E. Barba and Joy M. Perrin (Jefferson, McFarland & Co., 2017), 120–132.
28. Will Brooker, *Batman Unmasked* (New York, Continuum, 2005), 276, quoting Denny O'Neil's *The Bat-Bible*, an unpublished document used to standardize Batman at DC editorial offices.
29. Steve Brie, "Spandex Parables: Justice, Criminality and the Ethics of Vigilantism in Frank Miller's *Batman: The Dark Knight Returns* and Alan Moore's *Batman: The Killing Joke*," *Literature and Ethics: From the Green Knight to the Dark Knight*, ed. Steve Brie and William T. Rossiter (Newcastle upon Tyne, Cambridge Scholars Publishing, 2010), 205.

30. Carl Schmitt, *Political Theology: Four Chapters on the Concept of Sovereignty* (Chicago: University of Chicago Press, 1985, 2005); Schmitt, *The Concept of the Political* (Chicago: University of Chicago Press, 1996, 2005); Giorgio Agamben, *Homo Sacer: Sovereign Power and Bare Life* (Berkeley: Stanford University Press, 1998); Jacques Derrida, *Dissemination* (London, the Athalone Press, 1981); Giovanna Borradori, *Philosophy in a Time of Terror: Dialogues with Jürgen Habermas and Jacques Derrida* (Chicago, University of Chicago Press, 2003); Michel Foucault, *Power/Knowledge: Selected Interviews and Other Writings 1972–1977* (New York, Pantheon Books, 1980).
31. On sovereignty in Derrida and Foucault: Vincent Leitch, "Late Derrida: The Politics of Sovereignty," *Critical Inquiry* 33 (2007), 229–247; Marc Lombardo, *Critique of Sovereignty, Book 1: Contemporary Theories of Sovereignty* (Brooklyn, Punctum Books, 2015); Sergei Prozorov, *Foucault, Freedom and Sovereignty* (Burlington, Ashgate Publishing Company, 2007).
32. Schmitt (1996, 2005), 5.
33. Schwab in Schmitt (1985, 2005), xliii–xliv.
34. For a more thorough and nuanced interrogation of Schmitt's politics than is possible here, please see Tracy B. Strong's "Foreword" and George Schwab's "Introduction" in Schmitt (1985, 2005).
35. Agamben, 83; emphasis in original.
36. Derek Gregory, "The Black Flag: Guantánamo Bay and the Space of Exception," *Geografiska Annaler: Series B, Human Geography* 88 no. 4 (2006), 406.
37. Snyder.
38. Neal Curtis, "Superheroes and the contradiction of sovereignty," *Journal of Graphic Novels and Comics* 4 no. 2 (2013), 209–222.
39. Claudia Aradau, "Law transformed: Guantánamo and the 'other' exception," *Third World Quarterly* 28 no. 3 (2007), 492.
40. I summarize both Schmitt and Agamben; this necessarily lacks the depth and nuance of both theorists' work.
41. Curtis, 58.
42. Miller (1986), 172.
43. Frank Miller, et al., *Batman: Year One* (New York, DC Comics, 1987, 2005), 4.
44. See Brie.
45. Metropolis has never been Batman's city in comics or film; that he has established inroads there well before Superman's arrival may be read as an imperialist act, with Wayne Financial read as a colony. The destruction is thus a double assault on Batman's sovereignty: on territory he had claimed and on his right as sovereign to expand his territory.

46. Finger, et al., *Detective Comics* #33, 2.
47. Snyder; emphasis added.
48. Gregory, 415.
49. Aradau, 491.
50. Curtis, 77.
51. Snyder; emphasis in original.
52. Tina Managhan, "We all dreamed it: The politics of knowing and unknowing the 'war on terror,'" *Critical Studies on Terrorism* 10 no. 1 (2016), 1; Leigh Johnson, "Terror, torture and democratic autoimmunity," *Philosophy and Social Criticism* 38 no. 1 (2012), 111.
53. Johnson, 114.
54. Agamben, 187.
55. Johnson, 118.
56. Brie, 213.

Index[1]

A

Agamben, Giorgio, 221–223, 230n30, 230n40

Alfred Pennyworth, 83, 113

Anders, Charlie Jane, 19, 20

Aradau, Claudia, 222, 223, 225

Aristotle, 44, 56n16

Arkham Asylum: A Serious House on Serious Earth, 177

Arkham Knight (video game), 166, 169

Athens, 9, 13, 15, 36, 76–79, 83, 84, 104n16

Avengers, The, 59

Azzarello, Brian, 120

B

Bane, 20, 37, 51–55, 60, 67–70, 72, 74n25, 126, 141, 145, 151, 154, 155, 156n1

Barbara Gordon, 162, 198, 199, 202, 204, 205, 208–210

See also Batgirl/Bat-Girl; Oracle

Batgirl, 201, 205, 207

Batgirl/Bat-Girl, 5, 162, 195–211

See also Barbara Gordon; Betty Kane; Cassandra Cain; Nissa; Stephanie Brown

Batman (1960s television series), 182

Batman (1989 film), 178, 182, 183

Batman (Comics), 2, 108, 119, 183, 189, 191n17, 209

Batman and Robin (1997 film), 183

Batman Begins (2005 film), 183

Batman Beyond, 209

Batman: Cold Days, 118

Batman: Damned, 120

Batman/Daredevil: King of New York, 160

Batman: Digital Justice, 185

Batman Forever (1995 film), 183

Batman: Gotham Knight, 184

Batman Returns (1992 film), 183

Batman/Scarecrow 3-D, 164, 166

Batman: Terror, 161

[1] Note: Page numbers followed by 'n' refer to notes.

D. K. Picariello (ed.), *Politics in Gotham*,
https://doi.org/10.1007/978-3-030-05776-3

Batman: The Animated Series, 163, 165
Batman: The Killing Joke, 201
Batman: The White Knight, 13
Batman v. Superman: Dawn of Justice (2016 film), 5, 214
Batman: Year One, 92, 95–98, 100, 102, 112, 117
Batwoman, 197, 198
Benes, Ed, 204
Bermejo, Lee, 120
Betty Kane, 197
 See also Batgirl/Bat-Girl
Birds of Prey, 201–203, 206
Birzer, Bradley J., 7–10
Black Canary, 133, 202
Blackest Night, 168
Bloom, Allan, 84
Bob Kane, 91
Brooker, Will, 223
Burkett, Cary, 201
Burton, Tim, 9, 178, 180, 181, 183, 188
Bush, George W., 74n22, 226

C
Cassandra Cain, 202, 204, 205
 See also Batgirl/Bat-Girl
Carmine Falcone, 43, 61
Catwoman, 82, 85, 134
 See also Selena Kyle
Chiron, 108, 109, 113
Clark Kent, 81, 185, 219, 225
 See also Superman
Commissioner Gordon, 9, 33, 34, 37, 60, 65, 80, 99, 117, 137, 144, 181, 183, 186, 200, 205, 209
 See also James Gordon
Converse, Philip, 181, 182
Crisis on Infinite Earths, 201
Curtis, Neal, 223, 225

D
Daily Planet, The, 219
Danger: Diabolik (1968 film), 179
Dargis, Manohla, 25, 30
Dark Knight Returns, The, 2, 5, 80, 84, 92, 95, 98–102, 112, 117, 180, 183, 186, 188, 189, 214–216, 227
Dark Knight Rises, The (2012 film), 7, 20, 36, 37, 39, 42, 49–51, 55, 66, 182, 188
Dark Knight, The (2008 film), 4, 7–10, 14, 17–20, 23–37, 47, 48, 51, 55, 55n1, 58–60, 63–66, 86, 123–137, 141, 143–145, 150, 154, 155, 182, 184, 186, 187
Declaration of Sentiments and Resolutions (1848), 196
Democracy, 3, 13, 24, 27–29, 32, 37, 40, 160, 169, 217, 218, 227
Detective Comics, 18, 79, 161, 162, 167, 188, 199, 203
Diamond, Martin, 40
Dick Grayson, 123, 203, 208
 See also Robin
Dictatorship, 27, 93, 94, 100
Dixon, Chuck, 203, 206, 210
Doomsday, 217
Douthat, Ross, 39
Ducard, 61
 See also Ra's al Ghul

E
Eco, Umberto, 11

F
Fascism, 218, 221
Fear Itself (novel), 161, 166
Federalist Papers, The, 40

Finger, Bill, 197
Ford, John, 23
Fox, Gardner, 199, 200
Mr. Freeze, 85, 86, 118, 120, 129
Friedan, Betty, 199

G
Garbett, Lee, 207
Garcia, Anthony, 182
General Zod, 221, 223
Gibbons, Dave, 201
Gorfinkel, Jordan, 205
Gotham (television series), 159, 184
Gotham Cathedral, 183, 184
Gotham City Police Department (GCPD), 19, 116–118, 132, 137, 142
Gotham Free Press, The, 219, 221
Gotham Globe, The, 178
Gotham University, 161, 163–165, 184, 192n25
Graeber, David, 7, 8, 10, 21n8
Grayson, Devin, 138n3, 207
Green Arrow, 133, 134

H
Hamilton, Alexander, 40, 41, 55
Harley Quinn, 119, 184
Harvey Dent, 9, 13, 20, 27, 30–37, 48–51, 53, 57, 58, 60, 64, 92, 97, 102, 131, 141–145, 153, 154, 181
  See also Two-Face
Hobbes, Thomas, 16, 59, 62, 63
Holmes, Oliver Wendell, 133
Holy Terror, 189
Horrocks, Dylan, 207

I
Injustice 2 (video game), 159, 167
Irving, Washington, 165

J
Jack Napier, 118, 119
  See also Joker, the
James Gordon, 25, 35, 36, 42, 46, 47, 49, 50, 53, 54, 92, 95, 96, 102, 113, 117, 124, 142, 182, 186
  See also Commissioner Gordon
Jason Todd, 136, 164, 215
  See also Robin
Jean-Paul Valley, 88, 126
John (Robin) Blake, 53, 65
Joker, the, 25, 29–35, 38n4, 38n9, 47–50, 59–61, 63–66, 69, 70, 85, 98, 117–120, 124, 128, 143, 144, 152, 156n4, 178–181, 184, 186, 188, 189, 201, 202
  See also Jack Napier
Jonathan Crane, 159, 160, 164–166, 169, 192n25
  See also Scarecrow
Julie Madison, 81, 82
Justice, 1–4, 7–20, 26, 40, 58, 76, 97, 113, 123–137, 143, 152, 155, 163, 180, 198
Justice League, 135, 192n24

K
Kant, Immanuel, 125, 145–150, 152, 155
Kesel, Barbara Randall, 201
King, Tom, 82, 118
Klock, Geoff, 5, 214–216, 218
Knightfall, 88

L
Law, 2, 11, 24, 40, 58, 75, 93, 108, 123, 142, 169, 180, 199, 222
League of Shadows, the, 43–45, 47, 52, 55, 69, 141, 151, 155, 187
Legitimacy, 4, 24, 31, 57–72, 80, 137, 142, 144, 145, 227
Leviathan, 62

Lex Luthor, 217, 221, 224–226
Liberalism, 31, 33, 60, 105n41
Lucius Fox, 36, 38n4, 81, 152
Lyle, Tom, 206

M
Machiavelli, Niccolò, 4, 91–103, 107–120
Madison, James, 40, 41
Man of Steel (2013 film), 217
Man Who Shot Liberty Valance, The, 34, 35
"Matches" Malone, 114, 119
Metropolis, 117, 185, 217, 220, 221, 223, 224, 230n45
Miller, Bryan Q., 207
Miller, Frank, 2, 3, 5, 58, 70, 80, 84, 95, 112, 113, 180, 183, 186, 188, 189, 214–218, 223
Miranda Tate, 39, 52, 54
See also Talia al Ghul
Moldoff, Sheldon, 197
Moore, Alan, 120, 188, 201
Moreno, Pepe, 185
Morrison, Grant, 215
Murphy, Sean, 118
Mutants, the, 99–101, 183

N
Natural Born Killers (1994 film), 179
Necessary Evil: Super-Villains of DC Comics, 166
New Batman Adventures, 163
Nietzsche, Friedrich, 218
Nightwing, 207
Nissa, 195, 196, 202–209
See also Batgirl/Bat-Girl
Nolan, Christopher, 2, 4, 7–10, 19, 20, 23–25, 28, 30, 34, 36, 39, 42, 57–72, 104n39, 112, 141–145, 150, 152, 153, 155, 156n1, 159, 182, 184, 186, 188

O
O'Neil, Dennis, 191n24
Oracle, 196, 202, 203, 205, 208, 210
See also Barbara Gordon
Ostrander, John, 202

P
Perez, George, 201
Pericles, 36
Peterson, Scott, 209
Plato, 4, 76–79, 81, 83, 84, 86
Puckett, Kelley, 205
Punisher, the, 127
Putnam, Robert, 184

R
Rachel Dawes, 27, 31, 33, 42, 43, 46–49, 51, 54, 58, 61
Ra's al Ghul, 20, 42–52, 54, 61–64, 69, 120
See also Ducard
Republicanism, 55, 92–98, 100–102, 103n13
Retcon, 215, 218, 226
Ripstein, Arthur, 150, 151
Robespierre, Maximilien, 18, 19
Robin, 80, 82, 126, 127, 131, 136, 156n4, 160, 164, 166, 169, 180, 183, 197–200, 203, 206–208, 210, 216
See also Dick Grayson; Jason Todd; Tim Drake
Robin, Corey, 160, 169
Rome, 10, 27
Roosevelt, Franklin, 161

S
Sal Maroni, 30, 66
Scarecrow, 5, 60, 62, 159–175, 184, 192n25
See also Jonathan Crane

Scarecrow (*Villains*), 164
Scarecrow, Doctor of Fear (novel), 166
Schmitt, Carl, 59, 63, 66–68, 71, 72, 221–223
Schumacher, Joel, 183
Scott, A.O., 214
Scott, Damion, 205
Scott, Nicola, 204
Scott, Trevor, 207
Selena Kyle, 51, 54, 82, 189
See also Catwoman
Senator June Finch, 217, 218, 225
Shadow of the Bat, 164
Silver St. Cloud, 82
Simone, Gail, 201, 203, 204
Skinner, Quentin, 21n18, 21n20, 103n2
Smylex, 179
Snyder, Zack, 214, 216
Social contract, 60, 62, 125, 148, 149
Socrates, 9, 80, 84, 86, 87
Sons of Batman, the, 80, 85, 86, 88, 101
Sparta, 83
Spider-Man, 46, 185, 192n29
Stephanie Brown, 202, 204, 206
See also Batgirl/Bat-Girl
Strong, Tracy B., 221
Superman, 10, 11, 81, 101, 111, 117, 185, 214–218, 221, 223–227, 230n45
See also Clark Kent

T

Talia al Ghul, 69
See also Miranda Tate
Tarr, Babs, 204
Terrorism, 18, 68, 70, 74n26, 166, 167, 188
Tim Drake, 206, 208, 210
See also Robin
Torture, 30, 132, 135, 147, 207, 214, 218, 219, 222, 226, 227
Trump, Donald, 166, 169, 225
Two-Face, 13, 14, 49, 64, 65, 120, 130, 131, 136, 143, 144, 157n22, 181, 188
See also Harvey Dent

V

Vicki Vale, 179
Vigilantism, 17, 26, 30, 55, 59, 75, 76, 86, 88, 99, 100, 119, 125, 127, 214, 217, 218, 226

W

Watchmen, 120
Wayne Enterprises, 29, 45, 59, 67, 69, 117, 119, 152, 220
Wayne Financial, 220, 223, 230n45
Wayne Foundation, the, 81
Wayne Manor, 46, 95
Weber, Max, 32
Weeks, Lee, 118
Wertham, Frederic, 197
Wolfman, Marv, 137n1, 201
Wonder Woman, 217
World's Finest Comics, 159, 192n27
Wu, Annie, 209

Y

Yale, Kim, 202

Made in the USA
Columbia, SC
21 January 2021

31380364R00141